THE INTERNATIONAL OIL MARKET

Also by Alessandro Roncaglia

SRAFFA AND THE THEORY OF PRICES
WILLIAM PETTY AND THE ORIGIN OF POLITICAL ECONOMY

THE INTERNATIONAL
OIL MARKET

A Case of Trilateral Oligopoly

ALESSANDRO RONCAGLIA

Edited by
J. A. KREGEL

M. E. Sharpe, Inc.
Armonk, New York

Soc
HD
9560.5
R6313
1985

© 1983, 1984 Gius. Laterza. & Figli Spa, Roma—Bari
First published as *L'economia del petrolio* by Laterza 1983
First English edition 1985

First published 1985 by
M.E. SHARPE, INC.
80 Business Park Drive
Armonk, New York 10504

Printed in Hong Kong

Library of Congress Cataloging in Publication Data

Roncaglia, Alessandro.
    The international oil market.

    Bibliography: p.
    Includes index.
    1. Petroleum industry and trade. I. Kregel, J.A.
II. Title.
HD9560.5.R63 1985   382'.42282   84—5555
ISBN 0—87332—282—7
ISBN 0—87332—290—8 (pbk.)

Contents

Acknowledgements

I have had useful discussions on the topic of this work or on parts of it with M. Abdel-Fadil, L. D'Agostini, P. Davidson, S. Parrinello, P. Sylos Labini and M. Tonveronachi. The improvements in this English edition over the Italian one are largely due to suggestions by J. A. Kregel. Thanks, but not implication for the final result, are due to all of these colleagues.

A.R.

1 Introduction

I. THE RELEVANCE OF OIL

Over the past fifteen years, events in the international oil market have had a direct impact on the personal well-being of members of both developed and underdeveloped economies. They have also had a wide-ranging impact on the evolution of the world economy, an impact which varies widely from country to country.

As a result of the sharp changes that have occurred in the oil market over the last fifteen years, it is easier to identify the reasons why this sector occupies such a central role in modern economies. First, oil is an indispensable means of production, as a raw material for the petrochemical sector, and — above all — as a source of energy. In this respect, the fact that the price of oil was for a long period low, compared with available alternatives, and decreasing in real terms, helps to explain the impact of oil on the world's economies. Since changes in the direction of technological research and the adaptation and adjustment of production equipment require substantial periods of time, it is likely that, despite the recent large increases in its price, oil will be required for many years to come to satisfy a substantial, if decreasing, share of the energy requirements of all countries.

Second, the importance of oil as a commodity stems from the wide difference, especially in the short term, between its production costs and the price which consumers are willing to pay for oil products. Because of this, enormous wealth has been amassed and lost within the oil sector (and within related sectors) as a consequence of events in the oil sector. Political power has been converted into private or public wealth in the oil sector on a scale seldom seen in other parts of the economic system. At the same time, the economic strength — of countries as well as of private economic agents — can be defended and increased through the use of typically political instruments. Thus, in addition to the more specifically political elements, the economic characteristics of the oil market, e.g. the nature of the basic commodity oil, mentioned above, and the international nature of the oil trade play an equally important role in determining crude oil prices.

1

This latter fact represents the third, and possibly the most important explanation of the importance of the oil market. Trade in crude oil and in refined oil products represents a substantial share of total international trade. The largest oilfields are located in areas characterised by a low degree of industrialisation and a low demand for energy, such as the Middle East. On the other hand, oil is scarce in highly industrialised countries such as Germany, Japan, France, Italy, which account for a significant share of world demand for oil. Obviously in such a situation the working of the oil market depends on the political choices as well as the economic policy choices of both the oil-importing and the oil-exporting countries. As is also obvious, since the trade in oil is primarily unidirectional, flowing from one group of countries to certain other countries (apart from some exceptional reversals, such as that of Great Britain and Norway after the discovery and development of the North Sea oilfields), changes in crude oil prices have a great impact on trade balances of these two groups, and hence on economic performance of each country.

II. REASONS FOR THEORETICAL INTEREST IN OIL

Because of the central role of the oil sector in modern economies, it is important to study its particular characteristics, and to interpret correctly its method of operation, in order to understand past events, to forecast future ones, and to try to influence the course of economic events. Unfortunately, modern economic theory does not provide a consistent and generally accepted set of interpretative tools from which to choose those most appropriate to the analysis of the issue under consideration. Indeed, current debates in the field of economic theory concern its very analytical foundations.

There is a twin relationship connecting these debates to the problem of interpreting events in the oil sector. On the one hand, the adoption of a particular theoretical approach implies not only the utilisation of a specific set of analytical tools for dealing with the specific issue under consideration, it also, and more importantly, implies a specific conceptual and methodological framework, which produces specific interpretative hypotheses. On the other hand, while it is true that the very nature of the theoretical debates concerns issues of logical consistency, it is also true that a subsequent step in evaluating the merits of any approach (or 'research programme') refers to its interpretative power. From this perspective, comparison of the various interpretative hypotheses offered by the debates concerning the analysis of oil that have taken place in recent years is very useful. In fact, we can utilise this specific, but highly relevant, issue as a sort of proving ground for the relative explanatory power of contending theoretical approaches.

The relationship connecting economic theory to the analysis of a specific concrete issue would be of analytical interest even during periods of what Kuhn called 'normal science', characterised by the undisputed sovereignty of a specific theoretical approach. At the origin of any description, except for the simple accumulation of randomly experienced events, is an interpretative hypothesis formulated on the basis of a well-defined theoretical frame of reference. It is easy to lose sight of the simple fact that the underlying analytical structure must be kept in mind in order to avoid introducing logical errors which would invalidate any attempt to interpret events. In fact, such conditions occasionally arise, as we shall see in an example discussed in Chapter 3, Section IV, below. At the same time, the conflict between abstract theory and concrete reality can enrich theory by stimulating economists to enlarge their horizons and improve the internal specification of their analytical framework. Also, and a most important point, given the historical dimension of economic theory *qua* social science, such a confrontation provides hints as to the opportunity of modifying the system of abstractions on which theory relies, in order to follow structural changes taking place in reality.

III. OUTLINE OF THE PRESENT WORK

The study of a subject such as the international oil market provides insights into many different economic problems. The subject of investigation is thus of relevance not only to those operating within the oil sector, but also to those outside it. Because of this, the method of exposition adopted in this book is to attempt to make the problems of the analysis of the oil market comprehensible to those who have no particular expertise in it, as well as to provide a framework of analysis that may be useful to those with more detailed knowledge. To this end Chapter 2 presents a summary description of the structure of the oil sector, distinguishing its successive stages: exploration, production, transportation, refining, and distribution. A survey of the main interpretations of the working of the oil market, in particular of the factors affecting crude oil prices, is presented in Chapter 3. These interpretations are evaluated by checking their analytical foundations and their factual assumptions. An alternative interpretation, 'trilateral oligopoly', is then proposed. This interpretation is used as the basis for an analysis of the behaviour of oil companies in Chapter 4, the producing countries' behaviour in Chapter 5, and that of the consuming countries in Chapter 6. The main aspects of the evolution of the oil sector are also considered in Chapter 6. Finally, in Chapter 7, an attempt is made to identify possible short- and long-term scenarios for the evolution of oil prices and the structure of the oil sector.

The viewpoint of the present analysis is thus to consider the oil market as an instance of multilateral oligopoly. That is, as composed of three groups of economic and political agents, whose behaviour decisively affects the evolution of the oil market: oil companies, producing countries and consuming countries. In particular, the present analysis attributes a greater role to the latter than is generally the case in studies of the oil sector. The three groups are not, however, considered as three internally homogeneous units: each of them displays the typical characteristics of oligopolistic market forms, with a few big agents dominating the group, while operating side by side with a larger number of smaller agents, who are none the less autonomous decision-making units. We are thus in a situation which differs both from free competition (where prices are determined on the basis of production costs) and from absolute monopoly in which a single company or a single producing country determines prices. Rather, the situation in the oil market could be characterised as a 'trilateral oligopoly': the levels and changes of crude oil prices depend on those factors affecting the degree of oligopolistic control of each group over the market, and on the strategic choices of the 'leaders' within each group. The relevant factors can be identified by looking at the technical characteristics of the product, and at the institutional features of the international crude oil market and of the national markets for refined petroleum products. An analysis of the strategic choices of the leaders – for the sake of simplicity, Saudi Arabia among the producing countries, the US among consuming countries, and Exxon (or even better the 'Rockefeller group': see appendix to Chapter 4) among the oil companies – requires an analysis of their relative market position, the constraints on their action, and their political or institutional links with other agents in the market.

The analytical framework proposed for the interpretation of events in the oil market may appear to some so obvious as to be commonplace. In fact, it appears to be implicitly employed in the writings of many oil specialists, and in most newspaper accounts. However, the analysis carried out in Chapter 3 should make clear that the application of the 'trilateral oligopoly' interpretation can be distinguished from those who approach oil as a scarce natural resource, or point to decreasing returns as a dominating factor in the oil sector. In fact, these two interpretations (together with the simplistic one that explains everything in terms of OPEC's 'monopoly' power) today dominate the debate on oil. By distinguishing and comparing the various interpretations we are led to conclude that some explanations, which apparently rely on good commonsense and enjoy general acceptance, must be rejected as theoretically inconsistent and/or based on factual assumptions which are much more restrictive than they might appear at first sight, so much so in fact as to conflict with reality. In many instances, for example, when discussing the usefulness of national or State oil companies, or long-term trends in crude oil prices, our interpretation leads to results which differ substantially from analyses based on other interpretations.

In other words, while it might at first sight appear that different elements (such as scarcity, increasing costs, market power) may contribute to an explanation of movements in oil prices, deeper consideration, investigating the theoretical foundations of the behaviour of each of these elements, demonstrates not only the possibility, but also the necessity of choosing between them. Clearly, this has direct importance for any attempt to forecast the evolution of the oil market, or to devise optimal intervention strategies. In fact, it is precisely the debate on these issues which may lack clarity unless sufficient attention has been paid to the identification of the distinctive characteristics of the interpretative framework implicitly adopted by participants in the debate, and on the degree of logical rigor in each individual approach.

IV. SOME CUES FOR REFLECTION

In examining the vicissitudes of the oil sector, we shall see that the main events — and specifically the crises of 1973–4 and 1979–80 — do not stem from any single cause, but from a complex combination of different elements. The analytical approach adopted in the present work — 'trilateral oliogopoly' — does not by itself provide a direct explanation of the vicissitudes of the oil sector. Rather, our analytical approach is useful in that it allows us to assess the relative role of the various elements, and especially to identify some elements too often erroneously omitted because they are considered to be irrelevant. In this latter category we may include the energy policy choices of consuming countries, and the technological characteristics at the various stages of the production process in the oil sector.

In contrast to this, we shall not dwell upon the repercussions which the perturbations in the oil sector have had, and still have, on the international economy and on the economies of individual countries. In this respect, it should only be remembered that in addition to, and perhaps even more important than, the immediate impact effects (such as the dramatic shifts in the trade balance brought about by the increases in oil prices) there are other, more far-reaching effects, which have generally been given less attention than they merit. One example is the effect developments in the oil sector have on the relative competitive position of the various national economies. This effect is illustrated by the reversal of the relative position of the United States after 1973, when the availability of internal oil resources gave it a clear competitive advantage over other industrialised countries.

This situation should be compared to the one prevailing in the 1960s, when American industry experienced a noticeable competitive disadvantage, due to the higher cost of energy supplies in comparison to the Japanese and European economies. There is no doubt that the low cost of energy is to be included among the main factors of the 'economic miracle' of Japan and a number of European countries. It is now likely that the advantages of renewed energy competitiveness are helping the US economy, by counterbalancing the damages stemming from 'Reaganomics' and favouring a relative strengthening of US industry within the group of the OECD countries.

However, the most interesting aspect of the analytical approach advanced in this work lies in the possibility of utilising it to identify future tendencies in the oil sector. As we shall see in the concluding chapter, the analysis of market forms prevailing in the oil sector provides useful suggestions concerning the likely evolution of oil prices in the short as well as in the long run. While it is not possible to deduce a single most likely future course for oil prices, it has been deemed useful to single out three distinct short-term scenarios with a corresponding number of long-term scenarios, each case exhibiting very different patterns for oil prices. This notwithstanding, we shall see that our analytical approach, combined with factual elements, provides a sound basis for an evaluation of the relative economic profitability of some relevant strategic decisions. In this respect, it is instructive to recall the case of investment decisions in alternative energy sources.

In order to estimate the profitability of an investment in a solar, or nuclear, or hydroelectric plant we need, among other things, some estimates on the profitability of a 'reference' electric plant based on fuel oil or on coal. This implies the formulation of an hypothesis on the likely evolution of crude oil, coal and uranium prices over the foreseeable lifespan of the different plants. In the absence of reliable hypotheses, especially on the evolution of oil prices over the next ten to thirty years, a commonly adopted procedure has been to compute profitability estimates for different electricity production technologies on the assumption that the prices of all alternative energy sources are constant in real terms. Another widely adopted procedure relies on the simple linear extrapolation of past tendencies. As far as crude oil is concerned, this means assuming that crude oil prices in real terms will keep increasing for many years to come, at a rate of increase equal to the average over the past ten or twenty years. It has been suggested that this latter hypothesis is technically more refined than the previous one, which appears to be based in agnosticism; but in fact the two procedures are equally arbitrary, since neither of them makes any effort to take into consideration the elements which are likely to affect the evolution of oil prices in the future. It will be clear that profitability evaluations obtained by adopting such procedures give results that are very different from those which might be obtained with at least one of our scenarios — a crash in oil prices. While this may not be the most likely course of future events, it must still be considered a distinct possibility. Noticeably different results will also be obtained under the most likely scenario, the intermediate one, outlining a future course of oil prices in real terms lower than those prevailing at the beginning of the 1980s. From this perspective nuclear plants would turn out to be far less advantageous, in strict economic terms, than many analysts now maintain (and even more so if restrictive monetary policies persist in major industrialised countries, producing high interest rates which penalise investments with a relatively long gestation period). On the other hand, when we consider the scenario proposing the possibility of a sharp increase in oil prices (in real terms) as a consequence of political and military upheavals in the Middle East oil-producing area, we are confronted with the immediate scarcity of oil supplies as the most pressing problem.

Such a scenario should lead to investments which ensure a more generally diversified energy base, or even better to an increase in the flexibility of electricity production, for instance with bivalent thermoelectric plants, capable of using fuel oil or coal as inputs, or capable of being quickly converted to coal utilisation, rather than to invest in plants characterised by a rigidly predetermined technology, such as nuclear plants. This issue undoubtedly needs additional consideration; but enough has been said to point out how our analysis suggests caution should be exercised in the assessment of certain opinions, even if they are widely shared by experts in the oil sector.

This is but an example of the issues to which the analysis of the oil sector developed in the following pages can be applied. The importance of such issues may perhaps provide the necessary excuse for this addition to the already extensive literature on the oil sector.

2 The Structure of the Petroleum Sector

Petroleum is an oily flammable bituminous liquid that in a crude state often has a very disagreeable odor and may vary from almost colourless to black but is usually of a dark brown or greenish hue and sometimes fluorescent, that occurs in many places in the upper strata of the earth either in seepages or in reservoir formations from which it is obtained by drilling and pumping if necessary, that is essentially a complex mixture of hydrocarbons of different types with small amounts of other substances (as oxygen compounds, sulphur compounds, nitrogen compounds, resinous and asphaltic components, and metallic compounds), that is sometimes classed as paraffin-base, asphalt-base or naphthene-base, or mixed-base, and that is subjected to various refining processes (as fractional distillation, cracking, catalytic reforming, hydroforming, alkylation, polymerization) for producing useful products (as gasoline, naphtha, kerosine, fuel oils, lubricants, waxes, asphalt, coke, and chemicals) — called also mineral oil, rock oil.[1]

There are a wide variety of crude oils which differ in quality, just as the oil deposits which produce them differ in the quantity and quality of the oil that they contain, and in their geographical location, depth and geological structure. Crudes of different quality are produced by different conditions. The various grades of crude oil may be refined to produce a number of widely different final products such as petrol (gasoline), gasoil, kerosene, etc. Each particular refined product is destined for a particular employment or series of uses, petrol to power the internal combustion engines of cars, gasoil for heating or generating electricity, raw materials for the chemical industry and so forth. In fact, the productive structure of the modern economy has gradually developed on the basis of a combination of technological factors, one of the most important of which must be considered the availability and the particular technical characteristics of the different refined products of crude oil.

There are five distinct stages which comprise the petroleum production cycle, each with very different characteristics: exploration, production, transportation, refining and distribution. The intermediate stage of transportation from the point of extraction to the point of sale may occur either before or after the refining process. Transportation may thus be of either crude oil or of refined products. In this book we shall indicate the combination of these five stages as the petroleum sector.

The largest petroleum companies are vertically integrated. This means that they operate, either directly or by means of associated or subsidiary companies, in all of the above-mentioned phases of the production cycle. This fact, as we shall see below (Chapter 4, section IV), allows these companies to enjoy a degree of control over the totality of the petroleum market that is greater than that which would be given by any average measure of market power calculated as an average of the extent of control in each single phase of the production process taken in isolation.

Medium-sized companies, which are at least partially integrated companies, operate alongside the larger ones. Finally, there are small companies who operate in one single phase of the process. In recent years 'flagship' companies have taken on increasing importance. These companies are State-owned holding companies under governmental control. Those of the producing countries, such as Petromin in Saudi Arabia, are primarily involved in the initial phases of the production process. They are, however, increasing their role in 'downstream' activities. Those of the consuming countries, such as ENI in Italy, usually approach full vertical integration.

Public intervention can thus be seen to play a decisive role in influencing the make-up of the participants of the petroleum sector. In both the producing and consuming countries an ensemble of commercial and fiscal regulations, often very highly detailed in their specification, directly condition the profitability of the various possible lines of action of the participants. Government decisions in the area of mineral research and development policies have an even more direct impact on conditions of profitability. Even though the petroleum market is international in dimension, the positions of greatest influence are held by a few specific countries, such as the United States, on the side of the consuming countries, and, at the opposite extreme, Saudi Arabia on the side of the producing countries.

It should be kept in mind that the characteristics and the location of oil deposits depend on geological factors, while the consumption of petroleum products is linked above all else to the level of economic development reached by the various consuming countries. When per capita income rises it is generally the case that per capita consumption of petrolem also rises. Until 1973 the average elasticity of per capita consumption with respect to income was greater than unity, consumption rising more than in proportion to income, the increased consumption of petroleum being used as a source of energy in electricity-generating plants (coal and nuclear power are the main alternatives), for heating (gasoil and kerosene), for transportation (petrol and derv) and finally as a raw material for the vast petrochemical industry.

In the paragraphs that follow each of the five phases of production are examined separately in order to try to describe in very general terms the most basic technical characteristics and the complexity of the decision-making process of the petroleum sector. These aspects have a decisive influence on the conditions in the international petroleum market for they determine the distribution of power among the three large groupings, the producing countries, the petroleum companies and the consuming countries, as well as within each of these groups. As a consequence, these aspects are essential to any attempt to explain the long-term evolution of the petroleum sector.

II. THE SEARCH FOR PETROLEUM

The search for new petroleum deposits is technically a very complicated activity. Success is also highly random. First, it is necessary to locate promising geological structures. Then exploratory drilling must take place. If these tests confirm the existence of oil deposits it is usually necessary for additional test wells to be drilled in order to determine the size of the pool and its commercial viability. The expenses involved in such exploratory activities are substantial and may not produce any positive results. On the other hand, when a commercially viable deposit is discovered the profits (and/or government revenues) can be enormous and out of all proportion to the exploration and development costs.

The choice of the areas in which geological surveys should be carried out forms a part of the strategical decisions that must be taken by the large petroleum companies. In addition to those factors which make such decisions similar to playing geological roulette, considerations of a political nature will also have an important influence. The political complexion and the stability of the government that controls the area in which surveys are to be taken will be of particular importance. Commercial legislation and fiscal regulation, as well as the obligations and privileges of the company carrying out exploratory activity, will also enter the decision.

As far as those factors of a purely geological nature are concerned, we shall limit our discussion to pointing out that the existence of oil deposits requires two conditions: the presence of deposits of organic materials which have, in the passage of time, been transformed into petroleum, and the location of these materials in 'geological traps' which prevent the dispersion of the hydrocarbons. We might visualise one of these 'traps' as a gigantic inverted 'U' composed of impermeable rock. The interior of the trap is not composed, as one might imagine, of a cavern of crude oil, but of a mass of permeable and porous rock formations. The liquid and gaseous hydrocarbons are contained in the pores of these rock formations. The volume of the pores varies from 5 to 35 per cent of the rock formation. The technical characteristics of the deposit are therefore not only related to the total size, but also to the depth and the quality of the hydrocarbons, as well as to the internal pressure to which they are subject and the porosity of the rocks in which they are contained.

There are around 600 areas of the world which have been designated oil provinces, that is, zones with a high probability of containing deposits of crude. In at least a third of these areas preliminary exploration has only recently been started (see Colitti, 1981). The choice of the 'province' in which exploration activities will be carried out (and given the large size of some of the provinces, the zones within it) and the extent of the financial resources to commit to surveys and exploratory drilling is, as noted above, a 'strategic' decision for the petroleum company. Parallel to this decision, the country within whose frontiers the company decides to initiate exploration must also undertake a 'strategic' decision to grant permission on sufficiently attractive terms to be of interest. The government of the country may itself decide to carry out a more or less active initial exploration, usually by subcontracting to firms specialised in initial search activities which are generally limited to general geophysical investigations in order to evaluate the potential of those areas proposed for concessionary licence. This type of research is generally undertaken by small 'equipes' using geoseismic methods which allow identification of the most promising geological structures.[2] Such activity may also be undertaken by small 'service' firms who operate for the large multinationals on a commission basis.

At this point a second decision-making level is reached, that of the 'tactical' decision. This concerns whether or not exploratory drilling should take place, where it should be carried out, to what depth and to what extent. Indeed, there is only one way to discover whether or not a 'geological trap' contains hydrocarbon deposits — drill a small-diameter hole to a depth which may be several miles below the surface of the earth until it reaches the area of porous rock below the 'trap'.

In most cases the large petroleum companies consider the two decision-making levels — the 'strategic' and the 'tactical' — as logically distinct as well as temporally separated. They are normally taken by two separate decision-making centres within the company.[3] It is the 'strategic' decision concerning the initiation and the locality of the exploration activity of the large oil companies which has the greatest impact on the evolution of the petroleum sector, as well as on the entire economic life of countries and regions. The errors and the successes of these decisions are among the most important factors which produce changes in the relative market shares of the large petroleum companies operating in the sector. For this reason, especially after the increase in prices of crude in 1973–4, the large companies have tended to be present all over the world in order to avoid missing out on a 'big strike'. At the same time, the very high risks involved at this stage have led many companies to prefer to work in consortia, rather than independently, in order to share these high-risk costs.[4]

In this regard, a particular case is represented by exploratory activity on the mainland of the United States. Not only is this an area of political stability with minimal technical difficulties, it is also an area in which a particular form of property right exists. In difference from the legal conditions that are normally encountered in other countries, in the United States underground mineral rights are considered to be the property of the owner of the surface land. They may thus be leased to anyone by the private owner. This fact, along with fiscal regulations that are particularly favourable, has created that typically American figure, the 'wildcatter', an individual or very small firm looking for a 'lucky strike'. For a very long period (the situation changed after the 1973 crisis) the large oil companies in fact preferred limiting their own exploration activities within the United States, leaving the wildcatters to discover deposits which they then purchased.

Factors of an economic nature also play a role in the decision to make investments in exploratory activities. These include the expected movements in future demands and supplies for petroleum, and comparison between the expected future prices for petroleum products on the one hand, and the predicted costs of production for potential deposits and the costs of transportation to the area of final consumption on the other. The current and expected future prices of petroleum thus influence the decisions concerning search activities both directly, through the calculations of profitability just mentioned, as well as indirectly, through incentives to technological research and the introduction of more complex technologies. In this way they exert an influence, even if it is only after some time, on the 'proven reserves', the amount of oil that has already been located and which can be pumped and sold at a profit, given the existing level of technical knowledge, costs and prices. Proven reserves must therefore be considered as an output of the company's exploration activities and not as an exogenously given technological datum. They are a variable subject to economic factors. For this reason they should be distinguished from the amount of ultimately recoverable oil which is of a much larger order of magnitude than proven reserves, but much more difficult to estimate. The importance of this distinction will be further discussed in Chapter 3, section II, below.

III. PRODUCTION

Once the oil pool has been discovered, it is necessary to evaluate its dimensions and production characteristics in order to determine if production will be commercially viable. The test well which confirmed the existence of an oil deposit furnishes an initial body of information such as the quality of the crude and the underground pressure, but additional tests will usually be necessary. The drilling of additional test wells gives a more secure basis for evaluating the size and the characteristics of the deposit, determining the ideal location for the production apparatus and estimating the optimal rate of depletion.

With respect to the previous stage, the degree of randomness is here sharply reduced. The technical difficulties are, however, various. In the great majority of cases the technology which is required to put an oilfield into production is extremely simple and the minimum necessary capital requirements are relatively modest in comparison with the average capital investment in plant and equipment required in industrial manufacturing activity. There is thus little advantage to be gained by large-size firms over their smaller competitors in this stage. This has been evident even from the beginning of the development of the petroleum sector when the simple control of the transportation phase alone permitted John D. Rockefeller to carry out his successful strategy of industrial concentration in the petroleum sector (see below, Chapter 4, section II). This is also still evident today with the presence of a good number of very small operators in those countries where their existence has been made possible by means of granting property owners the rights to minerals found under their land, as in the United States, or by means of a governmental policy of dividing exploration licences and production permits for land areas which do not present particular technical production difficulties.

The technical difficulties are at a minimum for bringing into production deposits which are located in areas where petroleum is already being produced, for a technical infrastructure already exists to be used in support of the new production activities, for example, marine shipping terminals. Costs are obviously higher when a new area has to be opened up and the entire infrastructure has to be provided *ex novo*. The last fifteen years has seen the opening up of new production areas in particularly difficult areas such as Alaska and the North Sea. In the former case the high costs and the greater technical difficulties are above all associated with the transportation infrastructure. This is also the case for Siberian oil and gas. For the North Sea, on the other hand, the problems of cost and the technical difficulties occur in the production phase.

Whatever the particularities of a deposit in terms of the level of technical difficulty and the total average cost of production, the greatest proportion of costs occurs in the initial fixed capital investment; variable costs are very modest by comparison. This fact, together with the ease and rapidity with which it is possible to vary the rhythm of production within rather wide limits is, as we shall see in Chapter 3, section V, and Chapter 7, section III, of major importance to the determination of the dominant market form and an understanding of the behaviour of the operators in the oil sector.

The growth in variable costs is probably greater than that in fixed costs when production passes from the primary to the secondary, and then to the tertiary stages. The first stage is most common. The oil is extracted by means of the natural pressure of the underground deposit or by relatively simple pumping methods. For secondary production, water must be injected in the lower regions of the rock formation, or gas injected in the higher regions of the rock formation to increase pressure and push the oil towards the area of the well. On average such techniques allow the recovery of around a third of the oil present in the deposit (i.e. of oil in place, a concept that is thus different from the idea of recoverable reserves).

Tertiary techniques of production which increase the share of recoverable reserves are still in a relatively early stage of development and are not widely utilised. These techniques consist principally in the reduction of the viscosity of crude to facilitate its movement within the field towards the production wells. This is achieved by injecting water vapour or particular types of chemical mixtures into the deposit. For the present, the use of these techniques is limited mainly to the United States, but the rise in prices in 1973–4 has also had a large stimulating effect on their further development.

During the early life of a producing field, the primary production stage, the most important decision is the rate of depletion, or how rapidly oil should be pumped from the deposit. In this respect it is necessary to distinguish between 'installed production capacity', i.e. the number of barrels per day[5] which can be lifted with the existing production installation, the 'sustainable capacity' which is only slightly lower and is considered to be physically possible to maintain over a period of at least six months, and, finally, 'peak output capacity' which may be obtained over a few days or at most weeks. The depletion rates depend both on economic considerations, such as the expected future movements in prices for crude, and on technical considerations such as maintaining sufficient internal well pressure so as to be able to maximise the proportion of the deposit which is ultimately recoverable.

IV. TRANSPORTATION

The transportation phase has for a long time been of decisive importance for the oligopolistic control of the oil sector, as the experience of the Standard Oil Trust demonstrates. It is an essential link in the behaviour of a market which has global dimensions, and especially one in which the principal production zones are far distant from the primary areas of consumption.

It is possible to distinguish four different types of movement: (i) the transport of crude from the area of production to the area of consumption, or (ii) from the area of production to a refinery location which differs from the area of consumption; then, (iii) the transport of refined products from the refinery to the area of consumption, or (iv) from production areas with refinery capacity to the areas of consumption. This latter type of transport has been of major importance in the initial phases of the development of the petroleum industry. It is often the case that on account of the very long distances involved, strictly technical aspects of transportation technology make it less costly to move crude oil than refined products. In the period after the Second World War, for these reasons, and also possibly on account of the initial symptoms of a revival of political nationalism in a number of developing countries, the petroleum companies preferred the placement of their refineries in close proximity to the major centres of consumption. Transportation activity was thus primarily limited to movement of crude.

However, the attempts in recent years of a number of producing countries to link the initiation of an internal industrialisation process to the exploitation of their domestic petroleum resources has renewed the previous tendency to place refining capacity in or near the regions of production. But, whether it is a question of the transportation of crude or refined petroleum products, the central element for understanding the market structure relevant to this phase of the cycle of production is the necessity for highly specific means of transport: bulk ocean tankers, pipelines, road tankers, rail-tank cars, etc. In other words the petroleum industry is highly restricted in its ability to purchase and employ transportation services from firms outside the industry which do not depend totally on the petroleum sector for the demand for their services and which have alternative market outlets arising from the demand for transport from other sectors of the economy. It is for this reason that the transportation of crude oil or refined products, generally included in the statistical measures of activity in the transportation sector of the economy (and which represents a substantial proportion of the total — over half the tonnage in maritime transport), should rather be considered as an integral part of the petroleum sector. Only in a relatively recent period, and this only for the sector of maritime transportation, has it been possible to use multipurpose carriers (oil—ore and oil—bulk—oil (OBO)). But such vessels still constitute a relatively small proportion of the total tonnage committed to the transport of crude.

As has been indicated above, and as shall be seen more fully below (Chapter 3, section IX, and Chapter 4, section II), the transportation phase has played a major role in the formation of the existing oligopolistic market structure of the petroleum sector. In particular, in the case of pipelines the market comes to be automatically divided into a number of submarkets, each distinct from the other. The pipeline that carries crude from Alaska to the consumption areas in the Northern United States cannot be considered in direct competition with the Tapline put into place to carry crude from the Arabian peninsula to the Mediterranean. When the means of transportation are this specific and are represented by substantial amounts of immobile capital equipment, it is necessary that there should be a regular flow of supplies and a regular market for the transported products. In order for the investment to be considered sufficiently secure and profitable (the risk factor, given the dimensions of such projects, will be of particular importance) one must be certain of being able to control both the market regulating the inflow and the market regulating the outflow from the system. On the other hand, the acquisition of control of the extraction phase upstream, and of the refining and distribution phases downstream, will not be particularly difficult for whomever controls the transportation phase, for he operates as an absolute monopolist in a particular sector of the market. It was precisely this position which allowed the Standard Oil Trust in the United States (see below, Chapter 4, section II) to gain its overall position of control.

At the same time it is necessary to remember that the government agencies charged with enforcing anti-trust policies have been particularly active in this phase. This is the case, for example, in the United States where the classification of pipelines as 'common carriers' in 1906 placed them under regulations whereby they were obliged to assure services at equivalent conditions to all comers. Intervention of this type may be extremely effective in counteracting the tendency towards concentration that the objective technical factors produce in this phase of activity (see below, Chapter 4, section IV). The rapid expansion of the market also furnishes in this, as well as in other phases of activity in the oil sector, an important element in reducing the degree of monopolistic control exercised by the large firms (see below, Chapter 3, sections V and IX).

These latter points apply as well to the maritime transportation of crude via bulk tankers. Given the rapid growth and the current size of the market, this is an activity in which the high proportion of the market controlled by the large companies (but to a lesser extent than in the other phases of activity) can perhaps be considered as principally the consequence of the process of vertical integration. The growth in the average size of bulk tankers has indeed been accompanied in the post-war period by an extraordinary expansion in the quantity of crude transported by sea.[6] The economic importance of the transportation phase has sensibly diminished, with respect to conditions in the early periods, following the increase in crude oil prices in 1973–4 and 1979–80. From the strategic point of view the extent of the major oil companies' control over the market (just as for the producing and consuming countries) is more important in both the upstream and the downstream activities than in the transportation phase.

V. REFINING

The capacity of a crude oil refining plant is relatively small when compared with the total flow of petroleum in the combined process of production. However, in any particular country the output of a refinery may represent a significant share of the market for refined products, a share which is, of course, larger the smaller the size of the national market supplied.

In order to determine the extent of the large companies' control over this phase it is necessary to look to the height of the barriers that separate the various different national markets, from the costs of transport of refined products (generally higher than the cost of transporting crude) to fiscal legislation and commercial regulation. The rapid growth of consumption of petroleum products has not been accompanied by a parallel growth in the technologically optimal size of refineries.[7] As a result the level of concentration in most countries has thus diminished over time. Especially in periods of supply shortages, however, the difficulties encountered by independent refiners in procuring crude supplies has facilitated the increase in the level of control by the large integrated companies, even in this phase of activity. This has led to an increase in vertical integration which has not always been visible to the non-expert because it has in part taken the shape of long-period agreements under which the small refining firm, even though it remains formally independent, becomes an integral part of the sphere of control of the large integrated company.[8] For the same reason the direct refining activities undertaken by the producing countries is taking on an increasing importance. In fact, the technical characteristics of the refining process, with its limited investment in fixed capital and relatively low labour intensity, makes this type of activity particularly attractive as a means of reinvesting the income generated from oil sales by the producing countries with a low density of population. However, since refining activity is not only conditioned by the problems of crude supply, but also by the problem of finding final product markets, the petroleum-exporting countries which have recently created their own refining industries risk encountering a series of difficulties if they do not proceed to integrate vertically downstream through direct investments or with long-term agreements for distribution of refined products in the markets of the principal consumer countries, i.e. above all the industrialised countries.[9] (Kuwait has recently done this in Europe.) The acquisition and control of a regular market for refined products is of extreme importance in assuring the profitable operation of a refinery. In fact, even if technically it is possible to vary rapidly the utilisation rate of the installation, from an economic point of view it is rather costly to reduce rates of production because of the increase in unit fixed costs which this brings about, and because fixed costs constitute a very high proportion of the total unit costs (analagous to what occurs in the use of pipelines and bulk tankers).

Once in existence refineries are rather inflexible, both in terms of the quality of crude oil they can process, and in terms of the proportions in which the various final products are produced. Securing supplies of crude for all the refining capacity currently in operation thus presents a logistical problem of extreme complexity. It is necessary to assure a regular flow of the various qualities of crude, in the most appropriate proportions for each particular refining installation. When the composition of market demand for the various final products of the refineries changes, the composition of supply can be adjusted only within rather narrow limits, by means of changes in the utilisation rates of refineries with different technological characteristics and output mixes. An additional element of flexibility is to be found in international trade, as long as the composition of the various refined products differs in the final demands of each national market. For example, the share of petrol is particularly high in the United States.[10]

In any event the variations in the structure of demand for petroleum products are normally rather gradual. In the long term a tendency for the 'lighter' refined products to increase has become manifest. To meet this movement the technical characteristics of refineries can be adapted, both through the introduction of new plants as well as through the upgrading of already existing capacity.[11] After the petroleum crisis of the 1970s an impressive restructuring process was started which is still in progress and which is likely to continue throughout the present decade. Further, the entry of the producing countries into the refinery phase has been accompanied by the shutdown of the least-efficient refining plants in the industrialised countries,[12] as well as by notable financial efforts to increase the profitability of those plants that have remained in use. This has involved increasing the yield of light products as well as adaptations of the plants to ensure that they meet the recently instituted anti-pollution regulations.

It is probable that this process will lead to an increase in the level of concentration in refining within the industrialised countries. But this tendency should also be counterbalanced by the entry into the field of the petroleum-producing countries. Indeed, it may prove to be more than offsetting when the entire international market is considered.

VI. DISTRIBUTION

It is possible to produce over 100 different finished petroleum products by refining crude oil. They can be divided into six major groups: gaseous products (liquefied gas, polymers, acetylene, etc.), light distillates (kerosene and petrol), intermediate distillates (gasoil, heating oils, diesel fuels), heavy distillates (paraffin, lubricating oils), residual products (asphalt, waxes, coke, etc.) and waste products (sulphuric acid, which may be used in the production of some fertilisers).[13]

Here we are quite obviously confronted with a case of joint production, perhaps one of the most important from the economic point of view. We have already pointed out in our previous discussions the problems that this raises for any attempt to match the composition of demand for petroleum products to their supply. But, it is also clear that the extent of joint production also presents major difficulties for the setting of prices of the various products produced in the refining process. From the point of view of a vertically integrated company, the only calculation of importance is the relation between its combined receipts from the sale of all petroleum products and their total costs of production. The maximisation of their overall net receipts implies the maximisation of net receipts for each product taken individually.[14] But, the constraint on this maximisation problem faced by the vertically integrated firm takes the form of competition from the other producers already in the market and from potential entrants. It thus constrains the firm's total receipts and not the yield of any single product.[15] Thus custom, tradition and other institutional factors, as well as economic considerations, will play a role in the determination of the prices of each individual product.

Among the economic factors is the necessity of assuring that the 'lighter' products carry higher prices because the technical equipment required to increase their yield from the refining process necessitates a greater investment cost than for the other products. Their use is also considered more 'noble', which usually means a low price elasticity of demand. On account of this fact it will be necessary to examine the problem market by market to identify the available alternatives for each particular product (for example, coal may replace fuel oil in electricity-generating plants), above all in the long term given that the technical specifications may be considered as more or less given in the short term, that is, specifically oriented to the use of a specific product. Examples of this are the use of petrol (gasoline) in cars or the existing stock of electricity-generating plant. But the market form that prevails for the distribution phase of each of the particular products will also enter the determination of their relative prices.

In reality, in some cases such as fuel oil for electricity generation, a proper distribution network is not necessary, while it is an essential element for a product such as petrol. It is only in this second class of product that the prevailing market form in the distribution phase may be considered as an autonomous problem. From this point of view the principal cases to be considered are petrol and derv (gasoline and diesel fuel) which are primarily consumption goods sold to a myriad of diverse final buyers through a multitude of points of final sale. Here we have a case of differentiated oligopoly characterised by the existence of a small number of well-known brand names and in which advertising plays a major role. The 'barriers to entry' which inhibit entry of new competitors in this sector will in this case depend on the start-up costs which the new entrant must bear in order to assure himself a sufficient level of sales (cf. below, Chapter 3, section IX). The importance of advertising as a barrier varies from country to country. It is rather weak, for example, in the United States, while in other countries such as Italy where petroleum prices are administratively controlled by the government, the competition among different brands takes place primarily by means of advertising (see below, Chapter 4, section V).

For the other petroleum products, however, the problem is rather different. In the case of fuel oil for electricity generation, and to a lesser extent for the raw materials for the petrochemical industry and oil for industrial uses, it is the buyer who is in the position of being able to exercise oligopsony power. The direct purchase of crude oil, which is then sent to an independent refinery, is not uncommon in these activities. In such cases, as has been pointed out above, it is not possible to speak of an actual distribution phase. There may be intermediaries who operate in the market (such as those who deal in the 'spot' markets for refined products in Rotterdam or Genoa), but the largest part of the total sales are concluded by direct agreement between the major petroleum companies and the final buyers.

For heating oil the situation has changed over time and even differs by geographical location, depending on the size of the territory that can be served by a refinery of technologically optimum size. In this case, just as for various other petroleum products of secondary importance that it is not necessary to consider separately, the level of concentration is greater in the lesser developed countries and those of low population density. It is normal to find a small number of intermediaries who none the less exhibit a sufficiently high degree of competition, purchasing directly from the refinery and then distributing the products to the various final buyers.

While few important alternatives exist to petroleum products which serve as the raw materials to the petrochemical industry, there are a number of viable alternative energy sources ranging from coal to nuclear power and from geothermal to solar energy. The prices of these alternatives have an influence on the decisions taken on the prices of petroleum products. But it is also true, as has been seen in the period after the petroleum crisis, that the price of petroleum products may have a substantial effect on the prices of the alternate energy sources.

The market form prevailing in these latter sectors, as well as the actions of government fiscal and regulatory agencies, also has an impact on the relative profitability and thus indirectly on the prices of petroleum products (see below, Chapter 6, section VI). However, the prices of the other energy sources only set a maximum limit for the prices of petroleum products because of their competition with such products. A sufficiently high degree of competition within the petroleum sector should lead to prices that are substantially below such a maximum, making the other alternative energy sources of much less relevance to the analysis of the petroleum sector. As a consequence we shall concentrate our attention in the chapters which follow on the petroleum sector, making only passing reference to the other sources of energy when they are of particular relevance to the argument.

3 The Price of Oil: Main Interpretations and their Theoretical Background

I. INTRODUCTION

Various interpretations have been put forward to explain the long-term movements of the price of crude oil, and in particular to provide an explanation for the multifold increase which took place in 1973–4. In this chapter we shall examine the most relevant interpretations. As will be seen, the examination of underlying theoretical positions is very useful for the evaluation of the different points of view in this debate on a concrete problem in applied economics. Such an examination will provide useful elements for assessing the relative interpretative power of the different approaches. Such evaluations require a great deal of caution, however; different interpretations may be derived from a common theoretical approach, and conversely, similar results can be derived from differing theoretical approaches. None the less the usefulness of looking at the theoretical foundations of the various interpretations allows us to isolate crucial hypotheses, and locate weak links in logical chains of reasoning.

We shall start this chapter with consideration of the 'commonsense' explanation of the explosion in the price of oil based on its natural scarcity. This explanation ultimately rests on the idea that price is determined by the interaction between demand and a *given* supply, within the context of a more or less sophisticated marginalist framework. It is interesting to note that a substantially similar result, i.e. a long-term tendency for the real price of oil to increase, can be obtained from analysis in terms of the 'Ricardian' theory of rent.

A third interpretation, put forward by Adelman – a well-known expert on the world petroleum market – is based explicitly on a Marshallian framework. Adelman's approach is in direct contrast with the analysis presented in 1946 by Frankel, which will be the fourth approach considered in this chapter. The factor which separates Adelman and Frankel concerns

23

the degree of competitiveness in the oil sector. Frankel's contention that conditions in the petroleum market closely resemble oligopoly has also emerged from the 'managerial' approach developed by Edith Penrose. The remainder of the chapter will discuss Chevalier's 'Marxian–Marshallian' analysis and the work of a number of representative Arab economists (Abdel-Fadil, Al-Chalabi) which take the viewpoint of the petroleum-producing countries.

The concluding section of this chapter will summarise a number of useful elements which this survey has provided for the approach which will be utilised in the remaining chapters, namely, the interpretation of the oil market as an instance of 'trilateral oligopoly'. In this respect the oligopoly theory developed by Sylos Labini will turn out to be of particular importance.

II. THE SCARCITY OF OIL AND THE MARGINALIST APPROACH

The most generally accepted explanation of the increase in the price of crude oil in the 1970s – apart from the naïve position which simply blames OPEC – is based on the scarcity of petroleum resources. Indeed, scarcity is the factor most widely cited in analyses of long-term trends of oil prices. The importance of scarcity has been endorsed by officials of the OPEC countries and even by executives of oil companies; it also played a crucial role in determining US energy policy in the early 1970s. It should be recalled, at this point, that this theory need not be correct in order to have a direct impact on decision-making, and thus on reality by means of its influence on the strategic choices of the principal protagonists, in particular government agencies. If the theory is incorrect, its application will have consequences none the less; only the consequences will not in general be those that were anticipated, and thus may produce a sub-optimal situation, in comparison to what would have been the case had the policy choices been based on a correct theory. In this regard, it is interesting to note that the recent trend of declining oil prices has been accompanied by a sharp reduction in the number of statements stressing the basic scarcity of oil.

The 'scarcity' interpretation is based on the fact that oil, just as any other natural resource, is only available in finite quantity on earth. An increase in demand, confronting given supply, inevitably provokes a price increase.

A sort of cultural legitimacy to this rather naïve idea has been provided by the recent revival of Malthusianism, spurred by the application of computer models to forecasting. By extrapolation of the past trend of demand for any natural resource, by definition only available in a limited quantity, one must sooner or later arrive at a position where demand exhausts the natural resource. This limit will be reached more rapidly, the higher the ratio between current consumption and the ultimate resource availability, and the higher the rate of growth of demand.

The limit has been described as 'a world where industrial production has sunk to zero. Where population has suffered a catastrophic decline. . . . Where civilization is a distant memory'.[1] Economically induced technical progress — or technical change in general — that might reduce or eliminate the demand for scarce resources is implicitly considered to be insignificant. To the eye of less careful readers (a group which may contain those responsible for policy decisions) this implicit assumption converts an exercise in extrapolation into a reasoned forecast of actual future events. In this context, the apocalyptic tone utilised in describing the perspectives of human societies becomes part of the propaganda for specific policy choices. Yet the highly unsatisfactory results associated with a particular event cannot be considered as proof of a high probability of its occurrence.[2]

Leaving to one side the criticism of this approach based on the fallacy of predicting the future on the basis of the extrapolation of past tendencies, it can be shown that the concept of natural scarcity cannot be used to provide a direct explanation of the level and changes in the price of crude oil. In fact, the *stock* of oil ultimately available, both in already proven and in yet to be discovered fields, cannot be directly compared with demand, which is a *flow*, whose comparable magnitude can be properly defined only with reference to some given time period. Market prices are generally influenced by the relationship between flow demand and *flow* supply per unit of time. Even if ultimate reserves of oil are limited, the flow-supply of oil in any given time interval before its ultimate exhaustion can be increased to match demand, given the existence of unused productive capacity or sufficient time to allow the augmentation of productive capacity. When the price of oil exceeds extraction costs, under competitive conditions a rational economic agent will leave oil in the ground only if he confidently expects a rate of increase in the price of oil to exceed the rate of interest. The difference between the rate of price increase and the rate of interest must be sufficient to cover the high risk implicit in this kind of speculation (among other things, the producer must be confident that the oilfield will remain in his possession in future — which may be far from certain, for both multinational corporations operating in underdeveloped countries subject to the threat of nationalisation, and sovereign governments, who have already nationalised their oilfields and are subject to the threat of internal political upheavals or external invasion).

Other factors will also affect production decisions, such as minimum depletion rates per well, fiscal regulations, or the necessity of ensuring continuous supplies of oil in order not to lose customers. This latter element can have decisive importance in an oligopolistic market such as that for crude oil. But the relation between interest rates and expected rates of change in the price of oil remains the crucial analytical tool for the explanation of production decisions. This relation is the main element of the 'user cost' principle, developed by Keynes (1936, appendix to Chapter 6) and applied to the theory of natural resources by Davidson (1963, 1979c). It should be stressed, however, that the user cost principle does not in itself constitute an *interpretation* of oil prices and the oil market. It indicates the central role of expectations;[3] but the level of, and changes in, user cost remain to be explained, by identifying those objective factors which will influence production decisions through their effect on user costs.

It is here that the marginalist theory of exhaustible natural resources comes in. Assuming perfect competition, a known given amount of the scarce resource, and a constant state of technology, 'the exhaustible resource must appreciate over time at a rate equal to the rate of interest'. According to neoclassical theory, in which a given social rate of discount represents intertemporal preferences, 'the relative rate of change in the current price of the exhaustible resource along the optimal path must be equal to the social rate of discount'.[4] In other words, the price profile to the terminal price of the exhaustible resource is high enough to bring about its complete substitution by other means of production and other consumption goods. Complete substitution is attained simultaneously with the full exhaustion of the resource;[5] before that time the price path and the temporal distribution of consumption is determined by the above-mentioned rule.

This theory is based on very restrictive assumptions, the most important of which is the requirement that there exist future markets for all future dates to the time of depletion.[6] However, the existence of technical change and uncertainty over the actual amount of recoverable reserves deprives this approach of any heuristic content: 'in a world of uncertainty, we are left with a bootstrap theory of the time rate of exploitation of energy resources' (Davidson, Falk and Lee, 1974, p. 420).

The effects of such uncertainty could only be overlooked, and the natural scarcity of ultimately available petroleum would directly affect its current price, only if there was a widely held belief in the imminent exhaustion of oil reserves. Under such conditions rising oil prices would be confidently expected, so that traders in the oil sector would be induced to reduce current supplies. The scarcity of current oil available on the market would consequently generate a rapid, immediate rise in prices. However, barring cases of collective 'auto-suggestion' which can have a noticeable impact only for short time-spans in a competitive market, this situation of self-fulfilling expectations requires eventual verification which can only arise if oil exhaustion really is imminent. The process by which expected future returns are given a present value via a rate of discount, which is especially high when a large element of risk is involved, drastically reduces the relevance of events expected in the distant future on decisions to produce petroleum today. This especially appears to be the explanation of the forecast of the rapid depletion of oil reserves. The thesis that the price of crude oil depends on its scarcity as an exhaustible natural resource requires a precise factual assumption: that crude oil reserves will be exhausted within a short, and correctly predicted, period of time: within years, and not decades.

The assumption, however, is untenable, for even the most pessimistic forecasts predict the depletion of existing oilfields in the distant future. For example, the doomsday forecast of Meadows *et al.* (1975, p. 66), using 1970 as the base year, predicted depletion after twenty years, which exceeded that for gold (nine years: all gold mines should by now be exhausted!), mercury and silver (thirteen years), tin (fifteen years), and zinc (eighteen years). A less dramatic, and less incredible set of forecasts was arbitrarily constructed by the Meadows group by multiplying the existing reserves by five. Taking into account the expected growth in oil consumption this procedure gave fifty years of exploitable reserves.

These estimates, however, are based on a conceptual error. The MIT scientists confused estimates of proven reserves and estimates of ultimately available oil, two very different concepts. Their data refer to proven reserves, while the second notion is the more relevant to the discussion of the ultimate exhaustion of a non-reproducible natural resource such as oil. Proven reserves in fact correspond to a sort of 'shelf-inventory' of available product used by oil producers; the location, size and characteristics (quality of crude, depth and pressure of the field) of proven reserves are already known, and on the basis of such data it has been confidently decided that they are economically recoverable with known technology at prevailing price—cost relationships. (Hence when oil prices rise, *ceteris paribus*, the proven reserves of the oil companies' 'self-inventory' also increases.) The concept was defined to meet accounting requirements to report realistically the contribution of ownership of oilfields to equity value on the balance sheets of the oil companies. On the other hand, the second concept — ultimately recoverable oil — adds to proven reserves the known oil deposits that ultimately will be recoverable consequent upon improvements in extraction technology and/or in the price—cost relationship. The proven reserves should be considered as a producible means of production, since their production can be increased through investment in exploration (even if this is a stochastic process of production, where there is no guarantee of obtaining output). In fact, proven reserves are higher today than they were in 1970.

Estimates of ultimately recoverable oil are necessarily very tentative and display great variability. A conservative estimate for 1975 has been provided by a Rand Corporation research project sponsored by the CIA the results, after surveys of the giant oilfields, consideration of their geographical distribution, and the distribution over time of discoveries of new fields, are that ultimately recoverable oil 'is equivalent to 60 to 90 years of world consumption at current rates' (Nehring 1978, p. 89). This estimate has, however, already become suspect because its basic hypothesis i.e. that discovery of new giant fields has become even more difficult, has been disproven by the number of such discoveries since 1975.[7]

Other estimates are more optimistic. For instance Odell, a well-known independent oil market expert, puts the figure of ultimately recoverable oil reserves at double the Rand figure. Odell (1979) foresees oil to be available at least to the year 2020, even with consumption at five times present levels. If allowance is made for reductions in consumption induced by the increase in the price of crude oil and the trend towards substitution of gas for oil, annual consumption of crude oil should be stabilised at the present level. Oil would then be available well into the twenty-first century.

The more optimistic estimates thus announce a less alarming future availability of crude oil. But even accepting the more conservative estimates, such as one made in a recent AGIP study (Colitti, 1981), it is very doubtful that current market conditions should be influenced by the exhaustion of oil reserves at such a remote date.[8] It is hard to take issue with Adelman's emphatic statement (made just before the 1973 oil crisis) that at any price above $2 per barrel, 'the higher [than cost] crude oil . . . prices . . . reflect no scarcity of crude oil present or foreseen'.[9]

III. RICARDIAN RENT

Another way of approaching the idea that oil prices are determined by the scarcity of oil as a natural resource involves application of the Ricardian theory of differential rent. Every oilfield has peculiar individual character-istics: extraction costs vary widely from one field to another. There are different qualities of crude, and each implies a specific refining cost and supplies a basket of refined products of particular proportions. Finally, the geographical location of each field will imply different transportation costs to the final market. Under competitive conditions, therefore, there will be a tendency to start exploitation with those fields considered the most profitable, given extraction costs, the quality of crude (gravity and sulphur content), and transport costs. Only the relative exhaustion of such fields and the growth in demand will make it necessary to bring less profitable fields into production and/or to adopt more costly methods of secondary and tertiary recovery (see above, Chapter 2, section III). The increase in extraction and transport costs for any given quality of crude oil must then necessarily be connected with an increase in the price of oil on the markets of consuming countries. The 'owners' of the most productive oilfields will earn a differential rent (including a differential rent on the 'intensive margin of cultivation' when more costly secondary and tertiary recovery methods are adopted side by side with primary recovery). Rent can thus be considered as a phenomenon which levels the yield to producing firms to bring about a uniform rate of return on their investment.[10]

This theory, commonly applied in the analysis of natural resources, is of limited pertinence to the oil market. Differences in costs and quality between different oilfields can explain the existence of differential rents for the 'better' oilfields; but such differences do not explain the gap between crude oil prices and extraction costs (i.e. 'absolute rent') nor its changes over time.

A great deal of caution is necessary even in the application of this theory to the specific issue of differential rent for which it is relevant, since the assumptions on which it relies do not apply to the oil market for a number of reasons. First, the choice of the most 'fertile' oilfields among all alternative fields must be limited to those already located, so that a substantial element of uncertainty is represented by the possibility of future discovery of more productive oilfields. Secondly, there are substantial market imperfections both for the 'owners' of oilfields and the producing firms. Oilfields located in different countries are subject to different laws, often enabling more costly oilfields to compete effectively by means of custom barriers, as was the case in the United States from the late 1950s and the 1960s. Such conditions do not imply differential rents for less costly oilfields located outside the custom barriers. Analogously, producing firms, once they have acquired the right to develop a very profitable oilfield, often refrain from fully exploiting it in order to avoid disruptive consequences on the market and to increase profitability in more costly oilfields that they may operate. This behaviour was very common in the Middle East, due to the fact that all major oilfields were exploited by consortia of the big oil firms who, *de facto*, jointly planned overall production levels to avoid market shortages and gluts.[11] Factors such as these reduce the applicability of the theory of differential rent even within the context of 'static' analysis to which it normally applies. Still greater difficulties arise when it is used in order to explain the increases in crude oil prices in the 1970s.

In fact, many contend that the phenomenon of increasing costs and prices is not a 'static', but a historical phenomenon, since the discovery of big, profitable oilfields becomes ever less likely over time. Exploration costs per barrel of newly discovered oil thus increase, and the new oilfields will be more costly to exploit. But if the process is viewed in a historical context, technical progress should also be taken into account. There is no reason why technical progress, by reducing costs (obviously in real terms) in exploration and in production in both already exploited and in newly discovered oilfields, should not counterbalance any historical tendency to the exploration of less promising provinces and to the utilisation of more and more costly oilfields. In principle, the net result could be either a decreasing or an increasing price of oil. Indeed, this is what happened in agriculture, thanks to the dominating role played by technical progress. Notwithstanding the grim forecasts of Malthus and other Classical economists, worried by a tendency toward a stationary state due to the decreasing productivity of land, the cost of agricultural products (in real terms, e.g. in terms of the quantity of labour directly and indirectly necessary to produce them) displayed a strong downward secular trend. The same is true if we look at the 'real costs' (net of taxes and royalties) of oil products over the past century.

In particular, this 'Ricardian' explanation misses the mark in the sharp discontinuity evidenced in the oil price booms of 1973–4 and 1979–80. Certainly the price shock induced far higher investment than would otherwise have been the case, both in exploratory activity and in the exploitation of costlier oilfields and through the use of costlier secondary and tertiary recovery methods. But with equal certainty the price increases did not spring from the more costly exploration and production. It is a well-known fact that even at the price prevailing in 1970, i.e. before the first oil crisis, the exploitation of Middle Eastern oilfields might have been easily intensified not only to satisfy the current increase in demand, but also to replace a major proportion of production of the more costly oilfields in the United States and elsewhere (see, for example, Adelman, 1972; US Senate, 1974). Strategic investment decisions for more costly North Sea and Alaska oil, besides the rich Mexican 'Reforma Province', had already been taken before the first oil crisis, even though the activities in all these areas acquired a new momentum after it occurred — especially after the nationalisations in the Middle East and Northern Africa, and the experiences of disruptions in supplies from those areas due to political events. Even before the first oil crisis, strategic reasons, such as dispersion of political risk and fears of nationalisations in Middle Eastern and North African countries, were probably critical in the decisions to exploit more costly oilfields which were located in more stable areas. Expectations that technical progress would bring about decreasing costs in offshore production paralleled by stable transportation costs — a phase of activity considered technologically mature — also played a role in the decision to exploit North Sea oil, located near to important consuming areas (MacKay and Mackay, 1975). In any case, it is inappropriate to depict the recent events through the 'Ricardian' causal chain of (i) increasing demand coupled with given maximum supply from existing outlets, (ii) increasing price, (iii) exploitation of more costly new outlets.

IV. COMPETITION IN THE OIL SECTOR ACCORDING TO ADELMAN'S MARSHALLIAN ANALYSIS

An explanation of the tendency of oil prices opposed to that based on the Ricardian theory of rent has been suggested by Adelman. In his 1972 book he maintained that oil prices, then less than $2 per barrel, would be subject to a strong downward pressure. The wide availability of low cost crude oil would not only preclude the 'Ricardian' result of an increasing trend in oil prices, on the contrary it would foster an opposite trend. Adelman considered this downward trend strong enough to be ultimately bound to defeat any restraint on competition. This assertion is also supported by Adelman's analysis of the degree of competition in the world petroleum market: in Adelman's opinion, competitive forces would dominate, both among companies and among producing countries, much more than it would appear from writings such as those of Frankel (1969) and Penrose (1968).

This assertion about the degree of competition in the oil market is of decisive importance for Adelman's interpretation. His attempt at evaluating costs is meticulous and well documented, and constitutes a necessary reference for anyone interested in the field. But, when we are concerned with explaining the price of crude oil, it is of little relevance to establish that production and development costs in the major Middle Eastern oilfields are below 20 cents per barrel (at 1970 prices), if one is then forced to admit to the existence of substantial monopoly profit margins, and/or that agreement between producing countries enables them to extract an 'absolute rent' on their oilfields, with both elements larger in size than average full (variable plus fixed) costs.

In this respect Adelman vigorously disputes the earlier thesis of Frankel (see below), of a natural tendency to oligopoly. Frankel's theory is based on the premise that the oil market displays increasing returns to scale because of a high ratio between fixed and variable costs, giving bigger firms a strong cost advantage over smaller ones. Also, once investments in producing, refining, transporting, and marketing facilities have been made, any individual firm will experience lower unit costs as its production increases. A price higher than variable unit costs will generate sustained production up to full capacity utilisation, and the ensuing glut will depress prices. As soon as prices drop below variable costs, production will collapse. But before that occurs, when the price drops below average unit costs, the market will experience a more stable reduction in output distributed over a longer period of time, corresponding to the residual economic life of existing plants. As a result of the fall in production below demand, prices will again increase, and a new cycle begins. The market will avoid continuous instability only if regulated by direct government controls or by the development of an oligopolistic cartel.

These two basic features of Frankel's analysis of the oil market, i.e. instability and tendency to oligopoly, are both refuted by Adelman's rejection of Frankel's crucial assumption of increasing returns to scale. In Adelman's view, on the contrary, it is decreasing returns which predominate. Such an assumption, of course, implies competitive conditions and ensures market stability. Adelman refers to the theory of Alfred Marshall in support of his position;[12] but no matter how well documented Adelman's factual evidence may be, it is on less solid ground as far as analytical consistency is concerned.

Adelman (1972) declares that the situation in the United States 'is unique. Since the regulatory system has built up excess capacity . . . output could be expanded within those limits very cheaply' (p. 67). Yet increasing returns to scale in the United States oil sector are not relevant, since 'it can be stated that Persian Gulf development—operating cost today fixes the supply price of oil, *including necessary finding costs* . . . for the whole world' (p. 75; italics as in the original). It is clear from these explicit passages that the supply price must include not only the current operating costs of already drilled wells but also the 'necessary' developmental and exploration costs, for 'exploration is *needed to prevent an otherwise inevitable rise* in developing—operating costs' (p. 74; italics as in the original). On this Adelman elaborates the ingenious concept of Maximum Economic Finding Costs (with an analytical procedure recalling the equalisation of the intensive and extensive margin in differential rent theory):

> At the margin, development cost in known fields equals development cost plus finding cost in new fields. Higher finding cost drives up development cost. Zero new discoveries would eventually mean much higher development costs as old reservoirs were depleted. Discovery is necessary to stave this off. Hence the estimate of development costs rising as more and more of the oil-in-place is depleted gives us the Maximum Economic Finding Cost (MEFC), the penalty for doing nothing.[13]

As for transport, Adelman states that 'ship owners and operators are many and relatively small, entry is easy and cheap; it is a purely competitive industry' (p. 7). Nor does Adelman see any check to competition coming from integrated oil firms. A fringe of non-integrated firms will ensure competitive pressure on integrated firms in all aspects of their operation, since even if transfer prices on crude sales between a producing and a refining or trading affiliate of the same group can differ from 'true market' prices (due to the convenience, mainly from tax reasons − see below, Chapter 4, section 4 − of attributing most of the profit to the production stage), the final price of refined products must be the same for integrated and non-integrated firms.

From what has been said above it is clear that Adelman's theory of decreasing returns applies to the long term and to the industry as a whole. But instability can manifest itself as a result of short-term increasing returns to the individual firm. As was made clear in the theoretical debates of the 1920s over returns to scale and the theory of the firm, the elimination of a tendency towards an oligopolistic market form requires decreasing returns in the long run to the individual firm (see Sraffa, 1925, 1926; and for a survey of the debate, Ridolfi, 1972). The reason for this should be evident: according to marginalist theory, under perfect competition each individual firm must be so small as to be able to sell any level of output without producing an effect on the prevailing market price, and to acquire the necessary means of production in any desired amounts at the prevailing rates of remuneration. Adelman's support for his hypothesis of decreasing returns, however, rests on factors such as increasing development costs on already known oilfields and the decreasing probability of finding new giant oilfields, which refer to the industry as a whole. Under competitive conditions, these factors will cause an equalising differential rent to be paid to 'owners' of the oilfields and not to oil companies as such. Therefore, they should not constrain the production and investment decisions of the individual firm, even though they may affect the development of the sector as a whole. But precisely such a constraint on the growth of individual firms is necessary in order to prevent the emergence of a tendency to monopoly or oligopoly; and this constraint can only be provided by conditions of increasing returns to each individual firm. If the growth of individual firms is checked by increasing difficulties of discovering new oilfields or of developing already known ones, these factors should rather be taken as indicating the prevalence of non-competitive conditions in the sector, with firms being already so big that competition (as defined by marginalist theory) no longer prevails. Indeed, nothing in Adelman's wealth of data denies that bigger firms produce at a lower unit cost than smaller firms; Adelman only maintains that increasing quantitites of oil, *in the sector as a whole*, can be produced at an increasing cost. This assertion is not sufficient to exclude the existence of oligopolistic forces.[14]

V. FRANKEL AND OLIGOPOLY

The high ratio between fixed and variable costs stressed by Frankel (1969) is sufficient to preclude a stable competitive equilibrium. Variable unit costs will be roughly constant up to full capacity utilisation; it is very unlikely, anyhow, for these costs to increase sufficiently with short-term increases in capacity utilisation for the individual firm as to more than counterbalance the decrease in fixed unit costs. If competitive conditions exist, therefore, the individual firm will find it convenient to expand the scale of its activity up to full capacity utilisation, since, under competitive conditions, by assumption the individual firm's demand for additional factors of production will not influence their price, and the increase in its level of production will not affect the price of the product. The impossibility of a stable competitive outcome invites either regulatory intervention, as the pro-rationing system first established by the Texas Railroad Commission, or an oligopolistic structure. Frankel does not try to determine which of the two alternative outcomes is the most likely one. His central contention is a negative one, namely, the instability of competitive conditions in the oil market. Nevertheless Frankel emphasises some technological characteristics, related to the minimum optimal size of investment in fixed capital, that are conducive to oligopoly.

The oligopoly theory of Sylos Labini (1969), advanced some ten years after Frankel's book, is centred on a technological barrier to the entry of new firms whenever the minimum optimal size of new plants is large relative to the total size of the market. Hence the entry of a new firm into the sector will provoke a fall in the price of the product, due to the significant increase in total supply necessary to accommodate the new plant. (Due to the high ratio between fixed and variable costs, none of the already established producers will be prepared to reduce its own production to accommodate the additional supply of the newcomer.) Thus product prices and profits may (and generally will) be higher than under competitive conditions, without this inducing new firms to enter the sector, since potential competitors are discouraged by the change in price and profits that their entry would provoke.

According to Frankel — who however does not have a fully-fledged theory of oligopoly, and is thus prevented from deriving all the implications of his analysis — this is precisely the situation which prevails in at least two out of the four stages into which he subdivides the oil sector for the purposes of his analysis. Frankel suggests that small producers do not suffer from any size disadvantage in exploration, the development of newly discovered oilfields and production of crude, while in transport (especially where pipelines are concerned) and in refining there are strong discontinuities and increasing returns to scale which small firms cannot capture. Thus for technical reasons larger firms enjoy strong advantages, which enable them to exercise control over the market. Frankel does not appear to attach any particular importance to the final stage, the distribution of refined products. This stage, in fact, relates to an entirely separate set of markets (such as fuel oil, petrol, bunker oil, naphtha etc.), each with specific individual characteristics and hence better examined separately. For a large majority of these markets, the labels of imperfect competition or differentiated oligopoly must be considered as the most appropriate.

Frankel's interpretation is, in fact, supported by the history of the initial stages of the oil industry. The development of Rockefeller's Standard Oil Trust was originally based on the control of pipelines and transport in general, and secondarily on the control of refining. Production of crude — at least within the United States — was a very competitive activity, with many small producers; competition also prevailed in distribution.

Frankel, however, lacking a fully-fledged theory of oligopoly, did not recognise that a rapid increase in the size of the market is bound to decrease the strength of oligopolistic control, if the optimal size of plants does not grow in the same proportion as the total size of the market. Anti-trust rules can also be a very effective counterforce checking tendencies to concentration and the exploitation of monopolistic or oligopolistic market power. In this respect, it should be sufficient to recall the 1911 dismantling of the Standard Oil Trust, and — again in the United States — the regulation of 'common carriers' forbidding the imposition of differential prices to different customers.[15] Moreover, Frankel's analysis could not foresee the growing role of other producing countries and the possibility that they might exercise control of the market.

VI. PENROSE'S MANAGERIAL CONTROL

Frankel wrote his book before the Second World War, and it was first published in 1946. Since that time the oil market has experienced its most rapid growth. The change in the size of the market is implicitly stressed by Adelman, who does not find any empirical evidence of a relevant role played by barriers to entry due to technical requirements for a large optimal size of plants at any stage in the oil sector. How can we then explain the fact that the Seven Sisters have maintained their oligopolistic domination over the oil market?

According to Penrose (1968, 1971, 1975, 1977), from the 1930s to the 1960s major oil companies were able to exercise considerable control over the international oil market thanks to their joint control over Middle Eastern oil reserves through historical—political factors rather than through technical factors. If initially a formal cartel was necessary for establishing an oligopolistic equilibrium (the 'Red line' agreement of July 1928, and especially the 'As Is' or Achnacarry Agreement of August 1928), then the reciprocal knowledge of production plans ensured by the joint operation of the major oilfields was sufficient to ensure tacit collusion. In particular circumstances, such as the Iranian crisis of 1951 or Suez in 1957, the companies were allowed explicitly to organise the co-ordination of their activities through committees based in London and New York (on this see Sampson, 1975; Blair, 1976; Turner, 1980).

As far as the subsequent period is concerned, Penrose stresses the growing role of American 'independent' companies (see Chapter 4, section V, below) and of the State oil companies of some consuming countries. Their increasing share in the exploitation of North Africa and Middle East oilfields implied a growing competitive pressure on the oligopolistic system maintained by the Seven Sisters. This competitive pressure is shown by the downward pressure on the prices of crude oil and refined products after the Second World War. In turn, the 'multinationalisation' of the American independents (i.e. their growing sales of crude and refined products on non-US, especially European, markets) is seen more as a phenomenon due to specific changes in US customs rules (i.e. the introduction of a quota system for oil imports) than to the existence of a profit incentive superior to what barriers to entry might have guaranteed to existing firms.

The 1973 oil crisis is seen as the outcome of three concomitant, but distinct, historical tendencies: (i) the political conflict in the Middle East, centred on the existence and growth of the state of Israel; (ii) the growing will, and especially the growing capability, of oil-exporting countries to appropriate control of their oil industry; and (iii) the growing dependence of industrialised countries (particularly Europe and Japan) on Middle Eastern, especially Arab, oil (Penrose, 1977). In this interpretation of the 1973 oil crisis, political factors are given centre stage, while market structure and its determinants are allowed but a secondary role.[16]

This approach may be correct for assessing a quick succession of crucial events within a short time-span, but it does not provide a satisfactory basis for evaluating long-term trends in the oil sector. Everything, and anything, appears possible *if only* companies and governments had adopted one specific set of decisions or another. Yet, market forces ultimately will permit only a 'correct' set of decisions,[17] while generating losses for those agents in the sector responsible for 'incorrect' decisions. The fact is that the 'managerial' approach adopted by Penrose[18] can be very useful in interpreting the actual behaviour of the oil market step by step; but the absence of a general theoretical framework within which structural data (such as technological elements and the size of the market) can elucidate the possible equilibrium outcomes resulting from the interplay of market forces and policy decisions may limit its explanatory power for the long-term evolution of market structure.

A useful contribution of the managerial approach to the analysis of the oil sector lays in its stress on the role of the set of rules and conventions which constitute the framework for the operation of the big Middle East producing consortia, as being the decisive instrument for the oligopolistic control of the oil market by the major companies. Oligopoly is no longer a matter of technological discontinuities, but of specific commercial rules conducive to joint control, as well as to joint planning of the exploitation of major oilfields. Barriers to entry are no longer to be solely located in technological characteristics of the oil sector, but also in the managerial capability of devising and enforcing an appropriate institutional framework, inducing major companies to strict co-operation. These represent the most important changes which have arisen since Frankel wrote; but the managerial approach cannot be considered, nor was it intended by Penrose, to provide a general theory of the functioning of the oil sector.

VII. CHEVALIER: MARXIAN IDEOLOGY AND MARSHALLIAN ECONOMICS

Any theoretical approach for the analysis of a specific sector must be inserted into a wider framework depicting the economic system as a whole. Often there is resort to the marginalist or neoclassical framework centred around the notions of scarcity and choice, with the economic system portrayed as a 'one-way' avenue leading from scarce original 'factors of production' to goods and services utilised in final consumption. Much less frequent is the reference to the 'surplus approach', developed by Classical economists and by Marx, depicting the economic process as a circular flow of production and productive consumption.[19]

One 'surplus' account may be traced to the work of Chevalier (1975, 1977). Part of his terminology (surplus, exploitation, and so on), as well as the attention to the role of political strength in economic relations, comes from the Classical and Marxian tradition. Curiously, however, Chevalier's main thesis is fully grounded in a purely marginalist theoretical framework, and more precisely on the same argument — the Marshallian theory of the firm — used by Adelman.

Chevalier sees the oil sector as producing a 'surplus', which he defines as the difference between the realised value of the refined products in their final markets and the 'real' cost of production.[20] This surplus can be appropriated either by consuming countries through taxation, or by the oil companies, or by the oilfield owners, that is, the producing countries. The history of oil can thus be written as the history of struggles among the three contending groups, where relative success is determined by power relationships.

To fill the idea of the three contending groups with content, however, requires the identification of some objective basis for evaluating power relationships and the recognition that none of these groups is homogeneous, so that inside each group there is an internal oligopolistic struggle. Such an objective basis is identified by Chevalier in the sign of the first derivative of the 'cost in evolution' for the production of crude oil, entailing some historical or dynamic counterpart of the neoclassical notion of marginal cost (see Adelman's notion of Maximum Economic Finding Costs). For Chevalier (1975, p. 218) the market price of crude oil 'is equal, in theory and excepting some transitory crisis, to the cost in evolution of the last necessary field'. When the 'cost in evolution' decreases, we are confronted with a buyer's market and a 'natural tendency to a fall in prices'. When costs increase there is a producer's market, and the price of oil tends to increase.[21] Besides, under the latter circumstance 'the [average] cost of crude supplied is less than the world cost in evolution of crude', so that 'the market price necessarily includes a rent which is appropriated by producing countries through the fiscal mechanism' (Chevalier, 1975, p. 218). The oil crisis is thus explained, according to Chevalier, by the fact that 'since 1970 a period of increasing costs seems to have begun'.[22] This is the crucial element, while a subordinate role is attributed to what Chevalier (1975, p. 14) calls 'the degree of social consciousness', referring to the process of political and cultural decolonisation, which plays an important role in his reconstruction of events:

> with the evolution of productive forces, consuming and producing countries become conscious of the situation of exploitation to which they are subject. As a consequence of falling costs, such new consciousness can modify the strength of buyers (importing countries), but only by very little that of sellers (exporting countries). . . . In the phase of increasing costs . . . on the contrary, the seller prevails since prices tend to increase by more than average costs.[23]

Unfortunately, Chevalier's interpretation suffers from two fundamental misunderstandings, theoretical and factual. The theoretical defect in the attempt at utilising marginalist theory in analysing the working of the oil sector has already been exposed in reference to Adelman's writings. Increasing marginal costs are compatible with a competitive equilibrium, while decreasing costs are not; but reference should be made to marginal costs for individual firms, not for the sector as a whole (as Chevalier, following Adelman, does).[24] Unfortunately the tendencies of the marginal cost for the sector as a whole reveal nothing about the relative power of firms, consumers and oil exporters unless we add some unwarranted assumptions to the effect that increasing costs favour competition among firms and collusion among oil-producing countries, while decreasing costs correspond to collusion among firms and competition among oilfield owners.

Moreover, Chevalier's thesis of a transition from a long period of decreasing costs to a new era of increasing costs is far from satisfactory, as the author himself recognises. First of all, prices of crude oil are now well above typical extraction costs; second, the causal relationship is opposite to the one Chevalier maintains: it is because of high prices that costly fields are exploited and not vice versa, since existing demand could be satisfied by more intensive exploitation of less costly Middle Eastern oilfields. In other words, the historical evolution of average or marginal costs for the production of crude oil cannot be used as the basis for explaining trends in crude oil prices. Costs are themselves influenced by those economic and political factors which concur in determining the structure of the oil sector. Specifically, maximum costs, far from determining crude oil prices, are determined by them. As a matter of fact, it is also current and expected crude oil prices that are the basis of decisions to initiate the exploitation of more costly oilfields (or oil provinces), rather than intensifying the exploitation of less costly ones.

VIII. OPEC ECONOMISTS

The high cost of 'replenishing' proven reserves with new discoveries is often referred to by advocates of the OPEC position as a reason for a 'fair' (i.e. relatively high in comparison to costs) price of crude oil. But this reasoning, like the references to the natural scarcity of crude oil, is generally intended more as a justification of the relatively high prices of crude oil (compared to costs), than as a direct causal explanation of current price levels. OPEC economists are more interested in identifying a feasible — and optimal — pricing policy than formulating a theory of oil prices. They thus implicitly admit the existence of market power of producing countries, as well as of major companies and consuming countries. Even if it is only implicit, the 'vision' that lies behind the analysis of alternative policy options is similar to that of trilateral oligopoly which will be outlined in detail in the rest of this book. Thus we shall find it useful to refer to the contributions of OPEC economists at the appropriate places in the following chapters.

There are two points in their analyses that deserve separate treatment: the role of supply shortages and the behaviour of the spot market in creating instability, and the progressive change in the structure of the oil market represented by the increasing role played by the producing countries.

On the first point, a compact sketch of a rather widespread view is offered by Abdel-Fadil, with reference to a paper by the Kuwaiti oil minister (Al-Sabah, 1979):

One might be tempted to speak of the existence of a certain 'price-cycle' in international oil markets. Given the recent historical experience, the mechanics of this cycle may be depicted in the following schematic way: Supply shortages (Oct. 1973) → price increases (Dec. 1973) → shortfall in demand for oil due to curbs on oil consumption (1974—77) → freeze in oil prices (1974—77) → stimulation of demand for oil (1978) → . . . shortage of the first half of 1979 → . . . beginning of a new price cycle. (Abdel-Fadil, 1979, p. 5)

For Abdel-Fadil this 'regular' cycle is modified by the 'erratic shortages in the supply of oil' (such as the one following the Khomeini revolution in Iran), which immediately and strongly affect 'the behaviour of oil prices on "spot" and "future" markets'. As Abdel-Fadil (pp. 5–6) points out, 'oil companies were able to reap tremendous profits simply by being active operators in oil spot markets. . . . The early signs of higher prices [in 1979] came not from OPEC but from British and Norwegian companies with North Sea oil. They had short-term contracts and reacted more quickly to the market shortages.' On the contrary, 'OPEC countries are desperately trying to bring back a stable oil market' (even if 'they are equally keen to maintain the *real value* of their chief export against persistent world inflation and the falling dollar').

This points to the role of the spot market, which by-passes long-term contracts. Its growth since the 1960s, from the mere fringe of a largely vertically integrated oil sector to a minority but significant share of the market, is a phenomenon connected to the loss of the nearly full control previously exercised by the major oil companies on Middle East production consortia. The spot market is still relatively small (about 10 per cent of internationally traded crude oil and refined products), but it is no longer insignificant for the determination of world average crude oil prices, for it influences pricing decisions of producing countries. This is also shown by the development of speculative future markets for crude oil and oil products, which requires as a precondition a sizeable spot market. In principle, spot markets must display less price stability than the corresponding forward markets (see Davidson, 1972); but these latter can also be quite flexible.

The role and the relative stability of spot and future markets will obviously depend on the changing structure of the oil sector. The changes in this structure are specifically stressed by OPEC writers (in particular, see Al-Chalabi, 1980). In fact, during the 1970s there was a dramatic shift, especially in the Middle East, from the concession regime (by which oil companies determined production decisions) to joint ventures between companies and states, and finally to 'service contracts'. In this last stage, producing countries retain direct responsibility for pricing and production decisions, injecting a profound change into the structure of the oil market. The majors' 'system of control', up to the end of the 1960s, allowed them to link overall production, with a high degree of precision, to world demand (Blair, 1976, pp. 99–101). Now the overall planning of production through the allocation of quotas to individual member countries is exactly *the* issue on which OPEC is least successful. Thus the attempt at co-ordinating price decisions is undermined by the failure in planning the overall supply of crude. Exporting countries, when compelled to accept a reduction in their market share, or when confronted with pressing balance-of-payments problems, engage in some evasion, both of production quotas and of officially established price differentials, so that the degree of competition seems to have been growing in the past few years. As a consequence, major oil companies still retain a strong influence over production decisions, for they represent the only possible outlet for most of the oil produced by OPEC countries; their refusal to buy from any specific country can oblige it to limit production. As Al-Chalabi (1980, pp. 119, 141) stresses, 'with the OPEC take-over of price administration, market conditions or supply/ demand balances started to play a greater role in setting OPEC price levels', so that 'the present situation of almost totally uncoordinated marketing policies could, especially in times of a buyer's market, further strengthen the bargaining position of the buyers and thus add to potentially harmful competition among producers'. But Al-Chalabi, whose main interest concerns OPEC policy choices, does not explicitly consider other relevant elements of the new market structure, e.g. (i) the interests of the 'majors', coupled with their control over the markets for final products, and (ii) the interest of the biggest consuming countries. Both these elements combine to make the price of crude oil resistant to downward market pressures, originating in the conditions of supply—demand in the market. We shall consider these elements in the following chapters; here it is sufficient to stress that an analysis oriented towards the definition of optimal strategies for a specific group of actors in the oil market cannot fully substitute a more objective analysis of the oil sector and its evolution.

IX. THE OIL MARKET AS A CASE OF TRILATERAL OLIGOPOLY

The survey of the main attempts to provide a theoretical basis for explaining crude oil prices conducted in the previous pages leaves us with a number of useful elements, which we can use as the starting point for the attempt to construct a new interpretation. First, there are some negative factors. Neither the natural scarcity of oil, nor marginal cost, provides us with a satisfactory basis for the explanation of oil prices. Secondly, in the discussion of the prevailing market form, oligopoly rather than competition appears a better description of the international market for crude oil.

These elements suggest an interpretation of the oil market as 'trilateral oligopoly'. Agents in the oil market can be grouped as (i) producing countries, (ii) oil companies, and (iii) consuming countries. Within each of these groups a situation prevails which can be characterised as oligopolistic, including many individual agents, a few of which, by virtue of their size, have a direct significant influence on the market, while the bulk of the others can only do so by jointly entering or leaving the market.

Thus we can utilise the 'Classical' oligopoly theory developed by Sylos Labini (1969). It is grouped in the Classical ('surplus') approach, developed by, for example, Petty, Cantillon, Quesnay, Smith, Ricardo and Marx, and recently revived by Piero Sraffa. This approach is opposed to the prevailing marginalist or neoclassical one, which is based on the concept of scarcity and on the joint determination of equilibrium prices and quantities through a supply-and-demand mechanism.

Within the Classical approach, the economic process is one of continuous reproduction (and enlargement) of the material bases of human societies. At the beginning of the production period, specific quantities of commodities are advanced, as means of production or as subsistence for the workers employed. In a 'productive' system the utilisation of these commodities yields outputs in excess of the initial stocks: the excess constitutes the surplus, consisting of a heterogeneous set of goods. As a first approximation, production prices are determined on the basis of the competitive assumption of a uniform rate of profits throughout all sectors of the economy. Income distribution between wages and profits, as well as sectoral and overall rates of capital accumulation and of growth of output, are determined separately from prices. This analytic procedure leaves room for the consideration of the influence of historical and social forces on these variables. In the marginalist approach — reference is here made specifically to general intertemporal equilibrium models — all these variables are determined together with prices within the general model, as a straightforward deduction from consumers' tastes, technology, and initial availability of scarce resources.

From what has just been said, the Classical approach appears to be more flexible than the marginalist approach, especially with respect to the scarcity concept and on the existence of market forms different from competition.

As a natural resource, oil is 'ultimately' an exhaustible asset and marginalist economics claims to be the economics of scarcity, while Classical political economy on the other hand stresses reproducibility (see, for example, Pasinetti 1981). This might lead to the conclusion that marginalist theory is the most appropriate for the analysis of the oil sector. But the differences between the two approaches over the issue of scarcity are *not* those summarised above. Scarcity can be dealt with by the Classical approach, as in the case of land in the theory of rent. In addition it is explicitly considered as a prerequisite for a good to be considered an economic good, i.e. a 'commodity'. Conversely, within the marginalist scheme scarcity is not a simple prerequisite, but a quantifiable element which finds its expression in the price of the commodity. Embodied in its conception is the condition that the natural resource be available in a *given* quantity; this condition is not required by the Classical approach.

Something similar can be said with respect to the existence of non-competitive market forms. Marginalists usually dwell on the monopoly and competitive extremes, leaving an undefined intermediate ground to other market forms.[25] Within the Classical approach, on the other hand, free competition (perfect freedom of entry in a given sector, irrespective of the absolute size of firms or of the administered or market nature of prices) represents the analytic touchstone. The difficulty of entry, and the changes in the entry obstacles in time, explain the difference between the sectoral profit rate and the competitive one (which, according to a long tradition, can be related to the long-run rate of interest) and its evolution; this difference in turn, considering the 'difficulty of production', leads to the determination of commodity prices. Any movement in the price unrelated to technical change or to changes in the distributive variables (wage rate and general rate of profits) can be assigned to a change in the 'conditions of entry' in the sector under review.

These 'conditions of entry' depend on the specifics of oligopolistic market structure. Sylos Labini (1969) distinguishes 'plant', 'industrial' and 'financial' concentration, according to whether the oligopolistic unit is a single or multi-plant firm, or a financial conglomerate. Moreover, 'concentrated' oligopoly is distinguished from 'differentiated' oligopoly, in which trademarks are important in inducing a segmentation in the commodity market which comes to be subdivided into as many specific markets as the firms producing in the sector. Thus barriers that are internal to the sector will arise, which will increase not only the difficulty of entry, but also the difficulty of adopting competitive strategies to increase market shares by those firms already operating within the sector. Cases of differentiated oligopoly can be identified, in particular, in durable consumer goods production (e.g. cars, television sets), and some non-durables (e.g. gasoline), while concentrated oligopoly is common in the intermediate goods sectors (e.g. steel, fuel oil). In concentrated oligopoly with single-plant firms, a technological barrier to the entry of new firms into the sector arises when the minimum economically viable size is large relative to the total size of the market, making the after-entry product price lower as supply increases due to production from the new entrant.

Thus, in sectors where oligopolistic conditions prevail, equilibrium price depends on the technology, the prices of means of production, the general competitive profit rate, and the severity of the barriers to entry. Under 'concentrated' oligopoly, this latter element will in turn depend on technology (determining alternative plant sizes and the advantages of big plants over smaller ones), on the size of the market, price-elasticity and expected growth rate of demand. Other factors involved may be the effectiveness of advertising under 'differentiated' oligopoly, savings in overheads for multiplant firms or conglomerates, and the cost and availability of finance. All these factors allow for a number of possible equilibria, differing from each other with respect to the product price and/or the internal structure of the sector (number and size of firms). The strategy adopted by firms — especially the big ones — will determine which among the possible equilibrium outcomes will be achieved in practice.

Viewing the oil sector as a 'trilateral oligopoly', on the lines suggested above, provides an invaluable interpretative key which allows the identification of the elements which explain the degree to which the price of crude oil exceeds the theoretical minimum corresponding to a state of generalised free competition. This means that in order to explain the level and the evolution of oil prices we should look not only at production costs, but also and especially at those factors affecting conditions of entry and the internal power relationships of each of the three groups (producing countries, oil companies and consuming countries), as well as at interest relations (affinity or conflict) among the component members of different groups. The size of barriers to entry, and the degree of oligopolistic control of producing countries and oil companies over the market, will explain the excess of the price of crude oil over that which may be considered the minimum competitive level. As a first approximation, this minimum long-term competitive price can be approximated by the average cost of production (including an allowance for average exploratory and development costs) of the least productive fields necessary to meet world demand, plus the competitive profit rate. In the short term, the price can drop roughly to variable (direct) costs.[26] In oligopoly theory, these are described by Sylos Labini (1969, pp. 40–1) as 'exclusion price' and 'elimination price', pointing to the minimum price (expected to prevail after the entry into the market) at which a new producer will deem it convenient to attempt entry, and to the minimum price necessary to induce producers already operating within the sector not to leave it.

Thus the three groups should not be analysed as three internally homogeneous contenders — an approach very common in divulgative descriptions of events in the oil sector. Since conditions of perfect monopoly do not prevail within any of the three groups, the degree of oligopolistic control of the major agents over each group is a relevant factor in the explanation of their relative power. Events in the oil sector are not so much the result of greater or lesser diplomatic and strategic skill of each group of contenders, but rather the result of technological and institutional factors influencing the degree of concentration within each group, and the possible conformity of interests among groups. In this perspective, economic analysis becomes a powerful tool in deciphering events, and long-term trends, in the oil sector.

4 The Oil Companies

I. AGENTS IN THE OIL MARKET

The oil sector, as any other oligopolistic sector, is characterised by the presence of firms which are very different from one another. First and foremost are the 'Seven Sisters', as they were christened by Enrico Mattei,[1] usually referred to as the 'majors'. They are all very large, vertically integrated companies with affiliate companies in many countries. Their activities extend over the entire range of stages of production, from exploration to retailing of refined oil products. They are also widely diversified, currently present in such wide-ranging activities as nuclear energy and electronic office equipment. Then there is a myriad of small firms, generally operating in a single productive stage: geological prospecting companies, engineering companies, independent refiners, gasoline and service station chains, etc. In an intermediate position there are the 'independents' and the State oil companies such as ENI. The latter also tend to be vertically integrated companies, present in a number of different countries. Their characteristic feature, however, is their presence (often predominant) in their home market, which represents the largest share of their activities. Overall, however, none of these companies represents more than a very small share of the world petroleum market. Finally, over the past fifteen years there has been a rapidly increasing role played by the State oil companies of the petroleum-producing countries. These companies will be considered in the next chapter.

In such a situation, given the distribution of companies in the market, the major oil companies are capable of exercising a decisive influence on market developments. However, the existence of a large fringe of medium- and small-sized firms, which under certain circumstances ensure a margin of flexibility to the oil sector, implies a constraint on the major firms' freedom of action. In fact, major firms run the risk of experiencing a substantial and rapid erosion in their market shares (both as shares in the production of crude oil, and as shares in the markets of refined products), if in defining their strategies they do not recognise the constraint

47

on their freedom of action represented by the existence of other operators, less strong but competitors all the same.

Thus, the problems confronting us concern, first, the identification of those factors which may have led to the success of the majors; secondly, those factors present in the period following the Great Crash of 1929, which permitted the persistent prevalence of an oligopolistic market structure characterised by feeble competition, despite the fact that crude oil prices were higher than production costs (inclusive of exploration and development expenditures). Our third concern is the importance of the multinational structure of the majors, and in particular the vertical integration as found in most oil companies; fourthly, the causes and effects of the development of medium-sized oil companies ('independents' and State companies from oil-importing countries); and finally, the tendencies to diversification and the other changes which oil companies have undergone after the 1973–4 crisis. As we shall see, in dealing with these issues we shall find the obligopoly theory schematically summarised at the conclusion of the previous chapter especially useful.

II. THE FORMATION OF THE MAJOR OIL COMPANIES

The origins of the US petroleum industry are to be found in the clamorous successes and the silent failures of small crude oil producers, in the predominance of medium-sized firms active in the refining stage, and the activities of small- and medium-sized dealers engaged in retailing the various refined products. Generally, the transport stage involved operators (like railway companies) for which the oil sector represented a small proportion of their total clientele. In each of the main stages into which the oil sector can be subdivided (exploration and crude oil production, transport, refining, retailing: see above, Chapter 2), different operators were active, in continual and lively competition with each other and in persistent conflict with suppliers of the respective inputs and buyers of the respective products.

Competition was particularly fierce in the first stage, the production stage, for two reasons. The first is the 'rule of capture', a basic principle of US commercial law, which grants the landowner the exclusive rights to whatever might be found below the surface of his land. As it is generally the case that the confines of petroleum deposits do not respect the boundaries drawn on the surface above them, the 'rule of capture' constitutes a powerful incentive to each landowner to lift as much oil as possible as quickly as possible from wells discovered on his land, without concern for the damage which this might produce on the oilfield due to the excessively rapid exploitation (such as a premature decline in pressure). Nor were the supply consequences for the market of the discovery of an oilfield taken into consideration even though they would be concentrated in a short time period which would last as long as the price remained above variable unit costs. It has been observed that it was just as if a number of shopkeepers each had a key to a common warehouse, from which they could take supplies without charge until its contents were exhausted.[2]

The second reason, which is implicit in what has just been said, and which has been mentioned above in Chapter 3, section V, is the predominance of very low unit variable costs of production, compared to average full (variable plus fixed) cost. In a competitive market, the price of crude oil in the short run was determined by total demand and total supply, and was therefore independent of the quantity of crude oil produced by a single operator. As a consequence, as soon as an oilfield was discovered, it seemed profitable to engage in production as long as crude oil prices were higher — even if only by a very small amount — than variable unit costs. In the case of a relatively low price, higher than variable unit costs but not sufficient to cover depreciation of plant and equipment, and in particular amortisation of past exploration expenditures, there would be no new investments in exploration. Investors would experience losses on past exploration expenditures; but losses could be minimised, in such circumstances, by lifting as much oil as possible. There certainly was nothing to recommend a full-scale cessation of operations. Obviously the absence of new investments would lead to contraction of supplies, as a consequence of the gradual exhaustion of already known oilfields, and hence to an eventual rise in prices, until they reached levels high enough to induce a new burst of exploratory activity. In fact, because of the lags between the decision to start new exploratory activities, and the moment in which crude oil from the newly discovered oilfields reaches the market, there will be strong upward movements in prices during these intervals. The producers surviving the previous period of depressed prices and the first operators to strike new wells as a result of their exploratory efforts will thus experience very high profits. The market may be expected to exhibit large and rather frequent swings in crude oil prices, the larger and the more segmented is the market (due to high transport costs), with waves of bankruptcies followed by waves of excessive profitability.

Such a situation, characterised by persistent instability, can be overcome only if supply is regulated, and adjusted to demand. This is made possible by the erection of a monopolistic or oligopolistic price structure, and/or by the regulatory intervention of public authorities. The first condition gradually came into existence around the end of the nineteenth and the beginning of the twentieth century. The second was realised over a much shorter period of time, in the early 1930s under the pressure of a large glut produced, on the one hand, by the development of the Texas oilfields and, on the other, by the sharp reductions in demand consequent on the Great Slump.

The first condition, the transition from a competitive to an oligopolistic market, does not follow as a logical consequence of the pre-existing situation of inherent instability described above; rather it is due to the fact that certain elements inherent in the technology of the oil sector are conducive to the development of large firms and to the processes of industrial concentration.

John D. Rockefeller was the person who actually succeeded in exploiting these circumstances. The founder of the celebrated dynasty (the current position of the Rockefeller Empire is described in the appendix to this chapter) recognised not only that direct control over the production stage would be impossible since it was characterised by a large number of small operators, but that it was unnecessary in order to gain control of the oil sector. All that was required was control over the subsequent stage, transportation. Here the economies of large-scale operations are enormous. Transport by railway is less costly than transport by road tanker, and in either case the bargaining power that accrues to those controlling large quantities of crude oil for transport gives ample room for discounts and bargaining over terms and conditions. Transport by pipeline is even less costly, but only for inordinately large quantities of crude oil. Thus, the transport stage presents the potential for large economies of scale, accentuated by significant technological discountinuities, favouring larger firms. Furthermore, especially in the period of the oil industry's initial development, when consumption of oil products was still not very large, the refinery stage was also more liable to control by the major firms than the production stage. Rockefeller's strategy was to organise a consortium of refiners, which could obtain favourable conditions from railway companies for the transportation of his crude oil. In the year of its incorporation, in 1870, Standard Oil controlled around 10 per cent of the American market; Rockefeller alone owned 27 per cent of the shares of the company. In 1883 the Standard Oil Trust was organised on a nationwide scale. The Trust gained a presence in all stages of the oil sector, from exploration and production to retailing; and extended its influence overseas, through operation of an important tanker fleet.

The growth of the Standard Oil Trust appeared irresistible. In 1879 it already controlled 90 per cent of US refining capacity. Very high revenues, higher than those of many nation States of the period, allowed it to self-finance its own very rapid development. In the same period, however, criticism of large monopolistic companies became more and more frequent, and the Standard Oil Trust was one of the main targets. Among other things, a *History of the Standard Oil Company* was published in 1904. It was written by Ida Tarbell, who had been a representative of the crude oil producers in their clash with Rockefeller, thirty years previously. In the meantime the popular movement to limit the power of large monopolies obtained a most important victory. In the summer of 1890 President Harrison signed the Sherman Act (which derived its name from the Republican senator John Sherman, who had proposed it). The act forbad 'every contract, combination in the form of trust or otherwise, or conspiracy, in restraint of trade or commerce'.[3] Some years afterwards, in Theodore Roosevelt's presidency, a special anti-trust department was instituted. One of the first court cases that was brought by the department was against the Standard Oil Trust. The verdict, which was confirmed in May 1911 by a historic decision of the Supreme Court, ordered Standard Oil to be broken up into subdivisions. This decision reduced the Trust to 34 different oil companies. Those surviving today include Exxon, Mobil, Standard Oil of California, Standard Oil of Indiana, all ranking in the list of the top ten largest US corporations. Three of them — Exxon, Mobil and Standard Oil of California — are among the 'Seven Sisters' who have dominated the world petroleum market for more than half a century.

Despite the Court decision, the 34 companies that were created by the dissolution of the Standard Oil Trust kept an informal operating agreement. Senate documents from 1914 still refer to the 'invisible government' of Rockefeller and his partners, and in 1915 a commission of inquiry concluded that the concentration of ownership of the shares in the new companies born out of the Trust were so similar to the pattern of shareholding in the old Standard Trust that it constituted a restraint on competition.[4]

In the meantime, however, other companies succeeded in developing outside Rockefeller's control, thanks to the discovery of the rich Texas oilfields. Among these companies are another two of the 'Seven Sisters': Texaco, based in Houston, and Gulf, controlled by the Mellon family.[5]

Throughout the First World War these companies prospered within the continental United States, favoured by the rapid expansion in oil consumption, and they also started to expand their activities abroad.

At the international level they met competition from two large companies, Royal Dutch Shell and British Petroleum, who had been operating for some time in the Middle East, Russia and Europe, but also in the Far East and the two Americas. Royal Dutch Shell came into existence in April 1906 as the result of the merger of two giants, Deterding's Royal Dutch and Marcus Samuel's Shell. British Petroleum began its commercial existence as the Anglo-Persian Oil Company, and later became the Anglo-Iranian, before its final designation as BP. This latter company thrived under the tutelage of Winston Churchill, who was interested in securing oil supplies for the English Navy, which he had converted from coal to oil propulsion. In 1914, three months before the outbreak of the First World War, Churchill convinced the English government to buy the majority of BP's outstanding shares. In a famous speech in the House of Commons he firmly defended this decision. He argued that in this case the direct State intervention in such a crucial and complex sector as oil did not contradict the basic liberalist principles against interference in the operation of the economy, since the issue at stake was the struggle against a private monopolist, Shell Oil.[6]

In summary, the basis for the success of the 'Seven Sisters' in the major oil markets of the world can be identified in three sets of factors. First, a collection of varied chance elements, only partially connected to the personalities of their 'founding fathers'. Secondly, the technological elements favouring the development of major companies at the expense of smaller ones.[7] Thirdly, and finally, political decisions which sometimes favoured and sometimes hindered the development of major companies, e.g. the break up of the Standard Oil Trust or the British government's support for BP. We are mainly concerned, in this study, with the second and third group of factors. In this regard, it may be noted that chance elements diminish in importance with the development and integration of oil markets, and at the same time the 'fundamentals' gradually acquire a dominant role in determining the market structure and its evolution. It is however still true that the oil sector, in comparison to other sectors of the economy, is characterised by the relevance of political elements. This fact may be explained by the peculiarity of a typically international market, where (aside from the United States) the main producing centres and the main consumption centres are generally located in different countries.

III. THE INTERNATIONAL PETROLEUM CARTEL

In the second decade of the present century, the demand for oil products experienced an extremely rapid growth, especially in the United States. In addition to the requirements of war, this phenomenon can be traced to the development of the car industry. In 1911 petrol sales exceeded paraffin sales for the first time. In 1912 Henry Ford introduced the first assembly line to produce his famous model-T Ford. Confronted with the growth in demand, and with the needs of war, both the current production of oil and potential production as represented by proven reserves appeared insufficient. For the first, but not the last, time anxiety over an imminent exhaustion of oil supplies dominated the industry.

But within a few years, by the end of the First World War, the conditions of scarcity were replaced by an oil glut, in the United States as well as in the rest of the world. The development of low-cost production in Texas and, later, in the Middle East, was added to already existing sources, such as those in Eastern Europe. The result was a downward pressure on price and the periodic outbreak of price wars among the companies.[8]

US anti-trust law forbad collusive agreements among producers within the US territory, but had no application to events in foreign markets. As shall be seen below, the major companies soon reached co-operative agreements which included the partition of these markets. Within the United States, where the law forbids the creation of cartels for the control of the market, and where competition is brisk at the production stage, intervention to limit supplies is undertaken by public authorities. Initially, at the beginning of the 1930s, control over internal production was ensured through regulations which were officially intended to forestall an excessively rapid increase in production and to assure that only economically viable wells were brought into production. The result, however, was a system which produced the rationing of production, with well operation permitted only for a predetermined number of days per month (the so-called 'pro-rationing').[9] The number of operating days is determined on the basis of demand forecasts, so as to avoid supply gluts which would lead to falling oil prices.

Some years after this, when the competitive pressure of Middle East oil began to make itself felt in the market as a result of the foreign expansion of a number of the 'independent' companies, a quota system for oil imports was introduced. At the beginning the quota system was voluntary, but it later became compulsory. It was in operation from 1959 to 1973 in its most binding form (See below, Chapter 5, section II).

Within the international market, where US anti-trust regulations do not apply, the major oil companies made early and effective use of 'oil diplomacy', in a bid to ensure ordered markets by controlling the supply of crude and the distribution of refined products.

Among the first of such actions was the 'Red Line Agreement' which was finalised on July 1928 in Ostend, Belgium, by four of the 'Seven Sisters': two European companies, BP and Shell, and two American companies, Exxon and Mobil,[10] plus the newly born 'eighth sister', the Compagnie Française des Pétroles (CFP), and a 5 per cent interest to the Armenian businessman Gulbenkian.[11] The participants in the agreement pledged to operate together with the other partners in the whole of the ex-Ottoman Empire exclusively through the Turkish Petroleum Company, later to become Iraq Petroleum Company. The territories encompassed by the 'red line' included both Iraq and Saudi Arabia, but excluded Iran and Kuwait. But soon these countries were also brought under the agreement among the major companies.[12]

As already pointed out in Chapter 3, section VI, this organisational structure, based on joint participation in producing consortia, constitutes an institutional framework conducive to co-ordination of the activities of major companies jointly interested in Middle East oil. The rules determining the quantity of crude oil to be lifted yearly, and the shares of each member in the consortium's oil, are highly complex and vary from country to country. They all have, however, the same ultimate target: the balancing of the conflicting interests of 'crude long' companies, i.e. those with abundance of their own crude production, compared with their refining and distribution capacity, and of 'crude short' companies. The object of this balancing exercise is to limit supply so as to bring it into line with demand, and thus avoid downward pressure on prices.[13] With the pro-rationing schemes introduced within the United States, an organisational framework also emerged which allowed the companies to plan jointly the overall production of Middle East oil. Thus, the combination of the two elements ensured the major companies of the capability of planning the overall world supply of crude oil with remarkable accuracy.[14]

In addition to control over crude production, the nearly absolute domination of oil markets by the major companies also required control over the final phase of the production cycle, namely retailing of refined products, and a mechanism for determining crude oil prices in world markets. Starting in the late 1920s, even before the stock market crash in October 1929 which marked the beginning of the Great Depression, both elements, the co-ordination of crude oil prices and limits to competition in the national markets for refined products, were ensured by what is known as the 'As Is' or 'Achnacarry Agreement'.[15]

This agreement, finalised in 1928, remained a well-kept secret for a quarter of a century. Then, in 1952, it was made public as a result of the inquiry of US authorities into the activities of the 'oil cartel'.[16] Initially, the agreement concerned only Shell, BP and Standard Oil of New Jersey (now Exxon); but soon the other 'Sisters' and the Compagnie Française des Pétroles adhered. Member countries pledged to collaborate in order to preserve 1928 market shares; that is, to maintain the existing situation *as is* at the moment of the agreement. Member companies were allowed to expand only in proportion to the growth of the total market. This rule could only be violated in the event of an increase in market share being won at the expense of companies not participating in the agreement. The rules governing the agreement were extremely complex, covering shares on a country by country, and market by market basis. Co-ordinating committees were also instituted, and specific rules were devised, in particular to control the bidding at auctions for the public procurement of oil products.[17]

The Achnacarry Agreement also provides for a unique price of crude oil in each market, independently of the country of origin of crude, determined by means of a single criterion for the whole world. Crude oil prices at any point of entry to an importing country are calculated on the basis of crude oil prices in Texas points of export in the Gulf of Mexico plus transport costs to the country.[18] This system of base point pricing was known as the 'Gulf Plus System'. Its application implied that the price of crude imported into Italy from Mediterranean Arab countries (such as Libya) would be equal to the price of Texas crude, inclusive of transport costs from the Texas Gulf port to Italy. Clearly, monopolistic control over the Middle Eastern fields by the 'Seven Sisters' was a necessary prerequisite for the application of such a pricing criterion. It should be recalled, in fact, that the per barrel cost of production (inclusive of necessary exploration and development costs) of Middle East oil is only a fraction of the cost of oil from the Texas oilfields.[19]

During the Second World War and in the immediate post-war period, the 'Gulf Plus System' came under increasing pressure as a consequence of the continued rapid expansion of Middle East oil. Some commentators attach a great deal of importance to the pressure brought on the oil companies by the Commission responsible for the implementation of the Marshall Plan, which sought reductions in the price of crude oil for supply to Western European countries.[20] Thus, in the period after the Second World War a system with two base points was established: one base point was set in the Caribbean and the Gulf of Mexico; the second in Ras Tanura, in the Arabian Gulf. However, the prices of Arabian crude continued to be set at levels far higher than production costs. In 1946, for instance, when the 'Gulf' price was $1.56 per barrel of crude, the 'Ras Tanura' price was $0.90, while production costs in Saudi Arabia, including royalties, were about a third of that figure. Profits were obviously enormous. Iraq Petroleum Company's profit rate for the period 1952–63 was 56.1 per cent as a yearly average; the Iranian consortium's profit rate, over the period 1955–64, was on average 69.3 per cent per annum, while Aramco's average profit rate, for the period 1952–61, was 57.6 per cent.[21]

Some commentators considered the introduction of the dual base point pricing system as a demonstration of the existence of a competitive mechanism, for it moved westward the dividing line separating the area in which the price of Middle East oil, inclusive of transportation costs, was lower than the price of Texan and Venezuelan crude.[22] It should be pointed out, however, that this regulated 'posted price' was primarily used to determine the companies' transfer prices for Middle East crude sold to their affiliates. Large discounts were often granted on crude oil sales to third parties (such as independent refiners); but such sales involved only a small share of crude lifted by major companies. Discounts could take the form of easier payment terms, or the form of the computation of lower transport costs. But imputed transport costs differed from true 'market' costs even in the case of sales to affiliates, being based on AFRA freights, i.e. on an average of actual tariffs. In this case, however, the result could be an imputed transport cost higher than the one prevailing in the market, and above all higher than the effective transport cost for the producing companies, which generally utilised their own oil carriers, or rented them for very long periods. Competitive pressures were present even in such typically oligopolistic markets and were reinforced by sales of crude oil to third parties at prices lower than those used for sales to affiliates. Because of such competitive pressure, the profits of vertically integrated oil companies were generated nearly exclusively by production of crude oil; it was not uncommon for the affiliates in consuming countries, engaged in refining or in the distribution of oil products, to display losses in their balance sheets. The role of such companies can only be understood by recognising the vertical integration of the companies. Affiliates in consuming countries were intended to ensure market outlets for crude produced in the previous productive stages; and their losses could be considered from the viewpoint of the company as a whole as selling costs for its 'true' product, crude oil. A number of fiscal regulations which will be discussed more fully below (Chapter 4, section IV and Chapter 6, section III) supported this arrangement of artificially high transfer prices for crude oil, and made it convenient for vertically integrated companies to report the greatest possible proportion of their profits as originating in the countries of crude production.

The point is that by keeping crude oil prices far higher than production costs, integrated companies could maximise their profits, net of fiscal charges, while maintaining a satisfactory degree of control over the oil sector as a whole. This pricing arrangement also implied that the proportion of the companies' total fiscal liabilities was weighted in favour of the producing countries, whose fiscal revenues were calculated on the basis of the 'posted price'. Beginning in the second half of the 1950s, an increase in competitive pressure took place in the European markets, in particular from refiners and local retailers who were obtaining supplies of Soviet crude, and from 'independent' companies, who had acquired concessions in Libya, and State companies such as ENI. The increased competition made it necessary to reduce posted prices which caused a reduction in the fiscal revenues of the producing countries. This development was met with vehement protest. But then, as later, the producing countries were able to profit from the market power of major oil companies, which allowed them to pass on the increased production taxes in higher prices for refined products.

Thus, notwithstanding the existence of some competitive pressure in final consumers' markets, it can be argued that the control of the major oil companies over the producing consortia assured them oligopolistic control of the international petroleum market. Specifically, it is possible to agree with the conclusions of the Federal Trade Commission's Report, which found sufficient evidence to affirm that oil companies were operating a collusive base-point pricing system.[23] In other words, the price of crude oil was 'administered' by the major oil companies. In this their joint control over the main sources of supply was decisive. Such a control was nearly complete up to the mid 1950s, and although subsequently reduced it still remained significant. In turn, the existence of generally accepted criteria for 'administering' crude oil prices favoured the smooth functioning of the system of control over supply through the consortia established in producing countries.

IV. VERTICAL INTEGRATION AND MULTINATIONALISATION

For large integrated oil companies it is sufficient to control, by means of an oligopolistic cartel, but a single phase of the petroleum production cycle — be it production of crude or distribution of refined products — in order to ensure themselves control over the whole sector. If the control of the oligopolistic cartel over a certain stage is not absolute, obviously its overall control will be enhanced by more extensive control over other productive stages. As we have seen above, this is precisely what happened in the early stages of development of the oil industry. The building up of an oligopolistic (or even a tendentially monopolistic) cartel in the period of the Standard Oil Trust in the United States was initially based on the control over the transport and refining stages, from which it extended 'downstream', to distribution of refined products, while exploration and production of crude was carried on in strongly competitive conditions. Later on, with the development of the large Middle East oilfields, accompanied in the post-war period by the insulation of the US market through the quota system for imports of crude and refined oil products, the control over the international oil market by the major oil companies was mainly based on their joint control, through the Middle East consortia, over the stage of crude oil production. Finally, in the situation following the 1973 oil crisis, in which the degree of control of major companies over the market has been substantially reduced, the stage in which their market power is highest is probably that of distribution.

This rough sketch of the history of the oil industry clearly shows that vertical integration played a relevant role in allowing major companies to maintain an exceptional degree of control over the oil sector. Confronted with changed circumstances, and the gradual decline of the elements favouring their control over a specific stage in the production cycle, major companies were able to utilise their market power in the other production stages to at least slow their loss of overall control over the oil sector. By the end of this process, the major companies had succeeded in shifting the basis of their overall control over the oil industry to another production stage.

These factors explain how vertical integration can be useful to large companies in their efforts to preserve their oligopolistic control over the oil sector. It is also obvious why these factors will tend to be overlooked by those who maintain that a substantial degree of competition prevails in the sector. According to Adelman, for instance, 'because firms are effectively free to integrate into a particular part of the trade, there is no significance to the fact that many concerns are already heavily integrated into it. The decision to do so or not is purely a cost decision', and the obstacles to competition have to be located stage by stage, in the barriers to entry of new companies in that specific type of operation.[24]

But vertical integration adds nothing to what can be said independently about the market form prevailing in the sector, only if stage by stage we can deny the existence of barriers to entry for new firms. Thus, for instance, if there were no barriers to entry in the refining stage (such as the large optimal size of plants compared with the size of the market: cf. above, Chapter 3, section V), independent refiners could come in, obtaining their supplies of crude oil and transport services from other companies operating in the 'upstream' stages, and then selling the refined products to retail distributors. According to Adelman, the presence of independent refiners in the market should be sufficient to guarantee a free market, and a market price, for crude oil, with the large integrated oil companies obliged by such competitive pressures to adopt that price as a reference point in their profitability evaluations, even if fiscal reasons would still make it convenient to adopt a different transfer price for accounting purposes.[25] On the other hand, the fiscal authorities of importing countries could compel the vertically integrated companies to adopt the prevailing free market price as their transfer price. But even if this were not the case, and if integrated companies succeeded in setting transfer prices in relation to fiscal considerations at levels different from (higher than) the 'market' ones, since the prices of refined products to final consumers would be identical for either integrated companies or for a series of non-integrated operators, the larger earnings for integrated companies in the first stage of production of crude would have to be offset by correspondingly lower earnings in the refinery and distribution stage. Hence, vertical integration would be irrelevant as far as the degree of oligopolistic control over the sector is concerned, and would be profitable only in so far as it ensured some cost advantages and/or lower fiscal charges in comparison to non-integrated operators.

This reasoning, however, is only valid in the absence of barriers to entry into each of the different stages in the oil production cycle. Oligopolistic control over even a single stage of activity (such as crude oil production, through Middle East consortia) allows integrated companies, as noted above, to extend their control over other stages of activity. If the companies dominating the first stage (crude oil production) decide not to supply independent refiners, or to supply them only residually when their own internal demands for crude are satisfied, independent refiners would never be able to occupy more than the interstices of the market, without ever reaching a market share sufficient to ensure competition in the determination of crude oil prices. In other words, the barriers to entry can consist not only of technological elements (such as the relatively large optimal size of plants), but also to the existence of an oligopolistic market structure in the 'upstream' or 'downstream' stages of activity. In this latter case, vertical integration, even if it did not ensure other cost advantages, would allow companies to extend a certain degree of market control from one stage of activity to another.

We then have the issue of the cost advantages of vertically integrated companies over non-integrated ones. Those usually discussed[26] derive from the greater certainty of outlets and of supplies ensured by vertical integration, which allows better planning of production and transport, makes it easier to supply refineries with the desired mix of different qualities of crude, and helps in maintaining a high and stable degree of capacity utilisation. At the same time it ensures a higher flexibility in the face of unforeseen changes in demand or sudden accidental interruptions of activity in any stage of the productive cycle. The importance of these elements is uncertain, however. After examining them, Penrose (1968, p. 49) concludes that 'we have no way of determining in the abstract whether or not vertical integration is of superior operational efficiency'. However, it seems very difficult to defend the opposite thesis, of a lower cost efficiency of vertically integrated firms.

In any case there are two additional factors which favour the development of integrated firms. Penrose herself gives a hint of the first one (1968, pp. 48–9 n.), but does not attribute to it the importance which it deserves. Integrated firms will take into account a lower 'subjective risk' when deciding on investment projects in any stage of activity, because of their simultaneous presence in the other stages; thus 'coordinated planning might well have permitted a more rapid rate of expansion of the industry', in comparison to a situation in which non-integrated operators prevail. The lower 'subjective risk' may correspond to fewer errors in investment decisions and, if this information is taken into account by external lenders, to lower risk premium and thus to lower financial costs.

The second factor involves the possibility for multinational integrated companies to pay lower taxes, overall, than the series of non-integrated operators, since it is easy for multinational integrated firms to present their accounts so that the largest share of their combined profits are attributed to a stage of activity of an affiliate located in a 'fiscal paradise', or to exploit the opportunities offered by the rules on double taxation as in the case of the 'golden gimmick'.[27] For a given gross profit, integrated companies may then enjoy higher net profits, and hence easier internal financing of investment expenditures, which reduces the overall cost of finance and considerably strengthens the position and hence the bargaining power of large integrated companies.[28] Further, the greater financial stability favours integrated companies, even apart from any other advantage, should price wars occur.

As a whole, then, it must be considered an open question whether vertical integration is, or is not, a source of advantage stemming from increased efficiency and lower production costs. On the other hand, vertical integration is very likely to be a source of financial and managerial advantages. Finally, there can be little doubt that it plays an important role in consolidating the basis of market power of major companies. In other words, vertical integration may be useless from the point of view of collective welfare, if it does not bring forth a reduction in production costs; but it is undoubtedly useful to the large oil company, seeking to increase or consolidate its market power.

V. 'INDEPENDENT' COMPANIES AND STATE COMPANIES

As pointed out above, an oligopolistic market generally consists of a few large companies, some medium-sized, and a number of — even many — small companies. The 'majors' exert a decisive influence on the overall development of the oil sector; the entry or the disappearance of a large company produces not only quantitative changes in the market but also structural transformations, to the point of marking turning points in the history of the oil sector. The market power of major companies finds expression in their role as price-leaders, that is, in their responsibility for the choice of a price strategy (for crude oil as well as for refined products) to which medium-sized and small companies cannot but adhere. Small companies operate in the interstices of the market, and this is especially true in the case of an industry such as oil, segmented in productive stages displaying very different technical characteristics. Thus they can control neither prices nor quantities. A large change in their number is required to cause any noticeable effect on market conditions (or, more likely, on any segment of the oil sector).

Medium-sized companies, conversely, are large enough to influence market conditions by their development or disappearance and occasionally their influence may be appreciable on specific segments of the market (such as a specific country, or a specific stage of activity).

Medium-sized companies, therefore, deserve attention in an analysis of the oil sector. This class includes three groups of companies with widely differing characteristics. First, there are the so-called independents, namely large vertically integrated multinationals, which do not belong to the group of the seven largest companies (the 'majors', or 'Seven Sisters'). Secondly, there are the State companies of oil-importing countries such as the French CFP and the Italian ENI, which dominate this group. These companies are also often vertically integrated and operate on a multinational scale. Finally, there are the State companies of producing countries. In the past decade these companies have acquired a central role within the oil sector.[29] These latter companies were often formed in the wake of State companies of consuming countries, and the two classes are often considered jointly in the analyses of the oil sector [30] it is clear, however, that their strategic objectives are substantially different, if not opposed. In fact, in the case of State companies from importing countries, the main strategic objectives are the minimisation of the cost of imported crude oil, security of supplies, exploration and development of internal oilfields, where these exist.[31] Conversely, in the case of State companies of exporting countries, their objectives, their relevance and their strategic choices may be identified directly with those of producing countries themselves.[32]

The presence of State companies of the importing countries may have important repercussions on the internal markets for refined products, more than on the international crude oil market. There is no general rule, however, as to the direction of these repercussions on prices. In the French case, the near-monopoly of the State company in the internal market coexisted with higher internal prices for refined products than the corresponding averages for the markets in other countries. In the Italian case, conversely, consumers obtained at least some benefits from the competition of the State company with the Italian affiliates of the major multinational oil companies.[33] This was especially true for petrol in the 1950s, when Mattei adopted an aggressive policy on prices, quality and image, which allowed ENI to conquer a sizeable market share (see below, chapter 6, section VII, and specifically note 51).

But apart from any influence on the prices of petroleum products and more generally the development of the Italian oil industry, a company such as ENI also exerted a noticeable influence on the relationships between the oil companies on the one hand and the oil-exporting developing countries on the other. ENI was excluded from Middle East consortia, and experienced little success in its exploration within Italy. Thus, it was induced to establish an autonomous position in Middle East and North Africa. In its attempt to secure crude supplies it offered conditions that were at least apparently more favourable to the oil-producing countries than those common at the time from the consortia composed of the 'Seven Sisters'.[34]

However, the role of ENI in increasing competition among oil companies in their relationships with the producing countries has often been exaggerated. Of much greater relevance appears to have been the role of 'independent' companies. If we look at the history of the world oil markets in the years preceding the 1973 oil crisis,[35] the competitive pressure exercised by these companies is appreciable. It can be seen first in the final stage of the oil cycle (distribution of refined products) inside the US market, and was accompanied by an increase in the market share of small chains of non-integrated independent retailers in the post-war period.[36] It is also apparent at the opposite end of the oil cycle, in the exploration and production stages, in countries such as Libya, which only entered the oil market in the post-war period when the decolonisation process was well under way.[37] It is precisely by acquiring a modest, but noticeable and increasing, share of world crude oil production, that the group of independent companies modify the power relationships between the oil companies and the producing countries.[38] The latter are strengthened by the process of decolonisation; while the growth of independent oil companies at the same time weakens the first of these two oligopolistic groups, because independents often depend mainly or exclusively on a single producing country for their oil supplies.[39]

In summary, there can be no question that the importance of medium-sized oil companies, represented by State companies and 'independents', mainly from the US, increased in the post-war period. This reduced the degree of oligopolistic control exercised by major oil companies over the oil sector, even if it remained substantial. More specifically, there is little question that the growth of the medium-sized companies represented a necessary prerequisite for OPEC's successes in the 1970s.[40]

VI. AFTER THE CRISIS: DIVERSIFICATION AND VERTICAL REINTEGRATION

The 1973 oil crisis marked a decisive step in the process of gradual breakdown of the monolithic structure of control which had been organised by the Seven Sisters in the international petroleum market. These events tended to accelerate the process of internal diversification of the large companies. The tendency to diversify the companies' products was already evident in the 1960s, the 'golden years' for the conglomerate financial groups controlling companies operating in different, even unrelated, fields. Confronted with a decrease in their shares of the oil market, large oil companies increasingly utilised their internal funds to expand into other sectors, generally through acquisitions; previously these funds had been destined almost completely for internal financing of the investments necessary to maintain a constant share of a rapidly growing market. These new fields of activity were often connected to the oil industry or part of the wider energy sector, such as nuclear plants or the operation of coal mines. In a number of instances, however, expansion involved entry into sectors which were technically distinct from the oil industry. Investment decisions in these new fields were based on purely financial considerations or, perhaps more frequently, on the potential for exploiting the 'captive market' possessed by a large company (this is the case, for instance, for the entry into the office equipment industry, electronics, etc.).[41]

Yet, from the viewpoint of the present study, attention will be centred on the expansion of large oil companies into 'parallel' energy sectors. Neither expansion into electricity generation with traditional fuels and technologies, nor into the more modern field of solar energy, is of as much importance as the attempts to control the two key alternatives to oil, coal and uranium.[42] To a certain extent, in fact, it may appear that large oil companies, as a response to their declining control of their market of origin, are carrying out a progressive substitution of other primary sources of energy for oil. In this way they could keep an unchanged share of the wider market of primary energy production. This strategy would explain the benevolence shown by oil companies towards high crude oil prices. Higher prices would generate super-profits in the short term, even if coterminous with increasing overall costs of supply (inclusive of royalties to producing countries). But in the longer run such a strategy would certainly generate a progressive decline in the role of oil, through changes induced in the productive structure of the economy, in the choice of techniques, in capital endowments, and in the directions of technological research. In other words, a strategy favourable in high prices for crude oil would be a slow but luxurious suicide for the oil companies, if they did not have alternative possible lines of development at their disposal. This reasoning does not imply that the oil companies were induced to raise crude oil prices uniquely (or even mainly) by the possibility of favouring their own development in parallel markets; the super-profits obtainable in the short term can be considered, by themselves, a sufficient incentive to render the costs of a strategy of high prices acceptable.

On the other hand, it must be recognised that this choice was largely compulsory, a consequence of the changes in the power structure of the world petroleum market, and specifically of the increasing strength of the oil-exporting countries. In other words, the companies decided to make the best out of a situation which was difficult in any case. Thus they have themselves contributed to the realisation of breath-taking increases in crude oil prices, to the point where the increases allowed them to defend or increase their profits (especially due to revaluation of the proven crude oil reserves remaining under their control); energy diversification was only a by-product of their overall strategy. Furthermore, stress should be laid on the fact that this diversification process only took place in so far as the new sectors presented sufficiently high prospective profitability even when evaluated against crude oil prices much lower than those currently prevailing. As a matter of fact, even though the large companies invested huge sums of money in alternative energy sources, they showed noticeable caution in their investment decisions in these fields, and the recent trend of decreasing (especially in real terms) crude oil prices did not find them unprepared.

Some commentators, and noticeably the companies themselves, attribute the relative caution of large oil companies towards the process of energy diversification to the difficulty of financing the required investment with internal funds. In this respect it may be useful to refer to an issue in the theory of the firm which is the object of lively discussion, namely the relationship between profits and investment decisions. As is well known, according to the Classical economists there is a causal link which runs from the former to the latter, since realised profits represent both the best source of investment finance, and an objective element on which to base expectations of future profits, which represent the incentive to invest. According to a number of post-Keynesian economists, on the other hand, the causal link goes in the opposite direction, from investment decisions to pricing decisions. These latter decisions will be taken with the intention of generating a flow of internal finance sufficient to meet the needs of the firm.[43] This theory would appear to correspond to the position taken by the companies, who use similar arguments to justify a policy of price increases even in the presence of high profits (even if there is a significant analytical difference, since the 'post-Keynesian' relationship between investments and profits is mainly meant to be a macroeconomic relation, not directly applicable in its purest form to a single firm or industry). According to the companies' line of interpretation, in fact, a policy of price increases would only initially thwart the interests of the consumers; in the longer run the whole economy would benefit from the enlargement of the productive base created by the expanded investment which companies have undertaken with the increased internal funds. However, it should be noted that by itself a level of prices in any sector such as to generate a profit rate permanently higher than that prevailing in other sectors, can attract funds sufficient to finance the level of investments considered to be necessary for meeting the expected expansion in demand, whatever it may be. Recourse to internal financing, though the preferred way, is not compulsory, apart from the case in which there are barriers to capital movements among different sectors, namely the case in which the economy cannot rely on an efficient financial market. When in a certain sector existing firms enjoy significant market power, based on the existence of barriers to entry, these firms can enjoy a profit rate permanently higher than that prevailing in the competitive sectors of the economy; there are limits, though, determined by the size of barriers to entry, to the possibility of increasing profits. If the profit rate gets too high, such as to more than counterbalance the costs of an entry into the sector, new firms would come in, thus provoking a loss of market shares, a reduction in the degree of control and a fall in profits for firms already operating in the sector.

This pricing behaviour on the side of existing firms should thus be considered irrational, because the normal objective of a 'price-leader' is that of maximising its own profits in the long run, hence avoiding the entry of new competitors into the sector (see Sylos Labini, 1970). Whatever the factor, or the set of factors, which determine the level of investments, it is not possible to identify decisions concerning prices from these decisions, nor the subsequent profits, which will depend on the degree to which the oligopolistic structure of the market allows for an upward deviation from the profit rates prevailing in competitive sectors. Obviously, if this is true for investments concerning internal expansion, within the sector in which the firm already operates − say, the oil industry − this will also be true, and even more so, for investments concerning expansion into parallel activities and heterogeneous sectors. Thus, it is not the high growth rate of the sector − or, in recent years, of the energy sector as a whole − which determines the high profitability enjoyed by firms in that sector, but rather this high profitability is due to the oligopolistic market structure prevailing in the sector.

The results of extensive research into the investment behaviour of large oil companies (ENI, 1982) show that the diversification process has been largely concentrated in the acquisition of new reserves of crude oil in politically 'reliable' countries, in particular within the United States, in particular through takeovers of other companies. A second outlet for investments has been the modernisation of refining plants. Also, investment in infrastructure for the development of oilfields in the new oil provinces, particularly Alaska, required and still requires financial efforts of sizeable dimensions. Vice versa, in the distributive stage, major companies appear to have decided to limit their efforts, and to aim, above all, at rationalising their distribution capacity, through the closure or the sale of a number of retail outlets. Other companies, such as Occidental, have acquired relevant market shares in the coal industry.[44]

Overall, however, the investment strategy of large companies appears to be directed to re-equilibrating their own vertical integration rather than to horizontal diversification. As already noted, a dominant share of new investment is aimed at acquiring direct control of new crude oil reserves, through takeovers of companies owning such reserves (especially in the United States) and through an extremely resolute effort in new exploratory activities. In this way the oil companies compensate for the loss of control (often only partial) of their old share of reserves in the now nationalised Middle East consortia (see the Appendix on the Chronology of Principle Events at the end of the book for the timing of the nationalisation process). At the same time, the companies appear willing to accept some reduction in their market share at the retail level for a key product such as petrol, while extending their vertical integration into related petroleum products and to sectors such as the petrochemical industry. That is, major oil companies appear to attribute decisive relevance to the maintenance of a satisfactory degree of vertical integration; and this objective has a clear priority in their investment strategy.

In summary, oil appears to have remained an attractive investment opportunity for most companies. As far as an unprejudiced observer can tell, the large companies within the oil sector rely, in making their strategic choices, on the conviction that the oil sector will for a long period remain a key sector for world economic development. Notwithstanding some increase in the degree of competition resulting from the new role of producing countries, the market power of large, vertically integrated, multinational oil companies remain such as to offer perspectives for profit equal or better than those in other sectors.

APPENDIX: THE ROCKEFELLER EMPIRE

1. In the discussion of the development of the structure of the oil market in the period from the end of the nineteenth century, a crucial role was attributed to the break-up of the Standard Oil Trust, the creation of John D. Rockefeller. In 1911 it was divided into 34 formally independent companies. However, as might be imagined, this division was more formal than real as it concerned the autonomy of the new companies. The relative majority of share ownership in the new companies, and hence control over them, remained concentrated in the original managerial group. Thus the companies born out of the dissolution of the Standard Oil Trust

found themselves acting along co-ordinated lines, on the basis of a single strategy, worked out by the same controlling group. Increased autonomy gradually followed with the progressive enlargement of share ownership connected with the companies' development, and especially because of the pressures of anti-trust authorities. For instance, section 8 of the Clayton Act, passed in 1914, forbad 'interlocking directorates', namely the membership of the same person on the boards of directors of companies competing in the same market.[45] Furthermore, the spreading of share ownership brought about, or at least appeared to bring about, a decrease in the control of larger shareholders over full-time managers. This situation is aptly summarised by Berle and Means (1933) with the formula 'separation of ownership and control'; and it is bound to decrease the strength of the links between the various companies, for while they may have common shareholders, the full-time managers will necessarily be different from one company to another.

However, a number of things have changed since the Second World War. Specifically, in recent years the financial sector (banks and insurance companies) have rapidly increased their control over a whole range of publicly quoted companies. In addition to the direct ownership of large blocks of shares, the trust departments of large financial institutions manage other blocks of shares owned by retirement funds, investment funds, and private trusts, also exercising the voting rights. The importance of this element is often underrated by those who maintain that banks follow a passive policy, regularly voting in favour of the controlled company's management choices, and in the case of disagreement prefer 'to vote on Wall Street', selling the shares under their control. As a matter of fact, a substantial degree of control is exercised. For example, bank officers normally have seats on the controlled companies' boards of directors, and the companies frequently take counsel from the banks in anticipation of important decisions. The cases of bank representatives voting in opposition to management at meetings of the boards of directors are rare, and generally refer to secondary issues, precisely because there is generally *a priori* agreement on the main issues. In contrast to the situation described by Berle and Means, 'institutional investors' (the banks' trust departments, pension funds, insurance companies) have taken on increasing importance. In the post-war period the proportion of shares owned by institutional investors has increased — and keeps increasing — at the expense of the proportion of shares directly controlled by families, by large and small individual savers.[46]

The expansion of the share of institutional investors immediately raises the question of the links among large and apparently autonomous companies, stemming from the existence of large common shareholders. When shareholding is widely dispersed, and there is an absolute or nearly absolute separation of ownership from control, the strategic choices of any company are not influenced by any particular group of shareholders. But as soon as the degree of dispersion decreases, the larger shareholders are able to exercise decisive influence over the selection of management personnel and over the company's strategic choices, even when they control only a small proportion of the total shares outstanding – generally less than 5 per cent. The existence of a group holding large blocks of shares in more than one competing company, then, may be seen as the basis of a single decision centre acting as a sort of clearing house to soften competitive conflicts and co-ordinate, to a point, the operating strategies of a group of corporations present in a single sector or in connected sectors.[47]

2. Distinguishing between the owners of stock and those who control the voting rights, it is the large US banks which dominate the latter group. These institutions are themselves connected by cross-shareholding and by the existence of common shareholders. This opens the way to the formation of power groups which, through financial capital, exert substantial influence, if not complete control, extending over a wide range of differing productive sectors, from petroleum to electronic computers, from soft drinks to insurance companies, and from hotel chains to car factories.

The relevance of shareholding links was made apparent in an investigation conducted by a number of US Congressional committees over a number of years. These include publication of volumes of Congressional hearings, and of some specific investigations into the relevance of institutional investors. In 1978 two staff studies of the Subcommittee on Reports, Accounting and Management of the US Senate Committee on Governmental Affairs were published on *Voting Rights in Major Corporations* and *Interlocking Directorates among the Major US Corporations*. The data collected in the 1800 pages of the two volumes allow a reconstruction of the web of inter-related power. As an example we shall here examine the group which in all probability is the most representative of this tendency: the Rockefellers.

The Rockefeller family is the major shareholder in only two companies, the Chase Manhattan Corporation (the holding company of the Chase Manhattan Bank, which up to a few years ago was headed by David Rockefeller) and Eastern Airlines. It is the fourth largest shareholder in Exxon, the largest of the 'Seven Sisters'. These holdings do not seem substantial for the group which up to the dismemberment of the Standard

Oil Trust was in nearly total control of the US and world petroleum markets.

However, if indirect control is taken into consideration, the picture is drastically changed. With reference to the control of voting rights, rather than to direct share ownership, the picture turns out rather differently. Chase Manhattan Bank is the largest 'external' shareholder (that is, ignoring the 'internal' cross-shareholding with Citibank) in Morgan & Co., the holding company for Morgan Guaranty Trust, which in turn is the largest shareholder in Citicorp, which is the holding for Citibank, and in various other financial groups, such as Bankers Trust New York Corp., Manufacturers Hanover Corp., Bank-America Corp., Continental Illinois Corp. (also ignoring the 'internal' cross-shareholding connecting this holding and the Continental Illinois National Bank & Trust Co.).

An impressive web of financial inter-relationships emanate from these financial institutions. The Rockefeller group, which was only the fourth largest direct shareholder in Exxon, now turns out to be, indirectly, the first largest shareholder through the Chase Manhattan, the second through Morgan Guaranty, the third through Manufacturers Hanover, and the fifth through Citibank.

Analogously IBM turns out to be subject to appreciable indirect control. The sons of the founder, Watson, were still in control in the 1960s, but no longer as independent sovereigns. Their successors at the head of the computer giant are guided in decision-making by the representatives of a series of banks connected to the Rockefeller group: the first largest shareholder is Morgan, the second is Citibank, the third is Manufacturers Hanover, the fourth is Bankers Trust New York.

The same is true for ITT, the creature of Harold Geneen, still dominated by the personality of the ex-chairman: the first largest shareholder is Morgan, the second is Chase, the fifth is Manufacturers Hanover. The same phenomenon can be observed with respect to the largest shareholders of Pepsico; or of the steel giants, Bethlehem Steel and US Steel; or of American Express; or of the giant retail chains, from Sears Roebuck to Penney, from K-Mart to Federated Department Stores.

In the context of the present study, the situation of the petroleum market after the dismemberment of the Standard Oil Trust is of special interest. At first sight, everything appears straightforward: the largest shareholder of Exxon (previously Standard Oil of New Jersey) is different from the largest shareholder of Mobil (previously Standard Oil of New York) or from that of Texaco. But through the mediation of banks, here as in the case of other oil companies, the Rockefeller group often makes its appearance.

Exxon has already been considered above. As for Mobil, the largest shareholder is the Morgan Guaranty Trust, while the third largest is Chase. For Texaco, the largest shareholder is the Continental Illinois National Bank, the third largest is Citibank, and the fourth Morgan. Standard Oil of California (also known as Socal or Chevron), has Chase as its second largest shareholder and Morgan is the third. Of the three remaining 'Seven Sisters', for two of them the United States is not the home-country (British Petroleum and Shell), while the remaining one, Gulf, is controlled by the Mellon family group, which apart from being the second largest direct shareholder, is the first on an indirect basis, through the Mellon National Corporation and the Mellon National Bank. Even in the case of Gulf, however, the Rockefeller group appears, although in an indirect and secondary role: the Morgan Guaranty Trust is the second largest shareholder in the Mellon Corporation, with 1.86 per cent of voting rights, against 22.61 per cent of the Mellon Family.

3. The situation described in the previous section is represented in the following diagrams. Figure 1 depicts the Rockefeller group's web of shareholding connections in the world of finance; Figure 2 refers to oil companies, and Figure 3 to some large corporations in other industrial sectors. The three figures speak for themselves. Here it is only necessary to provide some notes of caution; other, more general, considerations will be set out in the subsequent sections.

First of all, let us note that here we have considered only control over voting rights, and not the percentage ownership of equity capital. Concerning the banking sector, we did not distinguish between bank holding companies and the banks they control in cases in which this was not necessary. In an instance in which this distinction was considered, that of the First Bank System, only one among the various banks of the group was explicitly considered, namely the First National Bank of Minneapolis, since it controls a substantial share of voting rights in the holding company.

Second, the figures only take into account the companies included in the inquiry on *Voting Rights in Major Corporations*. Not only does this mean that in all probability the web of the Rockefeller family group's influence is much wider than it appears here; it also means that our analysis cannot take into account the indirect cross influences reinforcing the links among the companies considered here, when these cross influences are mediated by companies for which we do not have comparable information on equity capital ownership and control over voting rights. As an example of the potential relevance of this gap, Figures

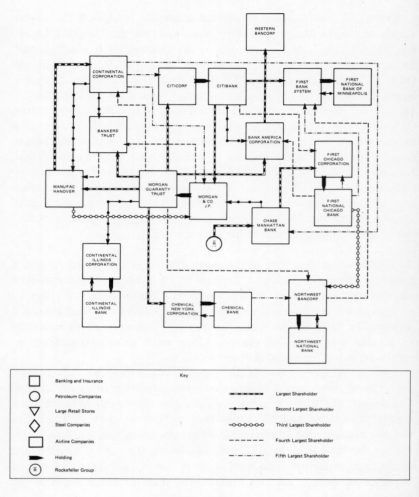

Figure 1

2 and 3 show the sphere of influence of one of these companies, the Prudential Insurance Co., which does not have visible links with the Rockefeller group, but has strict links with the companies considered here at the board of directors level ('direct' and 'indirect interlocking directorates').[48]

Finally, among the companies considered in the Senate inquiry, the figures only include those which appear to be most relevant. Otherwise excess detail would cloud the recognition of the main tendencies. In fact, Morgan Guaranty Trust alone is among the five largest stockvoters in 56 corporations (out of the 122 considered in the US Senate inquiry). For instance, together with Sears Roebuck and Penney's we should have included two other big retail chains, K-Mart and Federated Department Stores. But even with these limitations the figures should indicate with sufficient clarity the relevance of the issue of the structure of equity capital control in the system of big corporations.

4. The situation described up to now must obviously be interpreted with a great deal of caution. It is not necessarily true that the first largest

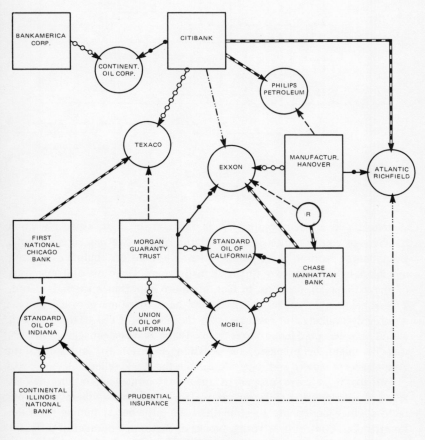

Figure 2

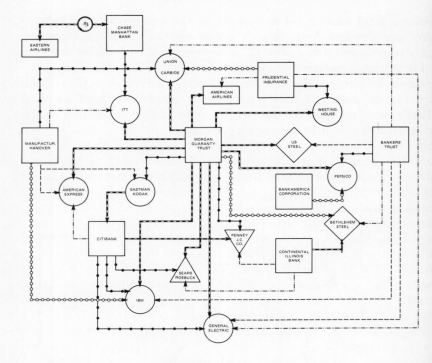

Figure 3

shareholder in a given company is in full control of it, especially when its share of equity capital is small, around one or two percentage points. Even more caution is required when we consider indirect control, mediated by one or two financial institutions. Directors and managers of the various corporations, in fact, attribute importance to, and defend, a personal margin of autonomy as the basis for some personal power: it is highly unlikely, for instance, that the 'father' of ITT, Harold Geneen would have accepted instructions from anyone.[49] We can imagine, however, that he might be prepared, on occasion, to listen to, and sometimes even to accept, advice and suggestions from the Rockefellers.

Perhaps it is more proper to speak of 'influence', rather than of 'control' or 'power'. However, as we shall see below, there are some factors which contribute to strengthen the influence stemming from the simultaneous control over voting blocks of shares in a number of different corporations. The discretion with which banks utilise their role as financial intermediaries, and the already recalled phenomenon of 'interlocking directorates', namely the presence of the same individual on a number of boards of directors simultaneously, both act in this direction.

But before considering these elements, another note of caution is in order here. The power, or more precisely, the area of influence of an individual or family group is not necessarily proportional to its wealth. The analysis above would suggest that the Rockefellers are the family group endowed with the largest influence within the American economy; but the situation turns out to be very different if we look at the ranking of the wealthiest men in the United States. For instance, running through the list of the richest men in the US (by wealth, not income) published by *Fortune* in 1968,[50] we find men like Paul Getty and Howard Hughes leading the list, with more than one billion dollars each. In the group holding between a half and one billion dollars we find three Mellons, together with a Hunt, Edwin Land (Polaroid), and the shipowner Ludwig: all persons with interests concentrated in specific corporations or industries. We must descend to the fourth group, that of holders of a wealth included between 200 and 300 million dollars, in order to discover five Rockefellers, together with two additional Mellons, a Ms Dupont, one Hewlett and one Packard, the 'patriarch' Joseph Kennedy, and about twenty others.

It is interesting to note, in this respect, that the Mellons turn out to be richer than the Rockefellers. Wealth in fact depends on the equity share directly owned by each family group; and the Mellons own (in terms of voting rights) 22.6 per cent of the Mellon National Corporation and 7 per cent of Gulf; while the equity capital owned by the Rockefeller family group corresponds to 1.85 per cent of Chase, 4.67 per cent of Eastern Airlines, and 0.87 per cent of Exxon. This obviously means that the Mellons' control over Gulf is much stricter than the Rockefellers' control over Exxon, not to mention their control over IBM or ITT, which is only indirect. But the Mellons' influence goes not much further than Gulf, while, as shown above, the Rockefellers' influence is much more widespread.

Obviously, the influence exercised over a given company is, *ceteris paribus*, the stronger, the larger is the proportion of a shareholder in equity capital. The control of the Ford family group over the Ford Corporation, for instance, is most secure, based as it is on the ownership of a 40 per cent equity share (again in terms of voting rights), against the 3.3 per cent of the second largest shareholder, the Manufacturers National Bank of Detroit. But the degree of influence may be very different for an equal proportional ownership of equity capital, depending on the degree of dispersion of ownership of the remaining equity capital.

In this respect, the Rockefeller group's web of direct and indirect share-holding is organised in such a way as to maximise the group's influence. For instance, it is one thing to control 3.3 per cent of equity capital when the first largest shareholder holds 40.3 per cent (as is the case for the Bank of Detroit with the Ford Corporation); and quite another when control of 1.6 per cent of equity capital represents nearly three times the voting rights of the second largest shareholder (as is the case for the Morgan Guaranty Trust holdings in the Westinghouse Electric Corp.). Above all, the indirect control mediated by financial institutions greatly facilitates the widening of the web of influence. Often the financial institutions, apart from their large direct shareholdings, manage other's blocks of shares and their voting rights on the account of pension funds or investment funds. Furthermore, banks exert a noticeable, sometimes a decisive influence, over corporations through their activity as financial intermediaries. Companies in need of financing are obviously subject to influence from banks. This influence increases in times of difficulty, and is reduced (but never disappears) only when profits grow, and internal financing becomes easier.

Let us consider an example (once again drawn from the 'staff studies' of the US Senate): the bank in which the Rockefeller family group is the first largest shareholder, Chase Manhattan, is by far the main creditor in the case of airline companies; and this fact undoubtedly reinforces the influence of the Rockefeller group by their direct or indirect control of the larger shareholdings in the sector.[51] In the case of various 'conglomerates', the banks played a still more important role, by favouring the development of protégé companies through mergers and takeovers, devised and managed by the banks themselves, who also provided the required financial support.

In addition to the intertwined network of shareholdings, and the institutional role of banks in the financing of productive activities, there is a third lever of control, represented by the phenomenon of 'interlocking directorates'. Often this phenomenon is but the counterpart of the influence exercised through shareholdings or through bank credits, but sometimes it constitutes an additional link among different companies. In all cases the result is obviously that of ensuring some co-ordination among the strategies of the companies concerned. Some meeting ground is also provided by the simultaneous presence of two persons, directors in two different corporations, on the board of directors of a third corporation, which also favours some co-ordination. US anti-trust laws (see above, note 45) forbid 'direct interlocks' connecting direct competitors. in other words, the law forbids the simultaneous presence of the same person on the boards of directors of companies active in the same sector, for instance banks. But anti-trust laws do not forbid 'indirect interlocks'; thus, for instance, directors of different banks may simultaneously sit on the board of directors of a corporation belonging to a different sector, such as an oil company. As we can well imagine, this provides an opportunity for comparing, and co-ordinating, the strategies of directly competing companies, which may prefer some degree of informal agreement and co-ordination of strategic choices to all-out competition.

This phenomenon was the subject of investigation by the US Senate (US Senate, 1978b). This inquiry brought to light a complex set of links undoubtedly favouring implicit, if not explicit, co-ordination of the strategic decisions of the largest companies in the various sectors; above all, the spreading of 'indirect interlocks' provides meeting grounds for the top personalities in the business world creating for them a common exclusive social basis.

Let us return to the Chase Manhattan Bank as an example. Its directors often sit at the same table with the directors of other banks: 'indirect interlocks' for Chase are: 2 with Bank-America Corp., 7 with Bankers Trust, 16 with Chemical Bank, 18 with Citicorp, 6 with Continental Illinois, 10 with First Chicago, 27 with Manufacturers Hanover, 17 with Morgan. Connecting Citicorp and Morgan, which as said above are linked by cross-shareholding, there are 30 'indirect interlocks'. There are 25 in the case of Morgan and Manufacturers Hanover, in which Morgan is the first largest stockvoter; and there are 26 in the case of Manufacturers Hanover and Citicorp.

As shown above, banks are among the largest stockvoters in the case of oil companies. No wonder, then, if in Exxon's board of directors (let us consider only the largest among the Seven Sisters) we find two directors from Citicorp and one from Chase Manhattan. Still more interestingly, the links among banks have repercussions in the petroleum sector. For instance, there are 4 indirect interlocks of Exxon with Atlantic Richfield, 6 with Mobil, 6 with Standard Oil of California, 5 with Standard Oil of Indiana, 2 with Texaco. In turn, Mobil has 3 indirect interlocks with Atlantic Richfield, 3 with Standard Oil of California, 3 with Standard Oil of Indiana, 4 with Texaco. And so on, with a network of relationships which mirrors and strengthens the network of shareholding relationships, and which are at one time the manifestation and the instrument of the influence exerted by a single financial group over the oil sector; in all probability we would find similar results if we were to examine other sectors.[52]

5. Thus we can say that some of the largest oil companies are directly

or indirectly subject to the influence of the same group. This fact may provide us with a useful key to understanding some events in the history of the petroleum market. Let us consider here, as examples endowed with a specific relevance, two key episodes in the evolution of power relationships within this market.

The first episode goes back to the immediate post-war period.[53] Two companies, Socal and Texaco, through Aramco, found themselves in control of Saudi Arabian oilfields, the size of which had become apparent only a few years earlier, at the beginning of the war. The two companies thus had available an excess of crude in comparison to their share of refined product sales. They thus found themselves in the position of being able to increase their production at a very low cost, but without having adequate outlets available. In such a situation two alternative strategies were available. On the one hand, Socal and Texaco could have taken advantage of the extremely low production cost of Saudi crude to acquire larger market shares at the expense of companies such as Exxon and Mobil by means of price rebates. On the other hand Socal and Texaco could have looked for an agreement with established companies such as Exxon and Mobil, accepting them into Aramco and obtaining in return an outlet for their crude with no need for price wars, either through direct long-term crude sales agreement, or through larger shares of the refined products markets. Many of Socal and Texaco top management involved in Aramco's administration would have preferred the first of the two alternative strategies;[54] but the New York headquarters of each of the two companies opted for the second strategy, agreement with Exxon and Mobil.

This was a decisive step for the stabilisation of a market structure with crude oil prices much higher than extraction costs in Middle East oilfields. But at the same time this was a step which nullified the expansionary desires of Socal and Texaco, since the two companies renounced the exceptional advantage they enjoyed relative to other companies in the market due to the discovery of the Saudi oilfields. How did this decision come about? One possible explanation is that Socal and Texaco on the one hand, Mobil and Exxon on the other belonged to the same sphere of influence, which attempted to eliminate conflicting strategic decisions before they occured.[55] In other words, it may well be that the war was avoided just because the opposing sides were both subject to the same sovereign authority, even if the generals and the colonels were different.

The second episode we shall consider here, in order to show the potential role of the areas of influence, is a more recent one, and is equally relevant for the history of the petroleum sector. As recalled above (Chapter 4, section V), the first OPEC country to score a victory over the oil companies was Libya in 1970. On that occasion Libya's premier, Gheddafi, ordered progressive cuts in crude oil production to one of the 'independents', Occidental, which unlike the major companies was completely dependent on Libyan crude. Gheddafi intended in this way to break up the unity of the companies. Before surrendering to Gheddafi's conditions, Occidental asked for Exxon's help: Occidental would have been able to resist Gheddafi, if Exxon had supplied it with crude oil, in quantities sufficient to compensate for the loss of Libyan supplies. Exxon refused. Soon after this refusal Occidental accepted Gheddafi's conditions. The way was thus open for a series of analogous surrenders on the side of other companies, marking the first important victory for OPEC. There are three possible explanations for Exxon's refusal to help Occidental: a big strategic blunder; a strategic choice to favour OPEC's success; or, finally, the fact that Occidental (unlike the other 'independents' such as Phillips Petroleum or Atlantic Richfield) was external to the Rockefellers' area of influence. As such, Occidental was to be treated as a dangerous competitor, to which all help should be denied. The first and second explanations may be more likely than the third one, but this latter cannot be excluded *a priori*.

In fact, this interpretation, like the previous one concerning the enlarged membership in Aramco, is but a simple hypothesis devoid of specific objective factual foundation. One should add, however, that this is true for other alternative explanations of these events. The two examples considered are thus sufficient to show how useful it can be to distinguish the oil companies belonging to a certain sphere of influence from those external to it, when looking for possible explanations for apparently abnormal events in the petroleum sector.

5 The Oil-producing Countries and OPEC

I. FROM THE DRAKE WELL TO MIDDLE EAST OIL

In order to investigate the structure of the oil sector we have to consider not only the number and size of firms operating within it, but also the shares in production and consumption of the various countries. In the international petroleum market, energy policies — and, more generally, economic and foreign policies — of individual countries play a significant role.

The position of each country is generally represented by the balance between national production and internal consumption;[1] those countries with a positive balance are then designated as producing countries and those with a negative balance as consuming countries. Actually, it would be more precise to speak of oil-exporting and oil-importing countries respectively. For instance the United States, for many years a very large importer of oil, has always been among the largest producers of oil in the world. Side by side with the size and direction of the flows of internationally traded crude oil and refined products, a useful second approximation to consider is gross national oil production and consumption. This measure is especially relevant in the case of the United States: relatively small percentage changes in its gross production and/or consumption may imply dramatic shifts in the balance, and as a consequence, in the whole structure of the international petroleum market.[2]

The set of oil flows from any one country to any other country, jointly with the set of individual countries' gross production and consumption, define the geographical structure of the oil market. Over the past century this structure has undergone substantial changes, due to two kinds of elements: the appearance on the scene of new producing areas, and the shifts in the United States' shares in gross production and consumption.

More than 120 years have lapsed since 28 August 1859 — the day Edwin Drake struck oil at Titusville, in Pennsylvania, with the first well purposely drilled for the purpose of discovering oil. Since then, the oil sector has experienced dramatic growth. In the age of Drake, oil derivatives were partly sold as medicines, and mainly utilised for illumination, gradually pushing whale oil out of the market. The first target for 'oilmen' was thus the control of this market. At the end of 1859, 'coal oil' was already used for lighting two million lamps in the United States.[3] Years later, when an international expansion for the US oil industry was being considered, the goal was 'oil for the lamps of China'. Only somewhat later was oil exploited as carburant for automobiles and then airplanes, gasoil and bunker oil for domestic heating and ships. It was quickly adapted for use as fuel oil for electric plants and as a source of energy in manufacturing plants, and finally — as virgin naphtha etc. — as a raw material for petrochemical plants (producing fertilisers and medicines, plastic materials and synthetic textiles).

At the end of the nineteenth century, European markets were mainly supplied with Rumanian and Russian oil; Persian oil only appeared in the market at the beginning of this century, utilised by British Petroleum for supplying the English Navy. Within the United States, the oil industry originated in Pennsylvania (which, as we saw in the previous chapter, is also the birthplace of Rockefeller's Standard Oil); but at the beginning of the twentieth century the centre of gravity shifted to Texas. The first super-giant oilfield in history was the 'Bolivar Coastal' field, discovered on the shores of Venezuela in 1917.[4] Better known, but much smaller in size, was the oilfield discovered at Spindletop in Texas on 10 January 1901.[5] 'East Texas' was discovered in 1930, when the Great Depression was already under way (but the identification of East Texas as a major oil province dates back to 1928).[6] The oldest among the major 'oil provinces' is the North Caucasus, which was already well known in 1848. The Middle East was recognised as an oil province in 1908; super-giant oilfields were discovered in Iraq and Iran during the 1920s.[7] The two largest known oilfields in the world, are Saudi Arabia's 'Ghawar' and Kuwait's 'Burgan', discovered respectively in 1948 and 1938. In the second post-war period, new oil provinces were added to the list: oilfields were discovered in Alberta in Canada (1947), then in Algeria, Nigeria, Libya (1956–9), in China and Western Siberia (1959–69); and, more recently, in Alaska and the North Sea (1969) and in the Mexican 'Reforma' province (1972). While it is certain that Middle East oil will remain dominant for many years to come, it is difficult to estimate the contribution to oil supplies which might come from the oil provinces discovered since the Second World War. Mexican oil reserves already appear to be much larger than earlier estimates, but Siberian and Chinese reserves still represent a conspicuous question mark.

In summary, we can say that crude oil production was initially located in the United States and near the Caspian Sea (Russia and Rumania).[8] Subsequently, in the 1940s and 1950s, the centre of gravity gradually shifted towards the Middle East (and within this area towards the South, from Iran to the Arabian peninsula). Finally, over the past twenty years there has been a new tendency toward geographical dispersion, with substantial new productive areas rivalling those of the Middle East.

As explained above, international oil flows and their evolution over time can be examined by looking at the balance between production and consumption of the individual countries.[9] From this point of view a dominant position may also be attributed to net oil consumption in the United States. In the 1920s, the United States exported between 15 and 20 per cent of the crude produced from their oilfields. This was enough to provide around a third of the oil consumption in the rest of the world. Things changed during the 1930s and as a result of the Second World War. In parallel with the reduction in the relative importance of the US economy in global terms, the US share in world oil consumption and production also fell. Up to 1973, the United States maintained its position as the world's largest producer of crude oil. Since that time, however, it has been surpassed by the Soviet Union. Except for the group of communist oil-producing countries, the United States was surpassed by Saudi Arabia in only one year, 1977.[10] In the meantime, however, internal US oil consumption grew much more quickly than production. As a consequence, after having been for a long period the first among oil *exporters*, the United States has become, in recent years, the largest oil *importing* country. Because of this radical change, US oil policy will be taken up in the next chapter devoted to consuming countries. Here, however, it is necessary to remember that the transition of the United States from the first among oil exporters to the first among oil importers in the world served as a backdrop to the increase in the market power of oil-exporting countries and their organisation, OPEC.

II. NAISSANCE AND DEVELOPMENT OF OPEC

The Organisation of Petroleum-Exporting Countries (OPEC) was born on 14 September 1960 in Baghdad, with Iran, Iraq, Kuwait, Saudi Arabia and Venezuela as its founding members. The weakness of oil-exporting countries became apparent in the 1950s, particularly on the occasion of Mossadeq's nationalisation of the Iranian oil industry. Oil companies were then able to adjust supply to demand, at first increasing and subsequently reducing the market shares of other producing countries (see above,

Chapter 4, section III). Furthermore, in the 1950s the pressure of abundant supplies with very low costs of production, and the increasing role of 'independent' companies (see above, Chapter 4, section III), had brought about a gradual decline, both in nominal and real terms, of the 'posted price' of crude oil. (The 'posted price' is the notional price which serves as the basis for computing taxes and royalties to be paid per barrel to producing countries.) Oil companies were induced to accept an increase in their payments to producing countries, at the beginning of the 1950s, only in response to the 'golden gimmick' (a fiscal regulation which will be examined in the next chapter): originally in favour of Saudi Arabia, but soon also to benefit other developing countries where the oil companies operated as concessionaries. On the whole, the share of the price of crude oil going to producing countries grew, but in a measure which was insufficient to cover the average increase in the prices of manufactured goods produced in industrialised countries. Total revenues of producing countries grew, but largely as an effect of the sharp increase in production. Moreover, major oil companies succeeded in increasing their liftings of crude more by intensifying exploitation of already known oilfields than through exploratory activity and development of new oilfields.

The countries which became members of OPEC display remarkable differences from an economic viewpoint (stage of development, population, density, etc.). Added to these, there are impressive differences of national culture and political institutions. The sum of these elements gives rise to strongly divergent long-term development strategies, so divergent as to make even a minimal degree of persistent cohesion within OPEC more than surprising. In actual fact, such cohesion is extremely limited: examples such as the Iraqi—Iranian war, or the Iranian backing of Israel before the Khomeinist revolution, are sufficiently obvious examples. Some commentators, stressing the limits of the unity of action of the OPEC countries — notably, the absence of complete agreement on a fully specified plan for the allocation of production quotas — maintained that OPEC could unify countries with such widely divergent interests only by means of guaranteeing the continual increase in their oil revenues. On such grounds, the success of OPEC might be better explained by reference to favourable external conditions, rather than by the definition and adoption of a common strategy by a unified group of member countries.[11]

The first decade of OPEC's life can be considered as a preparatory stage. The founder members were joined by Quatar in 1961, Libya and Indonesia in 1962, Abu Dhabi in 1967, and Algeria in 1969. The current composition includes Nigeria (since 1971), Ecuador (since 1973) and Gabon (since 1975).[12]

In the same period — the 'preparatory decade' — other economic and political circumstances were undergoing significant change, conducive to the exploitation of a stronger market position for OPEC in the 1970s in comparison to the 1960s.

On the political level, there was a speeding-up in the process of substantive decolonisation of certain important oil-producing countries.[13] Let us recall, for instance, the role played by Libya (see above, Chapter 4, section V and Appendix) since the military coup in which Colonel Gheddafi overthrew King Idris, on 1 September 1969; or the use of oil as a political weapon by the Arab countries immediately after the beginning, on 6 October 1973, of the fourth Arab—Israeli war.

As for the economic background to the greater strength of OPEC, we can concentrate our attention on three circumstances. The first was the transition of the oil market from a 'consumer's market' to a 'producer's market'. This transition was mainly connected to the abolition, on 18 April 1973, of the programme of oil-import quotas adopted by the United States in April 1959 — and to the subsequent rapid and large increases in US crude oil imports.[14] The second circumstance that is specifically relevant to an explanation of the speed of the general application, and the spectacular size, of the increases in crude oil prices, was the collusive behaviour of the major oil companies and producing countries that was induced by US fiscal regulations.[15]

The final factor strengthening the bargaining power of producing countries in relation to oil companies was the development of the 'independents' and the State oil companies based in consuming countries (such as ENI).[16] The bargaining power of the Seven Sisters was based on their simultaneous presence in a number of producing countries. As can be clearly seen in the case of Mossadeq's Iran, the simultaneous exploitation of many oilfields by the majors allowed them to consider the supply coming from each single producing area as dispensable. For the 'independent' oil companies, on the other hand, the situation was the reverse, for very often a single country represented their main source of supply. A producing country, where many independents operate, can thus dispense with any one among them.[17]

Many analysts also place emphasis as an essential element for any attempt to explain the 1973 oil crisis, on a circumstance which is simultaneously political and economic in nature, namely the crisis of the international monetary system, which can be represented by President Nixon's suspension of the gold convertibility of the dollar on 15 August 1971 and the shift in the subsequent years from a regime of fixed exchange rates to one of generalised floating.[18]

III. STRUCTURAL REASONS FOR OPEC'S STRENGTH AND WEAKNESS

Besides those circumstances reviewed in the previous section, a number of other elements positively influenced OPEC's success. These concern the physical and technical characteristics which distinguish oil from any other raw material.[19]

First, the storage costs for crude oil are different for producing and for consuming countries. In the case of producing countries, very simply oil can be left where it was when discovered ('oil in the ground', borrowing the motto of the conservationists), through reduced rates of production (liftings). Of course, this implies giving up potential earnings, but adds nothing to current costs. For the consuming countries, on the other hand, the build up of stocks of crude oil requires storage facilities which involve technical costs (i.e. aside from the interest charges on the value of crude oil held as stocks) which up to 1970 were approximately equal to the market price of crude oil itself. In addition, non-negligible risks are involved. Among other things, deposits of a highly imflammable liquid such as oil constitute a prime objective for terrorist actions. In the case of agricultural products, on the contrary, storage costs are equal — at least in principle — for both producers and consumers.

Secondly, in the case of oil it is easier to avoid gluts, by reducing the depletion rate of proven productive capacity. Even in the very short term, it is technically very easy to reduce extraction, when confronted with an unexpected fall in demand. In the case of agricultural products, as shown by the experience of the European Common Agricultural Policy (CAP), after the crop is produced supply can be reduced only by destroying it or by carrying large stocks, with all the costs involved. In the case of other minerals, especially metals, which quite often require relatively labour-intensive processes for their extraction in comparison with crude oil, a reduction in mining activity may be resisted, especially in the short term, because of social problems connected with the lay-off — even if temporary — of a large number of workers. In addition, in the case of metalliferous minerals there is the possibility of recovering scrap, which is widely practised and reduces the degree of dependence of importing industrialised countries from the developing exporting countries. In the case of agricultural products, a long-term dependence on a small number of countries is very unlikely, since crops can be grown in widely differing climatic zones, so that cases of natural monopoly in a restricted number of countries are generally impossible.

Finally, demand for oil products is — at least in the short run — very inelastic to price increases. Industrialised countries have developed on the basis of a set of technologies, now embodied in plants and machinery which cannot be rapidly replaced, and which relies on oil as both a major raw material and as an energy source. As a consequence, demand for crude oil and oil products depends more on the evolution of GNP in the major industrialised countries, than on petroleum prices, at least in the short run. Changes in demand, even in the face of dramatic price increases such as those of 1973–4 and 1979–80, can only be gradual. More precisely, the first signs of the process of adaptation to the new level of oil prices will appear in the decline of the ratio between changes in oil consumption and changes in GNP. The decline of the ratio between total oil consumption and total GNP follows much more slowly.

All the elements discussed above represent advantages available to OPEC in comparison with potential cartels of producing countries for other raw materials.[20] Certainly, the geographical concentration in the Middle East of a large share of world proven reserves of oil is an additional favourable factor; but contrary to widespread opinion, this element alone cannot constitute a satisfactory explanation of the successes of OPEC, since giant oilfields are currently present in a large number of independent countries. A similar geographical concentration of resources for many minerals already exists, without this fact bringing about producers' cartels.

IV. THE ROLE OF SAUDI ARABIA

Because a large proportion of total oil production occurs outside the territories of the member countries, and because of its low internal cohesion, OPEC cannot behave as a perfect monopoly. Attempts at establishing overall planning of production for OPEC oil have regularly failed, because of internal disagreements over the rules for the allocation of production quotas to the individual countries. It has been impossible to agree whether the quotas should be proportional to the quantity of crude oil produced over an average of past years (or a reference period to be determined), or proportional to proven reserves, or to the country's population. Agreement on a quota system based on pragmatic considerations is possible over short periods, but the definition of commonly accepted norms is a necessary prerequisite for maintaining a sufficiently stable degree of control in the long run over the quantity of oil brought to the market. It is this long-term control which is, in turn, a necessary prerequisite for the control of crude oil prices. Thus, for most of the life of OPEC (the period starting in early 1983 perhaps representing the first noticeable exception, despite widespread cheating and persistent pressures for modifications to established quotas), both in the periods of great and in those of lesser success, member countries have limited themselves to agreements — often difficult and sometimes unsuccessful — over price differentials for crude oil of various qualities (primarily in terms of density and sulphur content) and origin. The OPEC countries were often successful, in the periods of their strongest bargaining power, in co-ordinating their requests to oil companies, over both taxes and royalties, and their share of participation in production consortia. But even in this respect the agreements among OPEC countries have never been so detailed as to circumscribe the freedom of action of any individual country, so that a certain degree of competition has always been present among OPEC members. Thus each producing country, while adhering to officially agreed prices, retains freedom of control over payment conditions and accessory clauses (e.g. on the cost of harbour services), and even over the concession of discounts or the request of additional payments depending on the size of contracts or any other reasons.

Even in these conditions, one may be astonished at the success of OPEC both in assuring the permanence of price increases under conditions of a 'seller's market' and in resisting pressures for price rebates under conditions of a 'buyer's market'. As we have already noted, the receptiveness of oil companies towards the policy of high prices has played an important role in this respect.[21] However, as we shall see below, an important role is also played by the strategy adopted by the largest of the consuming (as well as among the producing) countries, the United States. But obviously it would be equally wrong to disregard the role played by OPEC and, within it, by Saudi Arabia.

Not only is Saudi Arabia one of the largest producers of crude oil in the world, surpassed only by the Soviet Union and the United States, it is also the country that produces by far the largest share of internationally traded oil (around a third of the total). Above all, it is the country with the world's largest proven oil reserves — and a majority of experts consider the official data to be a clear undervaluation of reality. Saudi Arabia has a very low density of population, and its political leadership is opposed to policies of accelerated industrialisation. As a consequence, receipts from oil exports by far exceed expenditures for import requirements. Moreover, because of its size, Saudi Arabian decisions influence those of the smaller states in the Arab peninsula, from Kuwait to the Arab Emirates, which are also characterised by circumstances substantially similar to those described for Saudi Arabia.

Like any oil exporter, Saudi Arabia obviously is interested in obtaining as high a price as possible for its crude oil. However, due to the high ratio between reserves and production (and also due to the absence of immediate internal investment outlets for financial resources acquired through the sale of crude oil), Saudi Arabia is also interested in a sustained stable demand for its crude oil and oil products in the very long term. In this perspective, Saudi Arabia is concerned not so much with the reduced share of low cost Middle East oil production in favour of higher cost North Sea, Alaska and Siberian oil, as with the prospect of a speedy process of technological change induced by 'too high' oil prices which would lead to a gradual but irreversible substitution of oil as the primary energy source in the industrialised economies. Such a process implies changes in the productive structure and in consumption habits of developed and underdeveloped countries alike, which even if slow and gradual are impossible to reverse once they occur. On the other hand, the increase in the market share of crudes from costly oilfields has been brought about by the persistence of crude oil prices much above production costs for oilfields in Saudi Arabia. The Saudis thus retain the power to recover their market share at will, by reducing oil prices. Even dramatic reductions in prices would still leave wide margins relative to costs and thus for substantial royalties on Saudi crude. We might say that the widening outlets for production from oilfields such as those in the North Sea are in the gift ('octroyée') of Saudi Arabia — obviously not as a magnanimous gesture displaying the Saudi leadership's friendship for high-cost producers, but as a rational and profitable strategy which produces the highest possible unit royalties at the expense of a noticeable but, given internal needs, acceptable reduction in the market share in contrast to a situation characterised by higher sales and lower prices.

Thus, on the one hand, Saudi Arabia is prepared to accept reductions in its sales, when supply has to be reduced in order to support prices against downward pressures. On the other hand, Saudi Arabia is determined to avoid dramatic explosions in crude oil prices, utilising its margins of unused productive capacity in order to avoid sudden sizeable supply gaps (as it did at the occasion of the Islamic revolution in Iran, or the Iraqi–Iranian war). Obviously the 'benevolence' of Saudi Arabia — based as it is on recognisable rational foundations — does not extend to the point of guaranteeing, even in periods of dramatic shortages, the supplies of crude oil as might be required by industrialised countries in order to increase their oil stocks.[22] The Saudis probably intend to use their control over the market in order to avoid persistent sharp fluctuations in supply, and to induce a stable trend in oil prices, which should grow in parallel or slightly more rapidly than the prices of manufactured goods produced in the industrialised countries. Such a goal seems to have motivated the 'Yamani formula' put forward in 1977, linking crude oil prices to the rate of growth of the national product (in nominal terms) of the industrialised countries.[23]

Another obvious target of Saudi strategy consists in preserving its position of leadership within OPEC, by keeping its market share large enough to be able to drive the market price up or down at will through changes in supply.[24] This target, however, implicitly constrains Saudi Arabia's willingness to accept reductions in its market share in periods of falling prices. At the same time, there are limits — which may be traced to technological factors — to changes in the opposite direction, namely to the size of possible short-term increases in production in order to offset sudden supply shortages due to upheavals in other producing countries.

These are the medium- to long-run guidelines for the Saudi oil strategy. In addition, account should be taken of the sizeable proportion of oil revenues that have been used to finance the 'forward' push to extend interests 'downstream', increasing vertical integration. This seems to be common to most of the oil-exporting countries in present conditions. Apart from the eventuality of internal political upheavals, this strategy could ensure OPEC a long-term role in oil markets, even if it is recognised that the role will be more limited than that in the 1970s. It also ensures Saudi Arabia its prime position within OPEC. In all probability, crude oil from the Arab peninsula will for some decades continue to play a central role in the international petroleum market.

V. COMMUNIST OIL

Oil exports by the Soviet Union were one of the most important elements contributing to the downward pressure on crude oil prices during the 1950s and 1960s. This crucial factor is often overlooked in summary analyses of the international oil market, because the bulk of Soviet crude oil production goes to meet internal consumption or is exported to other communist countries which, as a result, are largely isolated from the international oil market. However, as has been pointed out with respect to the United States, relatively small percentage changes in domestic production and/or consumption are sufficient to produce sizeable changes in net exports of Soviet oil. This helps to explain the large variation that exist in the published forecasts of Soviet exports which range from the pessimism of a recent CIA study,[25] depicting the communist block as a net buyer with rapidly increasing requirements for crude oil in future, to the more optimistic forecasts of an increase in the flow of Soviet exports of crude oil and especially of natural gas.[26] It is important to consider, even if briefly, the likely future tendencies of the Soviet oil sector and the main targets of Soviet oil policy.

Soviet targets are at one and the same time political and economic (with weights which change with circumstances).[27] On the one hand, are the obvious political interests encouraging strict dependence of other Comecon countries on the Soviet Union as their dominant source of crude oil supplies; and the use of oil exports as a means of obtaining leverage over non-oil developing countries, acting as buyers of last resort of crude oil from producing countries, which happen to be experiencing contractual disagreements with the major Western oil companies and thus deprived of their normal market outlets. On the other hand, the Soviet Union has an economic interest in acquiring hard currency with which to finance imports of machinery and know-how from Western industrialised countries. It also has an interest in taking advantage of its bargaining strength to impose a 'tax' on other Comecon countries, charging prices for crude oil which exceed those prevailing on the market.[28]

Political and economic motivations converge in the case of the intermediary activity which the Soviet Union occasionally plays in international oil markets. Due to its size, the Soviet Union increases its influence both by acting as buyer of crude oil in respect of exporting countries, and by acting as seller in respect of importing countries. However, even in this case it is possible to point to specific economic motivations, such as the potential for savings in transport costs (as, for instance, when buying oil in the Arab peninsula for meeting oil requirements of communist countries in Indochina), or the potential for commercial gains, when buying at a low price and reselling at a higher one. This is what has occurred, for instance, in the case of the Soviet purchases of natural gas from fields in Afganistan and Northern Iran. The Soviet Union may be considered a monopsonist with respect to these suppliers. The natural gas which is acquired from these sources is utilised within border regions of the USSR, and obviously allows increased natural gas exports from other Soviet regions to European countries.[29]

Political and economic motivations also converge in the case of Western attitudes to Soviet oil. It played the role of a sizeable and cheap supply source, outside the web of influence of major multinational oil companies, for some countries such as Italy. Soviet oil supplies were decisive to the development of the Italian State oil company. The creation of this company in turn helped to increase the degree of competition and reduce prices in Italian markets.[30] From the viewpoint of major oil companies – and this explains their active role in seeking to influence US and British foreign policies – Soviet oil has always been a disastrous calamity, as a supply source external to their control, and hence a most dangerous competitor. Since the Soviet Union is a 'marginal' competitor, suffering from technical problems, most of whose output is reserved for a group of 'privileged' priority clients (the Comecon countries) which must be supplied before going into the 'free' international oil market, its competitive influence is not great.

Undoubtedly, the presence of the Soviet Union in the international oil market, even if only marginal, constituted a competitive factor, which exercised a downward pressure on crude oil prices which has had more impact in some national markets than in others, but which on the whole has been neither decisive nor irrelevant.[31]

VI. THE NEW PRODUCING AREAS

Outside of OPEC but — in contrast to the Soviet Union — fully integrated in the international oil market, are the other producing areas which have acquired an increasingly important role after the 1973—4 oil crisis, noticeably increasing their market shares at the expense of OPEC. The increasing importance of these producing centres will be a decisive element in determining price trends and the structural evolution of the crude oil market in the years to come.

Some of these new oil provinces are characterised by very difficult technological problems (the North Sea) and/or very high transport costs (Alaska), and most require conspicuous fixed capital investments.[32] Concessions, even if subdivided into a large number of lots, are generally attributed to joint-ventures composed of a number of participating oil companies. In this way risks may be spread. This is necessary because of the size of minimum investment expenditures required for each venture. In the case of transportation infrastructures, particularly for Alaskan crude oil and for Siberian crude oil and natural gas, the size of the required investment effort is such as to call for the involvement of the political authorities of the various countries.[33] In some of the new oil provinces, furthermore, the proportion of natural gas to oil reserves is relatively high. As a consequence, the optimal exploitation of such provinces implies substantial changes in the productive technology of hydrocarbon-consuming sectors — changes which can be induced only gradually by an appropriate price differential favouring the use of natural gas relative to oil products, especially fuel oil. This creates the necessity of explicit energy policy choices by the consuming countries. An enlargement in the share of natural gas in total energy sources requires, among other things, large investments in 'service' infrastructures.[34]

In some cases, the development of new oil provinces has been delayed by specific circumstances. For instance, expansion of off-shore oil drilling in the United States was practically prohibited for a number of years after the ecological disaster provoked by an explosion in an off-shore exploration well near Santa Barbara, California in January 1969.[35] In Mexico it is nearly certain that one of the major causes of the delay in off-shore exploration, after the nationalisation of concessions held by foreign oil companies, was the lack of expertise of the State-owned company Pemex in the application of the most advanced exploration techniques.[36] In China, the main oil-producing area was devastated by earthquake. In Nigeria, as in Angola (and West African countries in general), wars and political instability were obstacles. In a number of cases (from Fire Lane in South America to the Sicilian Channel) exploratory activity has been halted by territorial controversies or by the absence of an agreement over international regulations on the exploitation of the ocean floor. In all cases, however, the increases in crude oil prices after 1970 (although occasionally and even more importantly due to the desire for more reliable supplies) favoured an increase in exploratory activity and a more sustained commitment to the development of the new oil provinces.

Increases in price and the search for greater reliability also induced an intensified exploratory activity in less promising areas, specifically a strong recovery in the drilling of exploratory wells inside and off-shore the United States. Increasingly, recourse was made to the exploitation of smaller oilfields. These efforts would appear irrational in the absence of internal political barriers in the international oil market; but they can be easily understood in the circumstances prevailing after the oil crisis, given the desire of each country to ensure independent internal oil resources. Normally, such resources are earmarked for the domestic market of the country of origin. Therefore, the development of these oilfields can be considered as a part of the usual adjustment process based on import substitution, i.e. as the response to the balance-of-payments difficulties caused by the surge in crude oil prices.

Thus, there has been a marked increase in the geographical dispersion of production, an increase in the share of self-consumption relative to world crude oil production, and a reduction in the flows of internationally traded crude oil and oil products. However, there are two notable exceptions to the widespread preference for internal utilisation of national crude oil reserves, relative to imported oil. First, since changes in the qualities of crude oil utilised in the refineries imply changes in the proportions in which refined products are obtained, it may happen that crude from national oilfields is not of the precise variety most suited to the country's pattern of internal consumption of refined petroleum products. In such cases it turns out to be more profitable to export domestic crude and to import crude of a more appropriate quality.[37] Second, national oilfields can be located far away from national refineries and consumption centres, which may be more central to foreign oilfields.[38] These elements hinder the tendency to a reduction in the share of internationally traded oil, but at the same time favour market segmentation. Both these tendencies imply a reduction in the bargaining power of traditional oil-exporting countries, particularly of OPEC members.

6 The United States and the Other Consuming Countries

I. THE CONCENTRATION OF CONSUMPTION IN THE UNITED STATES

As we have seen in Chapter 5, section I above, the petroleum industry first developed in the United States which for many years accounted for over half of the total world production. Until very recently it occupied the position of the world's major producer of petroleum. The United States occupies a similar position in relation to the consumption of petroleum. The United States has been and remains the world's largest consumer of petroleum despite the recent gradual decline in its relative position due to the worldwide expansion of industrialisation that has occurred in the post-war period.[1]

In the early period the United States share in worldwide consumption fell more rapidly than its share in world production, making the US the world's largest oil exporter. Then the position was reversed and the United States share in world production fell more rapidly than its share of consumption. The world's largest exporter thus became the world's largest importer. In both the early and the more recent periods it remains true that it is the internal changes in the United States economy which exert the most important influences on the development of conditions in the world's petroleum markets.

The United States petroleum industry developed side by side with the technological transformations and the changes in the social and productive structure of that country which created massive outlets for petroleum products. These transformations and changes were brought to fruition on the basis of a past experience, and the future expectation, of ample petroleum supplies at low costs. In particular, the expansion of oil consumption in the first half of the century was strictly linked to the growth of the automobile industry. Even today the share of United

States oil consumption accounted for by the transportation sector is much higher than in any of the other industrialised countries.[2] The evolution of technology, and above all of the life-style (with the rapid expansion of single-family dwellings and the suburban sprawl that it produced, both the result of the expansion of the 'affluent society') produced the world's highest level of per capita energy consumption, and highest ratio of energy consumption to national income of any industrialised country in the world.[3] Overall consumption of petroleum in the United States in 1978 was more than ten times higher than in Canada, seven times higher than in Germany and more than five times higher than Japan, and accounted for 28.8 per cent of worldwide consumption of petroleum.[4] This is why variations in the consumption of petroleum products in the United States are considered to have a decisive influence on conditions in the world petroleum markets.[5]

Among other things, the mere size of the United States economy is such that the technological decisions taken within the United States itself have a high probability of being adopted by the other industrialised countries. Economies of scale in research and development costs of new technologies and in the production of the resulting technical apparatus help to explain this phenomenon. Recognition of this predominance can be used to support the proposition that a determined American decision in favour of energy saving would have a multiplier effect which would spread over the entire industrialised world.[6] It can also be used, however, to explain the rapid post-war transition in Western Europe and Japan to energy technology based on petroleum.

In particular, European post-war reconstruction under the influence of the Marshall Plan was based on American production technology and represented a substantial expansion of the share of petroleum in total energy requirements. A number of separate elements combined to produce this fundamental change. First was the ready availability of existing American technology, primarily oriented towards petroleum as its basic energy source. Second was the existence of abundant supplies of low-cost Middle East oil which greatly simplified the task of those charged with assuring energy supplies to Europe in the chaotic post-war conditions. It also simultaneously explains the interest (and in all probability the pressure) of the major oil companies in developing European petroleum consumption.[7]

Finally, there is the question of political expediency. Although there is very little reliable information on this aspect, it is of greatest interest and deserves further investigation. The question concerns the benefits which might be gained by reducing the importance of the mining sector, above all the coal mines — the traditional centres of power of militant communist groups — replacing them with the output of an industry with low labour intensity. This choice helps to explain the firmness that the Marshall Plan authorities exhibited in opposing the interests of the major oil producers in fixing prices for petroleum supplied to the European market.[8] At present there is insufficient evidence to support this interpretation and there can be little doubt that on economic considerations alone coal would eventually have been replaced by petroleum. It should also be recalled that a number of European countries intervened to defend their own coal sectors or to slow the rate of their decline. Indeed, it was the role of the European Coal and Steel Community (the forerunner of the European Common Market) to support such delaying actions. But the fact remains that the dependence of Western Europe, as well as Japan, on petroleum as an energy source grew very rapidly in the process of post-war reconstruction. This was especially true in the use of industrial energy. The share of petroleum in total energy use in many European countries rose to a level far higher than in the United States, although, as noted above, United States per capita consumption remained far greater.

II. THE CHOICE BETWEEN INTERNAL PRODUCTION AND IMPORTS

Given the absolutely dominant position of the United States in the world petroleum market, its domestic decisions will have, as pointed out above, paramount influence. The most important of these decisions concerns whether or not demand generated by internal consumption should be satisfied by expanding internal production to the highest possible levels or whether national petroleum reserves should be conserved to as great an extent as possible, relying on imported oil to meet the difference.[9] The choice is one with both political and economic implications. The economic factors are perhaps the most evident, taking into account costs of production, including research and development costs for the discovery of new reserves, within the United States relative to production costs for foreign supplies including the associated transportation costs. In addition to the basic factors of relative costs, it is necessary to add the benefits for the major domestic petroleum producers of the possibility of obtaining stricter control over the oil market from choosing one source of supply rather than another. The benefits they hope to gain, of course, arise from the increased ability to exercise monopoly power in setting prices to the final consumer and increasing monopoly profits in the one case rather than the other.

The government, on the other hand, is more concerned with the implications for economic factors such as the level of employment (but given its low intensity of labour per unit of output the oil sector is of little importance in this regard) and the balance of payments.

The political factors are of two types. On the one hand is the influence of various private interest groups: in this case the multitude of small (but also a few large) domestic producers without foreign supply sources. On the other hand is the strategic necessity of assuring sufficient quantities of energy from stable and secure sources. This latter factor is the one which is most frequently raised in the debate over the political expediency of pursuing a policy of maximum preservation or exploitation of domestic supplies. But, the fact is that at least within certain limits, the concern over security and stability of supplies may be used in support of either side of the argument. Indeed, the development of internal reserves and the simultaneous reduction of imports is a necessary condition to assure isolation from those events which afflict foreign suppliers (such as war or revolution) and provoke the temporary disruption of imported supplies which may cause internal difficulties capable of placing national security in jeopardy.

On the other hand it is possible to argue that oil reserves in the United States, just as those in any producing country, are not unlimited so that the independence of the country in the long term is better assured by maximising the utilisation of the reserves of other countries. This type of reasoning does not, however, apply in the short or medium term because it is generally the case that limitations on internal production lead to associated reductions in domestic exploration activities and development of new domestic wells. A low effective level of domestic production thus implies a lower level of potential production as long as 'proven reserves' tend to vary more or less proportionately with domestic production rates.[10]

In the long term which we may define as the time necessary for exploration (which may include the development and construction of the necessary equipment such as marine drilling platforms) and bringing new reserves into production, i.e. around a decade, it should be possible in cases of absolute necessity to turn to other, non-petroleum sources of energy as well as to introduce modification in technology and the structure of production so as to allow for a substantial reduction in the consumption of petroleum. The compatibility of the twin objectives of assuring a sufficient domestic production potential and exploiting foreign supplies to the maximum is only possible within prescribed limits and requires very finely balanced policies. Above all, any changes introduced must be gradual in order to avoid conditions of uncertainty which might act as an impediment to investment in new production capacity at home and abroad, as well as to avoid sudden inequitable transfers of wealth and the tensions which such changes may exert on the efficient operation of the oil market.

History presents a very different picture, however. In reality, inconsistency was the characteristic feature of the important choices of energy policy in some of the most crucial phases of the evolution of the petroleum market both in the United States and internationally. After the United States became a net importer of petroleum in 1948 the combined pressure from those who feared that an excessive expansion in the share of total energy consumption satisfied from imports would constitute a danger to national security, and the concerns of the small- and medium-sized petroleum producers who possessed only or primarily domestic reserves, led first to the imposition in July 1957 of a system of voluntary controls and eventually in April 1959 to a complete system of import controls.[11] These measures did something to lift the 'sword of Damocles' constituted by the competition of Middle Eastern supplies, seemingly inexhaustible at very low cost, which threatened the survival of the domestic producers. It also meant, in practice, that the United States internal petroleum market was isolated from the international market. At the time even the most informed observers do not seem to have recognised the importance of this fact.

The first result was to accelerate sharply the process of 'multi-nationalisation' of the most important of the American petroleum companies. These companies had developed foreign reserves, primarily in the Middle East, with the immediate objective of using them to supply those markets which they had previously utilised as export outlets for their excess United States production. Given the rapid growth of the American domestic market and the exceptional estimates of available reserves in their foreign fields they were quite ready and willing to use these reserves to supply their own domestic US markets. But, faced with the restrictions on imports of oil into the United States these companies were forced to expand into other markets, in particular into Europe and Japan where the decline of coal was being accelerated and replaced with petroleum-based energy. Such policy led to some anomalous cases such as Italy and Japan, almost exclusively dependent on petroleum as an energy source.

A second and more obvious effect of the policy of the United States was to hold prices in the domestic market above those which prevailed in the international petroleum market. This differential was also reflected in the prices of refined petroleum products.[12] The result was a large transfer of wealth from domestic consumers to domestic producers. The most conspicuous damage was to be felt in those sectors of United States manufacturing industry with the highest intensity of energy consumption. Indeed, the higher cost of energy supplies to United States industry created for some years a competitive advantage for European and Japanese producers selling in American markets and competing with American producers in international markets.

It is perhaps just this factor, together with the decline in proven reserves, which produced the change in direction of the petroleum policy of the United States in the beginning of the 1970s. In fact, a decision to meet the very rapid rates of increase of internal consumption primarily from internal production would have accelerated the decline of proven reserves, which in addition to presenting a menace to the strategic objective of energy independence would also have been associated with an increase in the gap between international and domestic prices. The gradual, but increasingly rapid elimination of the restrictions on petroleum imports led finally in April 1973 to the definitive abandonment of the 'Mandatory Oil Import Program'.[13]

Thus, in the space of only three years, and with a sharp acceleration in 1973, the United States market was opened to imports of oil. The effects of this change on the international oil market were dramatic and of such import to justify the inclusion of United States petroleum policy among the primary causes of the petroleum crisis of 1973–4.[14] Between 1970 and 1973, imports into the United States of crude rose from 66 to 161 million tonnes per year in comparison with an annual rate of increase of 1 per cent for the preceding five years. The increase was especially marked in the period after April 1973 and continued unabated in successive years. Between 1973 and 1979 imports of oil into Europe declined by over 130 million tonnes; and in Japan imports fell by 12 million tonnes. Imports into the United States for the same period increased by 177 million tonnes.[15]

The United States abolished the regulations on imported crude only a few months before the outbreak of the Yom Kippur War.[16] The use of oil as an offensive political weapon by the Arab countries in the 1973–4 period is now well known,[17] and there can be no question of its crucial importance in bringing about the sharp increase in prices in that period. In particular, the dramatic atmosphere created by the Arab embargo led public opinion and many governments in the oil-importing countries to consider the disastrous increases in prices as the 'least of all evils' when faced with the catastrophic alternative of a significant shortage in energy supplies capable of bringing their industrial sectors partially or even completely to a halt.

The decisions to cut production taken by the Arab countries at this time[18] undoubtedly contributed to the consolidation of the 'seller's market' situation which had appeared at the beginning of the decade. But this factor, which many writers consider as the only, or the most important, explanation of the crisis is quantitatively much less relevant than the increase in imports to the United States. In the three years following the elimination of import restrictions in the United States, i.e. between 1973 and 1976, the reduction of United States internal petroleum production was three times as great as that of the OPEC countries. To a certain extent the size of the reduction in production in the United States may be explained by the decline in the size of US reserves, but the opening of internal markets to international competition from Middle East oil produced at extremely low cost by the very same companies which were reducing their domestic production rates in the United States should not be underestimated. The additional demand coming from the United States thus produced a decisive modification in the conditions prevailing in the international markets for crude oil, facilitating beyond all possible hope the economic success of those countries which in the same period attempted to use control over the supply of crude as an offensive political weapon.

It is instructive to confront this success with the failures of previous attempts by the Arab countries to boycott Great Britain and France during the Suez crisis in 1956, and the United States, Great Britain and West Germany during the Arab–Israeli conflict in 1969. On this latter occasion it was Iran in particular which increased its supplies of crude available in the market. On both occasions, it may be noted, the Soviet Union also attempted to increase its share of the market by increasing the level of its sales to the European countries.

All this is not meant to imply that the entire explanation of the development of crude oil prices during the 1970s is to be credited to the changes in American energy policies, but only that it is necessary to consider this factor alongside the behaviour of the producing countries and the petroleum companies if we want to gain a clear understanding of the events of the period. It is an indisputable fact, however, that the petroleum policies followed by the consuming countries, and in particular by the most important among them, the United States, were a decisive aspect, of much greater importance than is generally understood, in explaining what occurred in the international petroleum markets in the 1970s.

III. THE 'GOLDEN GIMMICK'

Another aspect of oil policy in the United States which has had a profound influence on the structure of the international oil market can be found in a seemingly unobtrusive piece of fiscal legislation which has come to be known as the 'golden gimmick'. This regulation, which was introduced shortly after the conclusion of the Second World War, was extremely favourable to the expansion of exploration of foreign oil reserves by American petroleum companies.

The 'golden gimmick' as it came to be known, was originally adopted in the early 1950s to allow Aramco to increase its royalty payments to King Ibn Saud of Saudi Arabia.[19] It involved granting petroleum companies a credit against their United States tax liabilities for production taxes (which were in fact royalties) paid to the governments of the foreign countries in which they were operating. Instead of being considered as costs of production to be deducted from gross income to determine net taxable income, royalties were treated as income tax paid to foreign governments and thus to be deducted from United States tax liabilities to eliminate any possibility of 'double taxation'.

Let us look more closely at the implications of this difference in the treatment of royalties.[20] Let us suppose that for Exxon, one of the four Aramco partners, the cost of pumping one barrel of Saudi crude is 20¢ and that the well-head price is $1.00. The royalty charged by the Saudi government on the 80¢ difference is 20¢. If the royalty payment is considered as a necessary cost of production (equivalent to a rental payment for the use of leased buildings or capital equipment) of the barrel of crude, the gross income of the company subject to United States corporate income taxes is 60¢. If the tax rate is 50 per cent, the Internal Revenue Service receives 30¢, leaving a 30¢ net profit to Exxon (see the example given in case I of note 20). If, on the other hand, the Internal Revenue Service considers the royalty payments made to the Saudi government as payment of income taxes to a foreign State and in order to exempt Exxon from double taxation of its income allows deduction of the royalty payments from Exxon's total United States tax liability, the situation is radically changed. The gross income of Exxon, that is the difference between sales receipts and production costs, is now 80¢. The tax due to the Internal Revenue at the 50 per cent tax rate is 40¢. But, Exxon may now deduct the 20¢ royalty paid to Saudi Arabia and thus its United States tax liability falls to 20¢. In this way Exxon's profit net of tax, which is the figure of concern to the company, rises to 40¢. The unchanged well-head price of $1.00, less 20¢ production costs, less 20¢ royalty payment, less 20¢ United States tax, leaves a 40¢ net profit under the new arrangement (see the example given in case II of note 20).

It should now be clear that if one wanted to increase the income of the Arabs this could be accomplished without changing the net profit per barrel received by the petroleum companies if, simultaneously, the Internal Revenue introduces a change in the regulations such as the one discussed above and the Arabs leave royalty payments unchanged, increasing their charges by creating a tax on the companies' operating income. This is essentially what occurred in Saudi Arabia where a new fiscal regulation was created *ex novo* (possibly with the help of the oil companies' tax lawyers) to conform with the United States tax laws.

The net result, of course, is to transfer the petroleum company's tax liability to the United States government to the Arab country, reducing United States tax receipts and increasing Arab countries' receipts. Indeed, as a consequence of the 'golden gimmick', petroleum companies were found to have much lower United States tax liabilities than companies operating in other sectors of the American economy. For example, in 1972 the proportion of net corporate income paid in United States taxes varied from 6.5 per cent for Exxon to 1.7 per cent for Texaco, from 2.1 per cent for Socal to 1.2 per cent for Mobil and Gulf (figures reported by US Senate, 1975, p. 92).

The United States government was led to accept this substantial reduction in its fiscal receipts in part by the pressure of the arguments presented by the large petroleum companies, but more importantly by political arguments. By adopting the 'golden gimmick' it was, in fact, possible to make an outright gift of $50 million a year to the Saudi king without having to obtain permission from Congress where strong pro-Israeli sentiment prevailed. According to the assessment given by an official Congressional report on the matter:

The foreign tax credit was an instrument of US foreign policy. US foreign policy objectives were threefold. First, the US desired to provide a steady supply of oil to Europe and Japan at reasonable prices. . . . Second, the US desired to maintain stable governments in the non-Communist pro-Western, oil exporting countries. Third, the US desired that American-based firms be a dominant force in world oil trade. These three US foreign policy goals were generally attained during the 1950s and 1960s.

(US Senate, 1975, p. 2)

However, the 'golden gimmick' contained a number of peculiarities which were to have a strong influence on the behaviour of the large petroleum companies during the oil crisis of the 1970s.

In the first place it made it more attractive for vertically integrated companies to attribute the greatest possible proportion of their earnings to the production phase, reducing the accounting profits of their 'downstream' activities, such as transportation, refining and marketing, by means of inflated 'transfer prices' for raw crude.[21] In the second place, but with even more important consequences, the 'golden gimmick' made the companies more receptive to increases in the royalties paid to the host countries as long as they were in the form of fiscal charges and accompanied by an equivalent increase in posted prices. In this way, the petroleum companies were not only made to play the role of tax collector for the petroleum-exporting countries, they were given a premium for the task, at the expense of the American taxpayer, which was larger the greater the success of the OPEC countries' policies to increase the rate of royalty payment and the price of petroleum. The United States Internal Revenue, acting for the US taxpayer, thus made a substantial contribution (among other things by foregoing several million dollars of tax receipts) to the success of OPEC. It is not surprising that one expert in the field has gone so far as to call the US Internal Revenue Service the 'fourteenth member' of OPEC.[22]

Let us go back to the numerical example to see how things work out in practice (case IV of note 20). Let us suppose that the taxes paid by Exxon to Saudi Arabia are increased from 20¢ to 40¢ or an increase of 100 per cent in the rate of tax and a 50 per cent increase in total per barrel receipts of the Saudi government. Let us also suppose that the well-head price of crude is increased by an amount equivalent to the increased payments, i.e. from $1.00 to $1.20, an increase of 20 per cent.[23] The difference between total receipts per unit and the 'real' costs of extraction rise from 80¢ to $1.00. Earnings net of taxes and royalties paid to the host country remain at 60¢. But now Exxon has no tax liability to the United States government, for while taxable income increases from 60¢ to 80¢ and the assessed United States tax increases from 30¢ to 40¢, the tax credit that the company can deduct from its United States tax liability as a result of the taxes paid to the Saudi government under the double taxation agreement increases from 20¢ to 40¢, cancelling the American tax liability. Exxon's profit, taking the tax credit into account, thus increases from 30¢ to 40¢. In other words, while the consumers of petroleum products pay higher prices to support the higher producer countries' incomes, there is also, via the 'golden gimmick', a transfer of wealth to the petroleum companies from the consumer through the agency of the United States Internal Revenue. Given the existence of such a mechanism it is not surprising that the 'seven sisters' reported consistent yearly increases in net profits during the years of the petroleum crisis.[24]

IV. ANTI-TRUST POLICIES IN THE PETROLEUM SECTOR

In addition to the regulation of petroleum imports into the United States and the tax treatment given to the American-based multinational petroleum companies, United States anti-trust legislation supplies an additional important instrument in the hands of the US government to influence the structure of the domestic and international petroleum markets. Indeed, it would be very difficult to exaggerate the importance of the first, and perhaps most decisive, application by the United States of its anti-trust legislation, the break-up of the Rockefeller Standard Oil Trust in 1911 (see above, Chapter 4, section II). The petroleum industry today is certainly far from the ideal of perfect competition, but one can easily imagine that in the absence of the historic decision taken by the Supreme Court, the situation would be very close to complete monopoly.

However, there have also been occasions, crucial for the development of the petroleum market, in which decisions were taken which moved in the opposite direction and the petroleum companies were given the guarantee that their combined actions would not be considered as a violation of the anti-trust act. These occurred primarily in conditions of crisis such as the Second World War and the war of Suez. But the importance of the petroleum sector for national security or, for a great power such as the United States, its importance in the area of foreign policy, has been such to secure special treatment for the major oil companies even for events which were purely internal to the oil sector, such as the creation of the Iranian consortium in 1953 or the bargaining with OPEC in the 1970s.[25]

In addition to its explicit official intervention in one direction or another the Federal government's continuous interest in, and investigation of, the petroleum sector has played an important role in conditioning the decisions taken by the major petroleum companies. The active oligopolistic collusion that existed after the 1928 agreements (the 'Red Line' and 'As is' Agreements discussed in Chapter 4, section III above) was first brought to light by a report of the Federal Trade Commission published in 1952 by the United States Senate under the title *The International Petroleum*

Cartel.[26] The report, a classic of its kind, might have been used as the basis of decisive legal action; but the attention that was drawn to the activities of the major petroleum companies by its publication, as well as the risk of penal action against the companies' American management seems to have been sufficient to induce the 'seven sisters', at the very least, to practice a greater degree of caution.[27]

It should be recalled, however, that with respect to the international oil market the jurisdiction and above all the active interest of the United States anti-trust authorities is limited to the actions of American oil companies and their implications for the price of petroleum imported into the United States and on the structure of the United States oil market. This means that the companies have much greater leeway to adopt collusive policies in their operations outside the United States. It appears that this is what has occurred on a number of occasions in countries where adequate anti-trust legislation and enforcement agencies were absent.[28]

More recently the attention of the United States anti-trust enforcement agencies (who could not take action against OPEC, an association of sovereign states and therefore outside their jurisdiction) has been drawn by the expansion of the petroleum companies into coal mining, nuclear power, and research and development activities in the energy sector. For the moment this interest has remained at the stage of preliminary discussion and exploratory studies (for example, see US House of Representatives, 1978) and sporadic intervention (in most cases not hostile to the petroleum companies) in cases of mergers or takeovers involving petroleum companies.

To a large extent the debates on the role of anti-trust policy in the petroleum sector are nothing more than a specific application of the discussion of non-competitive market forms already analysed in Chapter 3, section IX above, and we shall only briefly recall that argument here. According to the Classical economists the conditions of free competition are infringed when obstacles or 'barriers to entry' for new firms coming into the sector exist. Such barriers, which in the pre-capitalist era were typically of a legal character (the necessity of obtaining a licence or 'letters patent' in order to carry out a particular commercial activity) are, in today's world, generally linked to the advantages which the larger enterprises enjoy relative to the smaller producers with respect to such factors as technology, public image, managerial and financial superiority and greater 'weight' in influencing the government due to their large size.

If such advantages translate into lower unit costs of production (as occurs, for example, in the presence of economies of scale), it is possible to say that they also represent an advantage for 'the society as a whole', even if the larger firms are able to appropriate these advantages due to their control over the market. But it may also be the case that obstacles to competition give direct advantages to the firms with the greatest market power, permitting them to obtain higher returns, given costs, at the expense of final buyers (see Breglia, 1965, pp. 274–84). According to the traditional theory this should lead to a sub-optimal allocation of economic resources. The modern stagnation theorists (such as Steindl, 1952) have also stressed that firms enjoying such market power may also impede the process of diffusion of technical progress and thereby generate a tendency towards economic stagnation for the economic system as a whole.

On the other hand, defenders of large-scale structure for firms remind critics that in addition to the increased efficiency that results from economies of scale, the increased ability of large firms to undertake very large or very risky investment projects which small firms operating in conditions of free competition would be either unwilling or unable to undertake must also be considered. Some, such as Frankel (1969, and above, Chapter 3, section V) have also emphasised the increased stability that a sector dominated by a few large firms capable of regulating their production on the basis of demand would exhibit.

Finally, there is the advantage that would accrue to the home country when its own large firms are dominant in international markets. This is an aspect that is not to be underestimated in analysing the actions of the United States government with respect to its large petroleum corporations.

The existence of this complex of advantages and disadvantages associated with non-competitive market conditions means that it is difficult to stipulate general rules that should be followed in executing government anti-trust policy; each case must be judged on its own merits. In general, any attempt to re-establish small-size firms must be considered as utopian. In certain cases such action is rendered impossible by technological considerations alone. In the case of petroleum, for example, this is true of the construction and operation of pipeline systems which frequently, because of the size of the financial commitments involved and the necessity of co-ordinating operations both 'upstream' and 'down-stream' of the system, require the creation of consortia which are based on 'institutionalised collusion' among different companies. In such cases the government authorities can intervene by regulating the conditions which are required for provision of the service, such as the norms for 'common carriers' forbidding discrimination between affiliated companies and competitors. In the extreme they may even impose administered price schedules for the service.

In the search for and development of petroleum deposits in public lands or in the sea, government authorities may take into account the benefits of assuring that competitive conditions are maintained among the operators in the sector in the rules laid down for bidding for the exploration permits. But even this may not be beneficial in cases where particular technological difficulties are present (exploration of very deep water sites or in adverse climatic conditions such as prevail over the North Sea), or when a very rapid exploitation of reserves is a high government priority.[29]

The advantages of forbidding vertical integration are also a frequent topic of debate, and recommendations have been made to break up the highly integrated companies that exist at present into a number of smaller independent single-activity units. In this regard the opportunity of excluding petroleum companies from investments in associated energy sectors such as coal and nuclear power is also an issue.[30] The financial linkages between diverse petroleum companies is, as has already been pointed out in the Appendix to Chapter 4 above, a real problem. A partial solution was provided by the prohibition of direct 'interlocking directorates'. It can only be considered partial because it left open the possibility of indirect linkages secured through the boards of directors of the large banking and financial institutions.

Finally, as has already been mentioned above, motives of 'national security' or of political strategy have from time to time made it advantageous for the United States government to look with favour on the collusive activities of the large petroleum companies. It is not possible, on the other hand, to speak of a clearly enunciated anti-monopoly policy on the part of the European Community or of any single European country. They have in general left these matters to be resolved by the creation of State-owned petroleum companies. The restricted size of their domestic markets with respect to the technologically optimal firm size for the sector makes such a solution especially advantageous.[31]

All things considered, the very dimensions of the petroleum market and the character of oil as an essential commodity are sufficient to make it necessary for governments to exercise, at the very least, surveillance and control, if not direct intervention, over the market power of the large petroleum companies. Such control has undoubtedly conditioned the behaviour of the companies, and therefore the structure of the petroleum market, to a greater or lesser extent according to the period of time and the particular circumstances: greater at the beginning of the century with the breakup of Standard Oil; lesser, in particular in relation to the international market for crude and the national markets for products in countries other than the United States, in the inter-war period. Finally, control was less than what might have been desirable, but none the less present, in the period after the Second World War.

It cannot be said, however, that the emergence of the 'independents' and a greater degree of oligopolistic competition among the petroleum companies was determined, or even made easier in any decisive way, by the anti-trust actions of the United States government. As we have seen in Chapter 4, section V above, this was a process with autonomous economic causes such as the rapid expansion in the size of the market, the ample profit margins of the Middle East consortia and the decisions made by the producing countries. Notwithstanding its rather auspicious beginning it is not possible to maintain that anti-monopoly policies were exploited to the limits of their not indifferent potential. In this way the consuming countries gave up a key instrument of active intervention in the evolution of the petroleum sector.

V. THE BILATERAL MONOPOLY THESIS AND THE IEA

Faced with the market power of the major petroleum companies and the formation of what many consider to be a 'cartel' of the petroleum-producing countries, OPEC, it seems natural that the consuming countries might consider the formation of their own cartel in order to give a voice and bargaining power to the third group of protagonists in the petroleum sector. Indeed, after the first petroleum crisis of 1973–4 the United States government supported initiatives on an international level to form a common front of the principal importing countries. Pitted against the exporting countries associated in OPEC, the consumers' front was to have produced a situation of bilateral monopoly.[32] This proposal was met with a certain diffidence in some countries, in particular in France under Giscard d'Estaing who was very concerned to be seen executing a foreign policy independent of the United States and to conserve a privileged relation with the Arab countries who were of economic importance not only as suppliers of petroleum, but also as foreign markets for French exports.

The result of the United States' initiative was the constitution in November 1974 of the International Energy Agency (the IEA) which was joined by twenty of the twenty-four OECD countries.[33] The IEA is an autonomous institution, but it operates within the structure of the OECD. In addition to providing an information system on the petroleum market and to increasing co-operation among member countries in research on the conservation of energy and the development of alternative energy sources, it also has the charge to formulate an emergency energy plan to be adopted in the case of another crisis in oil supplies (new episodes of embargoes, revolutions or wars in the producing countries). Under this plan, aid is to be extended to those countries worst hit by those who are least affected. Its final aim is the 'co-operation with oil producing and other oil consuming countries with a view to developing a stable international energy trade as well as the rational management and use of world energy resources in the interest of all countries'.[34]

The diplomatic vagueness of its objectives leaves the IEA great freedom in interpreting its own methods of action; actions which are in any event subject to the foreign policy decisions of the governments of the member countries since the IEA is not a supra-national organisation. However, the idea of the three major interest groups remains clear: the industrialised countries of the OECD, the exporting countries of OPEC, and the non-oil developing countries ('the other consuming countries'). The common emergency plan prepared by the agency to meet, for example, an embargo, demonstrates the divergent interest of the OECD and the OPEC countries. However, in its actual operations the IEA has been limited to the role of a common research centre for the oil-consuming countries, principally because of the divergence of views on the opportunity of a strategy of all-out confrontation with OPEC. In this regard it should not be forgotten that some of the member countries of the IEA are currently important producers and exporters of crude (the United Kingdom and Norway), and of natural gas (the Netherlands). The only important agreement reached within the context of the IEA (in May 1976) concerned an emergency plan for sharing national stockpiles of crude oil reserves which was to come into effect automatically whenever the supplies of a member country fell by more than 7 per cent. The IEA countries also pledged to introduce rationing measures in case of an emergency and to set up emergency stockpiles equal to at least 70 days of their normal imports of crude oil.

The idea of the possibility and the opportunity of a direct confrontation between the consuming countries and OPEC has also been suggested by various American petroleum experts in the debate on United States policy on crude oil imports. According to these experts it should be possible to defeat OPEC by encouraging competition among its member countries. The implicit assumption behind this position (held in particular by

Adelman, see above, Chapter 3, section IV) is that the operation of the forces of the market will lead to a reduction in prices in the long run. The OPEC 'cartel' is thus the sole responsible agent for the vertiginous increase in oil prices that occurred in the 1970s. To break the cohesion of the OPEC member countries it would only have been necessary for the largest consuming country, the United States, to intervene actively in the oil market by means of a federal agency organised for the acquisition of petroleum and which would take the place of the multinational oil companies who are too disposed to act as the 'tax collector' for the producing countries. It would be the responsibility of this agency to auction import permits by means of a secret bid auction.[35] In this way, the United States, after having acted in support of the success of OPEC and the increase in the price of crude via the sharp expansion of their imports of petroleum after the cessation of the system of import controls,[36] was now to do an about-turn and defeat OPEC and produce the collapse of oil prices. All this was again to be accomplished single-handedly without reference to the complex and probably inefficient diplomatic mechanism of agreement available under the auspices of the IEA. These proposals, at least for the present, have not been accepted or put into practice as a part of United States oil policy.[37]

VI. THE MINIMUM PRICE THESIS AND ENERGY DIVERSIFICATION

Even if there are no doubts about the political expediency of a direct confrontation with the OPEC countries there are some objections of a specifically economic nature against any direct action which might lead to a sudden collapse of crude oil prices. Just as the increase in prices in 1973–4 and 1979–80 produced extraordinary gains for the petroleum companies by the revaluation of their proven crude oil reserves,[38] a collapse in prices would lead to equivalent losses with the risk of a collapse in stock market prices which even in the presence of positive results for the oil companies' current operations might lead to a global financial crisis.

At the same time, a reduction in prices would undermine the efforts that have been made by the United States and other petroleum-importing countries to diversify the sources of their energy supplies. All the economic calculations used to decide new investment projects would be rendered invalid and the decreases in expected returns that would result from lower prices would be such as to cause some projects to be scrapped immediately. Projects to produce off-shore and deep-water wells, and those of alternative energy sources would be particularly hard hit.[39] It is precisely this factor which makes it most likely that, in the medium term after a period of sustained economic recovery and renewed expansion of energy consumption unmatched by an equivalent expansion in supplies, a new phase of rising petroleum prices should follow. A sudden sharp reduction in prices would then be simply the prologue to a cyclical development which would greatly increase the instability of the petroleum market (see also below Chapter 7, section III).

It is considerations such as these that are at the origin of the proposals to set a minimum price for petroleum, possibly with the guarantee of all the IEA member countries, but at the very least of the United States alone.[40] The minimum price of $7.00 per barrel at 1974 prices which would be held constant in real terms was considered sufficiently high to encourage the development of the most promising of the alternate energy sources (in particular bituminous schist and oil sands)[41] and the continuation at an acceptably rapid pace of exploration for and development of reserves in technically challenging, but politically stable, areas such as Alaska and the North Sea. The public guarantee of a minimum price would greatly reduce the uncertainty surrounding the large real investment projects in the energy sector, limiting uncertainty to those projects which appear profitable at prices well above the minimum (and, of course, abstracting from any uncertainty concerning any potential revision of the minimum price itself).

Uncertainty would completely disappear for those investment projects in alternative energy sources which were already considered sufficiently profitable at crude oil prices below the guaranteed minimum. However, even in the case of a positive, but small difference between 'break-even' prices and guaranteed minimum, the possible loss in the worst possible case would be sufficiently limited to make the risk bearable, especially in conditions in which currently prevailing prices are substantially above the guaranteed minimum.

Such a strategy would certainly not have led to direct confrontation with the OPEC countries. However, given the open hostility it encountered in the industrialised countries, perhaps because it seemed to validate the producing countries' claims for a 'fair price' for oil, the proposal was immediately withdrawn and diplomatic efforts were concentrated on the strengthening of the powers of the IEA.

In fact, it appears that not even the Iranian revolution and the recent jump in prices in 1979–80 have offered sufficient incentives to the companies operating in the energy sector to make a guaranteed minimum price appear unnecessary. Indeed, various economists continue to foresee a collapse of OPEC in the near future, the price of oil collapsing with it. Even the high level of current prices does not appear sufficient to justify the principal investment projects for development of energy alternatives due to their large initial fixed costs and the excessive length of their recoupment periods.[42]

There are, however, other ways to provide the incentives necessary for the initiation of projects to develop alternative energy sources. Specific taxes on various petroleum products and/or the concession of fiscal exemptions to producers and users of such energy sources could, for example, be envisaged. Measures of this nature would also permit the selection of certain alternatives rather than others for special treatment, in particular the so-called 'soft' energy sources such as solar energy relative to the 'hard' sources such as nuclear power.[43]

Another instrument of energy policy which might be used to reduce dependence on oil is public funding of scientific research. In almost all countries which have instituted such facilities, however, they have been used in direct contradiction to the aims of fiscal incentives, i.e. mainly to support research into nuclear power generation.[44]

Notwithstanding the use of fiscal incentives on the one hand, and the public funding of research on alternative energy sources on the other, a number of countries have continued to give substantial support to the petroleum sector, in particular for exploration activities. This has come about both through the use of public funds, even to the extent of financing public enterprises operating in the petroleum sector, and via fiscal incentives to exploration for new petroleum deposits.[45]

The uncertainty which has, up to the present, surrounded the efforts of governments to encourage development of alternative energy sources to petroleum has been increased by the fact that these alternatives cannot be considered as having markets which are independent of the market for crude oil. This holds not only because of the possibility for substitution, even if limited, among the various sources of energy (it is difficult to imagine, for example, a nuclear-powered plane), but also on account of the relations that exist between the principal operating groups in each sector and therefore from the reciprocal interaction between the structure of the market and the prices of primary energy sources. Indeed, increases in petroleum prices have often been accompanied by increases in the costs of development and in the prices of alternate energy sources.

Further, when the same firms are operating in both sectors, the development of the second type of activity is conditioned by the company's overall strategy. It is not surprising that their activity in the petroleum sector preserves its dominant role (see above, Chapter 4, section VI). It is this fact which may lead to the consideration of the entire energy sector as a single market, subdivided into separate compartments with inter-relations sufficiently strong to consider the barriers that separate them as irrelevant.

This way of looking at the problem leads to the hypothesis that notwithstanding the massive investments of the major petroleum companies in the alternative energy sectors, the expansion of the limits of the energy market as a whole implies a reduction in the market control that can be exercised by the largest companies. Within the context of the more general market for 'energy' the 'petroleum' market should turn out to be more competitive than it appears when considered separately.[46]

In reality, the problem that confronts the authorities charged with the defence of competition in the petroleum sector is rather different. Even though they are linked one to the other, the various sectors of the energy market retain a sufficient degree of autonomy to make measures of their degree of concentration meaningful. The contemporaneous presence of the large oil companies in several sectors, even if it is only a minority interest, poses rather the problem of implicit co-ordination (or oligopolistic collusion) of the development strategies followed in each sector which has the effect of weakening external reciprocal competition between sectors and thus reinforces the barriers to entry in each of them.[47]

Finally, it is important to keep in mind that these questions became relevant only when the prevailing market structure within the petroleum sector (including here the power exercised by the producing countries) produced a divergence between prices and the costs of extracting crude of such a magnitude that other sources of energy became economically competitive. In the current state of technical knowledge, a price for crude oil such as that which prevailed during the 1960s would drastically reduce the relevance of alternative energy sources in any discussion of the structure of the petroleum sector. In other terms, it is only the permanence of a non-competitive market structure in the petroleum sector which has made necessary the study of the interconnections with the market forms prevailing in the other energy sectors. It is thus absurd to argue that it is the existence of these other sectors which has increased the degree of competition in the energy sector as a whole.

VII. THE EXAMPLE OF ITALY

Up to this point our attention has been concentrated on the United States, the largest and most important of the consuming countries, and on the discussions and strategies for energy policy originating in that country. This should not imply that the United States can be considered as the typical case among the consuming countries or as representing an average sufficiently representative of the various particular conditions of other countries. It has already been pointed out that the consuming countries may be considered as an oligopolistic group. Each one enjoys autonomy of decision, although it is only natural that each takes the decisions of the others into account. This may lead, as in the creation of the IEA, to collusive behaviour. A certain degree of co-ordination among the various countries is also assured by the fact that the largest of them, the United States, plays a dominant role within the group and by the fact that its decisions have direct and immediate effects on conditions in the international petroleum market. The other countries are free to exploit the margins of autonomy which they possess in determining their own national energy policies; yet, none of them taken by itself would be able to influence in any significant way the structure of the international petroleum market which they must consider as being exogenously given by forces outside their direct control.

Italy can be classed among the principal consuming countries of average size. With respect to these it presents the following characteristics: a high degree of dependence on imports as a source of energy (second only to Japan); a high degree of dependence on oil as a source of total energy requirements (higher than Japan); refinery capacity in excess of domestic needs, the result of policy outlined in the 1950s which was to lead to the consideration of Italy as 'Europe's refinery'.[48] Finally, Italy possesses an extremely active State-owned petroleum company, ENI, created in the immediate post-war period.

Just as in other European countries, Italy was converted to petroleum in the years of post-war reconstruction by means of policies encouraged, as we have seen in section I above, by the strategic decisions implemented by the United States through the Marshall Plan. Italy was to remain the most faithful of all the Marshall Plan participants to these policies during the 1960s and found it extremely difficult to move away from them even after the petroleum crisis of 1973.[49]

The evolution of Italian energy policy in the post-war period can be examined by distinguishing three separate periods. The first covers the time up to the disappearance of Enrico Mattei, the second closes with the beginning of the oil crisis, and the third covers the post-crisis period.

The first period is marked by the creation of the State-owned Ente Nazionale Idrocarburi (ENI) and by its acquisition of a significant share of the domestic market in competition with, and at the expense of, the large multinational companies operating in the Italian market.[50] It was a period in which ENI found it necessary to create a political base within Italy to support its plans for economic expansion. This action included the ownership of a daily newspaper, *Il Giorno*, and the formation of a new segment of the Christian-Democratic Party, 'Forze Nuove'.

The most immediate causes of ENI's rapid expansion were an inspired marketing strategy[51] and the abundant financial resources derived from the so-called 'gas rent', that is from the fact that the difference between the selling price and the cost of production of the methane gas which ENI had discovered in the Val Padana was not absorbed by royalty payments to the government. The principal factor in ENI's rapid expansion is to be found, however, in the aggressive strategy adopted for the provision of crude oil supplies. Indeed, it was in this period that the control of the market by the large multinationals united in consortia was particularly pronounced (see above, Chapter 4, section III), while the failure of exploration activity in Italy made it necessary to look for foreign sources of supply.

Two courses of action were followed. The first was an attempt to secure concessions in the Middle East and then in Northern Africa by offering conditions which were, at least on the surface, more attractive than those traditionally conceded by the 'seven sisters' (see above, Chapter 4, section V and in particular note 34). The second was to purchase crude from the Soviet Union.[52] The price paid for the Soviet crude of around $1.40 CIF per barrel was markedly lower than the 'transfer prices' charged by the major companies supplying their Italian affiliates. This price difference in addition to, and perhaps of even more importance than, the 'gas rents' favoured the rapid, financially secure, expansion of ENI despite the growing costs of maintaining its political support and some strategical errors.[53]

The second period is characterised by the cessation of direct conflict with the major petroleum companies. On the one hand, ENI's presence in the market was accepted (and consecrated by the signing of an important contract for the supply of crude from Exxon). On the other hand, ENI ended its policy of low prices in the domestic market and tempered its drive to expand into international markets. There has been a good deal of speculation about whether this shift in strategy had been decided before Mattei's death in a mysterious plane crash.[54] There has been much less discussion of the more important issue of the opportunity of such changes in policy.

It was in this period that the 'seven sisters' were constrained to accept the operation of the 'independents' in the international petroleum markets. The oligopolistic structure of the petroleum market thus saw a marked increase in the role of medium-sized companies (which were also multinational and vertically integrated, see above, Chapter 4, section V), and ENI found itself in a position similar to that of the American 'independents' with regard to supplies of crude from the producing countries: subordinate to the 'major' companies, but with a not insubstantial degree of autonomy which allowed them to pursue an agressive policy leading to expansion at a rate which was above the average for the market as a whole. The period was not, however, marked by the 'intemperance' that was present in the first phase of ENI's expansion.

After the petroleum crisis ENI found itself in great difficulties. In the first place, the administrative control over the prices of the various petroleum products produced delays in the adjustment of prices of refined products to their increased costs of production. These delays were further aggravated by attempts to use such controls as an anti-inflationary tool and, on occasion, for political advantage. The gross operating margins of the petroleum companies operating in the Italian market were reduced in a much greater proportion than occurred in other consuming countries. The reduction was such as to cause a number of the major companies to withdraw completely from the Italian market.[55] The government thus gave ENI the ultimate responsibility for securing sufficient oil supplies to the domestic market and ENI found itself in a position in which it had to increase its share of the market in a period when the additional quantities of oil it had to procure could only be found at a cost that was substantially higher than the average for prevailing long-period supply contracts.

In the second place, the economic crisis which followed the petroleum crisis had detrimental effects on a number of ENI's subsidiary activities, in particular those in the chemical sector (ANIC). At the same time, the fact that ENI was the strongest of the State holding-companies led to decisions to involve the company in a number of particularly onerous life-saving operations (a part of EGAM, Liquichimica, SIR, etc.). Both of these factors indicated a change in ENI's behaviour relative to the political authorities, the active confrontation of the Mattei period being replaced by a more acquiescent posture. This was due to objective external factors and internal subjective factors (greater weakness of the managerial staff), which when taken together meant that the rapid expansion of ENI's market share in supply, refining and distribution in Italy could not be considered as the response to favourable market conditions.

ENI's expanded role should have occurred in the context of at least a relative decline in the share of energy consumption satisfied by means of petroleum, such as occurred after the oil crisis in the majority of the consuming countries. However, the specification of a national energy programme for Italy took a number of years,[56] primarily because of the polemical discussions that went on concerning the security of nuclear power. As a consequence, the reduction in the use of petroleum was achieved primarily through the simple effect of the increase in prices via the automatic mechanisms of the market which, as noted above, require a substantial period of time and are in any case not capable of overcoming certain decisive technological discontinuities. In particular, the relative price difference between oil and the alternative energy sources must be sufficiently large and considered to be sufficiently permanent to induce the substitution of fixed capital necessary to modify the composition of energy consumption.

It is not our purpose to go more deeply into these problems, for they are more closely linked to the particular developments of the Italian economy and the influence that petroleum imports exercise via their impact on the balance of payments, than to the structure of the international petroleum market. It will be sufficient to observe that it is most probable that the greater demand for petroleum generated by the slower process of diversification to alternative energy sources has been counterbalanced by the lower energy demand, and thus the lower demand for imported petroleum, caused by the slower growth of the Italian economy necessitated by the absence of an efficacious energy policy to substitute for imported petroleum alternative sources of energy or plans for savings in energy consumption.

None the less, as we have pointed out above, in the case of a medium-sized economy such as Italy, only a sharp real turn-around in its own presence in the international oil market will have a significant effect on its structure. To take another example, the transformation of the United Kingdom and Norway from crude oil importers to medium-sized exporting countries seems to have occurred sufficiently gradually so as to produce no sharp disruptions in the international petroleum markets. Thus, as a first approximation, the behaviour of the producing countries may be analysed by concentrating attention on the United States alone, both because of the size of its own oil sector and because of the dominant influence of the United States economy and oil sector on the other industrialised countries.

7 Some Likely Future Scenarios and the New Oligopolistic Equilibria

I. HOW TO ANALYSE THE PROSPECTS FOR THE PETROLEUM SECTOR

In this chapter we shall draw on our previous analysis to formulate some indications of the prospects for the petroleum sector, and in particular the likely evolution of crude oil prices. Of special importance in this endeavour will be the interpretation of the international petroleum market developed in Chapter 3, section IX. It will also be useful for these purposes to distinguish between short-term and long-term prospects. As we know from the theory of oligopolistic markets (Sylos Labini, 1969, pp. 57ff.), in the short term product price depends on variable production costs, which in the case of crude oil are much lower than the price, and may be considered relatively stable. Changes in demand will thus provoke oscillations around the 'normal' level in the degree of utilisation of available productive capacity. But this is true only when changes in demand are both foreseen and of limited size, or when they are considered to be transitory by the main agents in the sector. Moreover, the initial market structure must be considered to be an 'equilibrium' one. However, as shown in chapters 4 and 5, the petroleum market can at present be considered to be going through a 'transition stage', following the breakdown of the old equilibrium based on the control of crude oil supplies by the major oil companies. In this 'transition stage', there is no guarantee that crude oil supplies will steadily and continuously adjust to meet changes in demand. The struggle for wider market shares can induce sudden changes in supply by major producers. Such instability in the petroleum sector is at one and the same time the cause and effect of more general political instability. Analogously, on the demand side, changes in agents' expectations concerning the political stability of producing countries and the energy policy and fiscal regulations of consuming countries, may influence decisions on crude oil inventories, inducing significant changes in demand even in the short term (as happened in 1979: see above, Chapter 5, note 22). As a consequence, the short-term perspectives of crude oil prices largely depend on demand and supply movements.

Paradoxically, these factors appear to suggest that the traditional neo-classical models are valid instruments for analysis of market conditions. In fact, these models rely on the interplay of demand and supply to determine price, both in the short and the long term, and for competitive and non-competitive market forms alike. However, the main reasons why crude oil prices depend on demand and supply in the short term is the dominating role of 'political' instability, especially after the 1973–4 oil crisis. This fact prevents the identification of 'regular' crude oil demand and supply responses to the usual values of the price and income variables. The random nature of these events are such as to deprive them of any usefulness for forecasting purposes based on econometric estimates of price equations based on demand and supply, which constitute the traditional neoclassical instrument for the analysis of primary commodities markets.[1] Furthermore, there are also substantial differences at the analytical level.

Within the traditional supply and demand approach, crude oil demand is generally made to depend on the national income of oil-importing countries and on the price of crude oil. This latter element, possibly jointly with other exogenous factors — namely, factors which are independent from demand — determines the quantities supplied. The equilibrium condition of equality between supply and demand is then used within small econometric models to determine the future path of prices. In simpler, qualitative evaluations, the comparison of the future paths for supply and demand allows one to predict whether there will be a seller's market, with an upward pressure on prices (when demand exceeds supply), or a buyer's market, with a downward pressure on prices (when supply exceeds demand).

However, this approach can be criticised on at least two accounts. First, (as Al-Janabi (1979) stresses) the demand for crude oil has but an indirect link with its price, because it is a derived demand, depending on that for refined products, the prices of which do not necessarily follow the same path as those for crude oil (because of movements in transport costs, refining and distributive margins, and especially taxes on refined products[2]). Second, and even more importantly, as already noted above, under non-competitive conditions it is incorrect to consider supply as independent from demand. As often happens under oligopolistic conditions, in the petroleum sector there is currently a wide margin of unused productive capacity. This allows crude oil producers to adapt supply to changes in demand, with no need for price changes. As stressed in Chapter 3, section III, notwithstanding the natural resource character of oil, even in the medium and long term supply can be adjusted to demand, with no need for price changes. In fact, new capacity can be added in a number of areas (think, for instance, of the oil potential in Iraq, China and Western Africa) at costs that are no higher than those prevailing in the most costly oilfields now being exploited (such as Alaska). It is even likely that supply will be increased more than strictly necessary, so that a downward pressure on prices will persist in conditions of increasing demand. This will happen, for instance, if the rise in demand is the result of a period of falling prices countered by attempts to reduce supply by at least some producing countries, so that supply can 'bounce back' to meet the increasing demand, leaving a persistent downward pressure on oil prices.

In general, changes in demand and supply must be inserted within the framework of the 'oligopolistic game' which characterises the oil market. What really matters, in determining the price path, is the degree of oligopolistic control over the market exercised by each of the three contending groups. A given path of supply and demand can derive from different sets of circumstances, corresponding to different — even opposite — changes in the relative power of the three groups.

Because of the high degree of uncertainty, and especially because of the high interdependence between events in the petroleum sector and events, especially political, outside of it, the recourse to sophisticated analytical tools of game theory appears pretentious. It may be more useful to sketch out some likely scenarios, pointing out their links with events external to the oil sector, and their likely consequences. In doing this, we must distinguish short-term from long-term prospects. In the first case, the problem will be to identify possible developments in a sector undergoing deep structural change. In the second case, we shall have to identify possible final equilibria for the market structure of the oil sector. As already pointed out, the structure of control based on production consortia jointly managed by the major oil companies for the exploitation of Middle East deposits was swept away by the nationalisation process initiated by the producing countries in the 1970s. Over the last dozen years we have thus witnessed a process of transformation in the structure of the sector, which is still going on and which involves not only the distribution of power among the main operators, but also their very nature. Only at the conclusion of such a process will the petroleum sector reach a relatively stable new equilibrium. In this respect, it is important to notice that the forces in the field, while sufficiently evident to allow us to discard the hypothesis of indeterminacy of the final outcome, are open to a multiplicity of possible equilibria. In other words, the final equilibrium is not indeterminate but plurideterminate, as so often happens in oligopolistic markets. The strategic choices adopted by the principal operators in the sector during the transition stage are decisive in determining which, among the different possible outcomes, will be realised.

II. THE SHORT-TERM SCENARIOS

For even the most immediate future it is impossible to identify a 'model' path, the most likely one to which all other possible paths can be confronted, attributing to them a probability which decreases with the increase in the size of the distance from the reference path. Rather, it will be more fruitful to concentrate our attention on three possible lines of evolution: the central one will be the most likely, but we must also consider the other two paths, which may deviate widely from the central path, but are none the less far from unrealistic. In fact, these two 'extreme' paths appear to be more likely than a number of those intermediate between them and the central path.

The first scenario – which we might call the *crisis scenario* – corresponds to the outbreak of political upheavals in some of the main oil-producing countries; particularly in the Arab peninsula, and to the drastic increase in ecological risks connected with deep-water technological problems, such as, for instance, to provoke the halting of crude production in Mexican and North Sea off-shore oilfields, or the interruption of the Alaska oil pipeline. More recently, an ecological disaster – the blowing-up of some off-shore wells in the Persian Gulf, near Abadan on the Iranian coast, and the subsequent oil spills – may, according to the more dramatic accounts of the situation, reach the point of provoking massive problems, notably the suspension of navigation in the Hormuz Straits. This outcome, however, must be seen as a likely outcome of political upheavals. The interruption of shipping through the Hormuz Straits would alone halt about two thirds of OPEC exports (the proportion would progressively fall, but remain substantial, with the coming on stream of the recently completed Saudi Arabia pipeline to the Red Sea). An 'Islamic revolution' in Saudi Arabia, extending to Kuwait, Qatar, and the Arab Emirates, which disrupts crude production in the area might halt more than fifty per cent of OPEC exports for a relevant time-span, especially if production installations are damaged.

In such circumstances, as shown on a reduced scale by the Khomeini revolution in Iran and later by the Iraq—Iran war, the market would immediately switch from a potential glut of wide dimensions to a state of absolute scarcity. Not only would the price of crude oil explode, the security of supplies would also be severely affected. Countries such as Japan or Italy would run the risk of finding themselves with dramatic gaps in their fuel oil supplies for conventional thermoelectric plants, and feed-stocks for the petrochemical industries. The reciprocal assistance agreements within the IEA (described in Chapter 6, section V) would in all probability only be partially applied. The countries most heavily dependent on crude oil imports would certainly not be able to deal with the difficulties involved simply by rationing petrol or forbidding the use of cars on Sundays, since petrol is obtained in the refineries in more or less fixed proportions with the other petroleum products required in order to keep the economy going. A series of more wide-ranging interventions would be required. Limits to petrol consumption would have to be accompanied by limits to the use of fuel oil for private heating, and especially for electricity production, and this might mean the need for rotations of temporary stoppages of supply to manufacturing plants and to household users, such as were applied in Great Britain in the winter of 1971—2 during the miners' strike. As we can see, this is a very dramatic perspective. Even if this is not the most likely scenario (and even if it is becoming less and less probable, with the building up of crude oil production capacity in politically more stable areas, and more or less everywhere in the world), the potential gravity of the problems obliges us to consider them carefully.

The second scenario — the central one — might be called the 'Saudi hypothesis' or the 'downward stability scenario'. It foresees the persistence of present trends. The petroleum market would evolve within a framework characterised by the following elements: the absence of dramatic events such as wars or revolutions, a relatively moderate pace of development in industrialised countries, a gradual entrance into the market of the new sources of crude (such as the Mexican 'Reforma Province', the Ivory Coast, Angola, etc.), and persisting difficulties for two potentially very large producers such as Iran and Iraq, keeping them on the margins of the market. Under these conditions, the market would be kept in a state of small but perceptible excess supply, such as to be manageable by Saudi Arabia, thus facilitating control of a gradual downward trend in crude oil prices. In fact, the strategy adopted by Saudi Arabia is central to this scenario. This strategy appears to be based on three elements. First, the enormous size of Saudi oil reserves (both proven and probable) which should allow, in contrast to Iran, large oil exports for many years to come. (There is a general consensus among oil experts on the fact that official

Saudi reserves are grossly underestimated: see, for example, Davidson, 1979b). Second, Saudi Arabia's low population density and political considerations prevent a very rapid process of industrialisation. Third, the cumulative surplus of the Saudi current account balance which has been reinvested in industrialised countries (especially in the eurodollar and domestic US markets), is of such magnitude as to guarantee capital income inflows, which at current levels of interest rates would be sufficiently large to finance necessary commodity imports in the event of any sharp decline in revenues from oil exports.

As a consequence of these three circumstances, Saudi Arabia is not interested in short-term maximisation of oil revenues; but rather prefers 'moderate' crude oil prices, in order to prevent excessively rapid implementation of energy conservation programmes or of alternative energy sources (from tar sands to coal, from solar to nuclear), or intensive exploitation of high-cost oilfields (such as off-shore in deep waters, or in internal areas in China and Siberia). At the same time, Saudi Arabia is interested in the stability and development of industrialised economies, because of its large investments, and resulting interest income.[3] Above all, Saudi Arabia is interested in defending its dominant leadership position in the international petroleum market. As the largest oil-exporting country, it is able to do this by the threat of speeding up or slowing down the daily rate of crude production sufficiently to influence market conditions. As oligopoly theorists stress, excess capacity is inherent in market leadership, as a deterrent to potential competitors even more than as a prearrangement to meet growth in demand. In our case, the possibility of increasing production is not only conducive to 'keeping order' among its OPEC partner—competitors; it is also a guarantee for the Western world that events such as the Iranian crisis in other countries would not provoke a dramatic shortage in oil supplies. Still more importantly, it is in the interest of Saudi Arabia to keep its oil production at levels sufficiently high so that a sudden withdrawal from the market would be considered a disastrous occurrence by the United States and their Western allies, thus assuring that survival of the present Saudi government is considered vital. All this means that Saudi oil production and exports should remain substantial. Thus the Saudis will be prepared only to a limited extent to accede to the pressures of other OPEC countries to decrease their share of OPEC exports.

According to this scenario, there should be a gradual fall in prices, over the next few years. In money terms, oil prices may even remain constant, or bounce back after periods of rapid decrease; but in real terms the fall should be more or less continuous and perceptible. The subsequent path of prices would then be guided by means of the 'Yamani formula', indexing crude oil prices to nominal national income of industrialised countries, but starting from a lower real price of crude oil, closer to that prevailing before the Iranian crisis. This path would be compatible with a gradual increase in demand for oil over the medium period, and thus with full exploitation of the large Iraqi resources by the end of the 1980s and the introduction into the market of oil from Eastern Siberia and internal China in the 1990s. Shale oil could capture a growing share of the market, but without substituting traditional oilfields at least before the year 2000 (except in the case of a renewed protectionist spur to North American internal markets). The picture would be completed by a gradual, non-dramatic, fall in the share of energy coming from oil.[4] As can be seen, this scenario seems to have an internal long-run consistency, and to be compatible with a global scenario of persistent economic growth, in the absence of large-scale military conflicts. This makes it acceptable for large industrialised countries as well, which increases the likelihood of its occurrence.[5]

All this does not mean that the third or 'breakdown scenario' can be excluded. A collapse in crude oil prices could occur if peace were re-established in the Middle East allowing Iran and Iraq to return to normal production thus flooding the petroleum market; and/or if some oil-exporting countries such as Mexico and Nigeria were obliged to make distress sales, with Saudi Arabia unwilling to balance such increases in supply with further production cuts. In addition to all this, there is also the possibility of a collapse in demand, due to continuous stagnation in industrialised economies caused by the persistence and extension of restrictive monetarist policies, or very rapid substitution of oil by other energy sources, backed by a strong trend towards energy conservation. Changes in the composition of final demand, induced by the changes in relative prices, may also contribute to a reduction in energy consumption. The excess supply of crude oil might be further accentuated by the rapid entry of new producers (such as Angola or Egypt) into the market. Such an event, analogous to the processes of oil substitution and energy conservation, would not occur by mere chance but would rather be the logical outcome, with a lag, of the substantial oil company investments in new programmes of exploration for oil reserves, and in the development of energy sources alternative to oil: investment programmes which had been decided after the crude oil price increases in 1973–4 and 1979–80 had rendered them profitable.

Faced by a fall in crude oil prices, oil-exporting countries with large populations, important industrialisation programmes already under way, and large international indebtedness would be strongly pressed to increase their level of production in order to ensure an unchanged amount of foreign earnings through higher export volume. These countries would find it very difficult, both socially and politically, to interrupt a semi-completed programme of accelerated industrialisation. But with a number of producing countries simultaneously pushing for higher export volumes, there would be no way of avoiding competitive cuts in crude oil prices. Under such circumstances, oil prices would fall, in a short time span, and the fall might even be of very sizeable proportions, to below $10 a barrel. In fact, once exploratory costs have been sustained, and once production capacity has been installed, producers will find it convenient to keep production going, unless oil prices fall below variable costs, which for oilfields all over the world are generally much lower than $10 per barrel. Rather, a fall of crude oil prices below average production costs (inclusive of amortisation for exploration expenses and fixed production installations), implying only partial recovery of fixed costs already sustained, would probably induce producers to increase the production level so as to minimise their losses. As a consequence, the fall in prices would provoke an increase rather than a decrease in supply.

If we assume that Saudi Arabia would not be prepared to keep reducing her oil exports, for reasons pointed out above, the large oil companies would take on a decisive role in determining the speed and limits of the reduction of crude oil prices. In fact, one of the main reasons why the 'breakdown scenario' cannot today be ignored is that, with the transition from a concessionary regime to a regime of service contracts, the companies are losing the ownership of crude oil, and more and more often are obliged to buy it from the State companies of oil-exporting countries. As a consequence, the companies which in earlier times could increase their profits by increasing crude oil prices and, even if not in the same proportion, the prices of refined products,[6] today may consider a reduction of crude oil prices more desirable, if the prices of refined products fall in a lesser proportion. However, we should recall that even after the widespread nationalisations of producing consortia in Middle East countries during the 1970s, all major oil companies own directly large proven reserves in the United States and elsewhere, so that a fall in crude oil prices would provoke large losses on capital account. In addition, they would also experience large losses because of the rigidity of prices fixed by long-term agreements with producing countries. Each company individually might find it profitable to get crude at cut-rate prices, after the nationalisations which drastically reduced the degree of vertical integration in the sector; but a fall in crude oil prices would not be in the interest of the major oil companies as a group.

A number of economists (the most notable being Milton Friedman[7]) consider this scenario a distinct possibility, and have been predicting it since the 1973–4 crisis. Other economists (Adelman, Davidson, Safer, etc.; see above, Chapter 6, section IV and note 35) maintain that consuming countries, above all the United States, should adopt policies conducive to this outcome, such as a very high excise tax in consuming countries or an auction scheme for oil-import permits. This scenario, however, goes against the interests of producing countries, as well as against the interests of the oil companies as a group. It also goes against the interests of major industrialised countries. This was shown, among other things, by the behaviour of the United States in the recent case of the Mexican currency crisis, in August 1982. A first consideration is the dramatic fall in the imports of manufacturing goods and services on the side of oil-exporting countries; but there are also other, even more important, considerations. In fact, the 'breakdown scenario' would reproduce a mirror image of many of the problems experienced in the 1973 crisis. Because of the sudden change in the relative prices of the various energy sources, a large number of investment projects (e.g. in energy sources alternative to oil: solar, shale oil, tar sands, coal, nuclear, etc.) would suddenly become unprofitable; the ensuing losses might be substantial, with chain repercussions, so as to produce a noticeable negative effect on the stability of the international financial system. At the same time, the drop in exporting countries foreign earnings would put some of them in a very difficult position as far as the servicing of their international debt is concerned. Both internal and international financial markets would be affected, with the risk of a confidence crisis and a collapse of the international financial system.

Since 1981, the oil market has by and large conformed to the 'downward stability' scenario. Crude oil prices are still much higher, even in real terms, than those prevailing before the Iranian crisis; and downward pressures persist. The decrease in crude oil prices up to the present has been sufficiently gradual, even if obviously its speed has not been constant. There have been a number of small crises; in each it seemed as if a 'breakdown scenario' might emerge, but the joint interest in price stability on the side of the main agents in the market induced strategic choices sufficient to avoid a price collapse. Here we will consider briefly the three most representative of these crises: the 'Nigerian' crisis of early 1982; the 'Mexican' crisis of August 1982, and the OPEC crisis of early 1983.

In the first of these occasions, a potential crisis situation was defused by the 'leader' among exporting countries, Saudi Arabia. At the beginning of 1982, Nigeria was experiencing heavy financial strains, and came under strong pressure from oil companies to accept a sharp reduction in oil prices.

Saudi Arabia intervened, fixing a minimum target for Nigerian sales, and threatened an embargo against those oil companies who would not fulfil their quota of liftings of Nigerian crude. This was sufficient to stop the companies (which were to gain individually, as pointed out above, but to lose collectively, from a fall of crude oil prices) from boycotting Nigerian oil, and a relatively slight reduction of prices was sufficient to avert the crisis.

In the second example, the potential crisis was averted by timely action by the United States. In August 1982, Mexico experienced a dramatic currency crisis. Even a heavy devaluation of the peso and drastic internal deflationary measures were insufficient to solve the problem, given the size of its international indebtedness, and the large number of long-term investment programmes under way. Because of the recent development of the oil-producing 'Reforma' province, Mexico — which is not a member of OPEC — was already striving to expand its market share in international crude oil markets. There was thus a clear risk of distress sales of crude oil, breaking the price front and starting a general price war, with the inevitable outcome of a price collapse. However, distress sales were avoided thanks to US readiness to concede a large emergency loan in exchange for an increase in Mexican crude oil supplies to the internal US market. The price was lower than the then prevailing 'market' price; but the timing and size of the agreement (also considering the 'collateral help' of the US with the IMF and other international financial institutions) was sufficient to avert the application of such prices to other crude oil sales.

The latest, and the most serious, crisis took place in February–March 1983. OPEC had reached the verge of collapse. However, an internal agreement was finally reached, calling for a substantial reduction in the official price of 'reference' crude oil (from \$35 to \$29 per barrel of 'light Arabic' crude at 34° API). In the weeks immediately following the agreement, the market prices for the crude oil of non-OPEC producers also fell; but the general impression was that these price rebates were aimed more at reestablishing pre-existing price differentials, than at initiating a much-feared price war. In fact, the price rebates were large and concentrated in a short time-span. A price war would have been far more dramatic.

A price war would imply a decision, on the side of the stronger producers (those enjoying lower production costs), to set prices so low as to oblige competitors to leave the market. For example, Saudi Arabia and the other producers in the Arabian peninsula might reduce crude oil prices to less than \$5 per barrel, or around a sixth of the present price, so as to prevent companies operating in the North Sea and Alaska from covering their current production and transportation costs. In the Arabian peninsula (but also in Iran and Iraq, and in a number of other producing countries as well) current production costs are less than $1 per barrel. Thus, in the case of a price war, there would be a tendency to go back to the situation prevailing in the 1960s, as far as the geographical distribution of the large producers is concerned (and, as happened then, the United States could revert to closing its internal market, in order to defend its internal production). However, it is clear that at present a price war is considered a threat to be avoided by all producers. Apart from any consideration of political risks or the risks of an international financial crisis, it is more profitable for Saudi Arabia to sell 2 million barrels of crude per day with an overall 'royalty' of $28 per barrel, than to sell 13 million barrels per day but with a 'royalty' reduced to $4 per barrel or less. Recourse to a price war is only conceivable as the final weapon.

III. STRUCTURAL CHANGES IN THE OIL MARKET

In the absence of sudden and drastic crises, the long-term trends in crude oil prices will be determined by the structural changes now taking place in the oil market. These changes are taking place within each of the three groups of agents in the market (the producing and the consuming countries, and the oil companies) and their inter-relationship.

The main element of change has been the process increasing the direct role of producing countries in the exploitation of their oil resources. This process became much more pronounced in the period after 1973. This policy was discussed above (Chapter 5); here we shall develop its consequences for the structure of the petroleum sector.

First, this policy implies a partial, but substantial, reduction of the degree of vertical integration of the major oil companies. In turn, this produces a reduction of the companies' market control in their downstream operations as well, from the marketing of crude oil to refining, transport and distribution of refined products. As recalled above (Chapter 3, sections V and VI, and Chapter 4), once the stage in which market power due to those technical factors described by Frankel had been overcome, a stage of 'managerial control' was reached, even before the Second World War, based on cartel agreements and especially on the joint ownership of Middle East consortia. The control of major oil companies over the international petroleum market was later slowly eroded, during the late 1950s and 1960s, by the growing role of the American 'independent' oil companies (such as Conoco, Occidental etc. operating especially in North Africa) and of State companies such as the Italian ENI. It is precisely this erosion which explains the reduced cohesion within the group of oil companies, and hence their reduced power in the confrontation with producing countries in 1970–3. Now it may seem that the acquisition of direct control over the production stage by producing countries would rapidly bring to an end the oligopolistic control of major oil companies over the market, so that the only relevant question becomes the rapidity with which producing countries exercise the dominant role previously held by major oil companies, not only in the production stage but over the petroleum sector as a whole. However, by now it is clear that this simple interpretation of current trends does not correspond to actual events.

The most important element in this respect is the 'realisation problem': a sudden change in traditional channels for selling oil products would imply a disruption of the market, with losses on the capital account for some firms and the necessity of surviving a prolonged price war for any newcomers. A drastic fall in the prices of oil products would bring about a parallel fall in crude oil prices. Producing countries, therefore, have a vested interest in preserving established channels, i.e. in acquiescing to the persistent dominance of the major vertically integrated oil companies. The very transition in the control of Middle East consortia is based on a shift to long-term agreements for oil sales to the old proprietors (see above, Chapter 5, note 17). Correspondingly, the absorptive capacity of other buyers of crude oil is limited, at least in the short term, by the difficulty they would encounter in increasing their shares in the refined product markets.

The shift in ownership of sales networks, from major oil companies to medium-sized companies, and the parallel increase in the degree of competition among crude oil buyers, must of necessity be gradual, its effect felt in the long term. But such gradual change can only occur if the producing countries also favour such a trend, by modifying their present practices. However, they might not consider it to be in their best interests, for while it is true that competition among buyers of crude increases the bargaining power of producing countries, the same competition may also produce downward pressure on final prices. The first effect implies increasing, and the second decreasing pressure, on crude oil prices. The net effect may be negative: the competitive reduction in the margins in the intermediary phases − refinery, transport and distribution − would not be in the interests of producing countries, if the price of refined products falls by more than the margins in the intermediary stages. In such an event, the downward pressure on the prices of refined products would be transmitted directly on crude oil prices. This outcome may be considered as likely, because of the degree of competition that exists among crude oil producers. The final result would be the disappearance of oligopolistic super-profits for both oil companies and producing countries, to the advantage of final buyers (or possibly to the tax authorities of the consuming countries, if taxes on petroleum products are gradually increased so as to counterbalance the fall in refined products' pre-tax prices).

In addition to this, it should also be noted that producing countries will be increasingly interested in defending profit margins in downstream operations, because of their growing stake in them. This tendency is already well under way. Thus we may formulate the general hypothesis that in the absence of traumatic events, the consolidation of producing countries' control in the 'upstream' stages of the petroleum sector will not be accompanied by a drastic reduction in the power of the group of oil companies as a whole, with respect both to producing and to consuming countries. Rather there may be a limited, gradual reduction of the market power of major oil companies in favour of the 'independents' and the smaller oil companies; but this process will also be more limited and gradual than one might suppose at first sight on the simple basis of the proprietary change of producing consortia.[8]

As far as the group of oil companies themselves are concerned, it is possible to identify the consolidation of a tendency already apparent in the post-war period, which has strengthened after the 1973 oil crisis. This is the tendency to a greater role for the State companies, even in oil-importing countries with a low internal production of crude. These companies (such as ENI in Italy) are the instrument for the energy policy of the consuming countries, but in practice they enjoy a substantial margin of autonomy. Their market power in the 'downstream' stages of activity is generally concentrated in the country of origin; the presence in other countries, with 'service contracts' in the exploration and crude oil production stages is limited to a few cases, notably ENI. Even in these cases, relevant bargaining power cannot be attributed to the State companies. Their contracts are either acquired in open competition with the large multinational oil companies, or result from bilateral government-to-government negotiations. In this latter case it is more correct to speak of bargaining power on the side of the producing country. On the other hand, the growing role of State companies makes necessary at least one qualification: the 'downstream' expansion of producing countries will imply a gradual withdrawal of vertically integrated companies located in consuming countries, and especially of State companies, from refining in particular, and possibly from transport as well. In fact, it is precisely in the direct bilateral relationship between the government of the producing country and that of the consuming country that an easy transition may occur from agreements on crude oil sales to agreements on refined products sales, preserving the long-term nature of the agreements, possibly based on the exchange with technical services (such as project evaluation and building of refineries, and training of related personnel in producing countries).

A growing downstream stake in refining (and more generally in the basic petrochemical industry) and in the transport stages by the State companies of large producing countries is a suitable outlet for 'petrodollars', especially in Arab countries characterised by low population density and persistent current account surpluses. Refining and shipping of crude oil and oil products are in fact capital intensive activities, requiring a well-established technology and a small labour force; the profitability of these investments, moreover, is indirectly guaranteed by the market power of large crude oil producing countries in the petroleum sector. The acquisition of direct control over the distribution of petrol (generally refined products) in industrialised countries appears less likely. This might be more likely in non-oil developing countries, while there is room for minority participations in developed countries, the main result of which would be to ensure long-term stability of commercial channels. Analogously, financial investment in peripheral activities (possibly the same as the diversification investments of major multinational oil companies) are possible and profitable. Such investments will not in general be made by the State oil companies, but by other institutions of the producing countries and by private organisations.

In general, it seems that the growing role of oil-exporting countries in the international arena, and specifically in the petroleum sector, need not produce a corresponding increase in their market power, leading to a parallel decrease in the power of major oil companies. Recent events would rather suggest that the degree of competition among producing countries is higher than that which existed among major oil companies, connected as they were through Middle East consortia. As has been shown above (Chapter 4, section III), the consortia were endowed with institutional mechanisms conducive to the joint planning of production and to the avoidance of price wars. Such mechanisms do not exist within OPEC, nor even within OAPEC, and cannot be substituted by a generic political solidarity — assuming there is such a linkage among OPEC countries, not to mention the important exporting countries outside of OPEC, such as Mexico, Great Britain, Norway.

At the same time, the oil crisis of 1973—4 brought about a growing consciousness of the relevance of the oil sector on the part of consuming countries. Events in the consuming countries affect the international petroleum market today just as before the 1973 oil crisis; but the economic authorities of consuming countries now take these repercussions much more seriously. By itself, this increased consciousness favours, at least in principle, the avoidance of counterproductive choices, and thus favours the interests of consuming countries. In particular, this should produce greater care in formulating economic policies that do not favour higher oil prices, and increased stress on active intervention encouraging energy diversification. None the less, it is difficult to foresee any significant increase in co-ordination of energy policies among industrialised countries, such as to make it possible to consider them as a single monopsonistic block. The scope of the International Energy Agency (IEA) is mainly to provide for exchange of information and to provide a safety net in case of dramatic disruptions in oil supplies. But it should also be stressed that the simple exchange of information is by itself conducive to greater consciousness of the problem, and suggests better ways to deal with it, especially for those countries in which public administration is less qualified.

As already pointed out, the influence of consuming countries over international petroleum markets can also manifest itself through State companies. The interaction of political and economic relationships may favour consuming, especially industrialised, countries on the strict economic level, for they can obtain better conditions for their supplies of crude oil or refined products in exchange for concessions concerning political, strategic or military elements (for instance, the sale of sophisticated weapons). The experience of 1973 and the years immediately following should not deceive us: the use of oil as a political weapon on the side of oil-producing Arab countries was possible at the time because of the then existing disequilibrium between supply and demand of crude oil, which was produced by the re-opening of the US market to imports (see above, Chapter 6, section II). In a situation of greater equilibrium, and especially in a situation characterised by large margins of unused productive capacity, the bargaining power of consuming countries may be substantial.

Consuming countries will also be affected by inroads into downstream activities, especially refining, by producing countries. This will specifically affect countries such as Italy, which in the 1950s was chosen by the major oil companies for location of refinery centres (due both to greater political stability in comparison to producing countries, an element brought to the fore by the 1951 Iranian crisis, and the lower costs of shipping for crude than for refined products: see above, Chapter 6, section VII, and note 48). The development of better direct bilateral relationships with producing countries may favour an orderly reabsorption of excess refining capacity in consuming countries. However, this issue needs to be explicitly considered in government-to-government agreements; and direct State intervention is needed in the consuming countries to ensure the co-ordination of the various companies operating refineries inside their territory: large (foreign) multinationals, the State company, small independent refiners. If these conditions are not met, it is likely that producing countries will enjoy a stable competitive advantage, since they can ensure their own refineries a high and stable degree of capacity utilisation (the problems concerning the transfer of technology are extremely limited for refinery plants). The same will be true for basic petrochemical plants.

The new trend in the location of refineries and basic petrochemical plants interact with a diversification policy adopted by major oil companies, as a reaction to their reduced control in the stage of exploration and production of crude oil. As shown above (Chapter 6, section III), because of the turn taken by events during the 1973–4 oil crisis, there was an extraordinary increase in the oil majors' profits. Initially, at least, some part of these profits were due to accounting conventions, stemming from inventory revaluations (including proven reserves directly owned by the oil companies). These profits provided the financial basis required to accelerate a diversification programme which had already been encouraged by the changes then in progress in the proprietory arrangements of producing consortia. This diversification programme seems to follow two main lines: expansion into petrochemicals and then into chemical production in general; and expansion in the sphere of overall energy (including coal, nuclear, etc.). However, as already noted above (Chapter 4, section VI), it should be stressed that, contrary to widespread opinion, by far the largest share of investments by the large oil companies is still directed to the oil sector (more than 80 per cent, in value terms). Emphasis appears to be on exploratory activity (or on financial acquisitions of firms with large proven reserves of oil) in politically friendly environments, mainly the United States, Canada and the North Sea; and on the restructuring of refinery activities, with closure of some plants and upgrading of others. (On the investment strategy of oil companies in recent years, see ENI (1982) and ENI (1983); according to ENI (1982) vol. I, p. 42, 63 per cent of total investments of large oil companies are in the exploration and production stages). The stress on the acquisition of new proven reserves is explained by the desire to re-establish a satisfactory degree of vertical integration, while the restructuring of refining plants can be seen as a reaction to the downstream expansion of producing countries, and to changes in the composition of demand for refined products (a fall in the share of 'heavy' products, such as crude oil; and an increase in that of 'light' products, such as petrol). Large amounts of financing also go into the necessary infrastructure for bringing new oilfields on stream in difficult areas such as Alaska and the North Sea. Very large infrastructure investments will also be required to develop the utilisation of natural gas, which will in fact constitute the main alternative to oil (see IEA, 1982; Aït-Laoussine, 1980a; Jensen, 1980).

According to a number of commentators, the growing relevance of the international trade in natural gas does not substantially modify conditions in the international petroleum market, both because the commercial links for natural gas largely reflect those of commerce in crude oil and petroleum products, and because gas and crude oil can be considered to be joint products (even if the technical coefficients are not fixed). Natural gas production is largely associated with crude oil production, in the form of natural gas dispersed in crude oil. Especially in OPEC countries, a large proportion of the natural gas thus obtained is burnt, after its separation from oil, or reinjected into the oilfield in order to preserve internal pressure and facilitate the production of crude. The transport of crude is much easier than natural gas, and requires a much lower capital outlay in infrastructure. However, OPEC countries are gradually acquiring the capital endowments necessary for the *in situ* utilisation of natural gas (mainly as a source of energy for their manufacturing industries, and as a raw material for petrochemical plants), and above all for export. Thus the share of natural gas which is utilised, relative to its total production, increased in the OPEC countries from 37 per cent in 1973 to 55—6 per cent in 1979.[9]

Natural gas can be transported either through gas pipelines, or through special ships, in liquefied form (LNG — liquefied natural gas — carriers). In this latter case there is also a need for liquefaction plants in the exporting countries, and regasification plants in importing countries. In comparison with oil, natural gas enjoys the important advantage of being 'cleaner', that is free of combustion residuals, in particular sulphur. However, greater technical difficulties and higher transport costs have up to now hindered its utilisation. Even today it is difficult to say whether a fully fledged market for natural gas really exists. In reality there exist a series of bilateral long-term agreements, connecting a specific exporting country to a specific importing country, which are required to justify investment in the necessary infrastructure, and which vary widely from country to country. In June 1980 OPEC officially declared a unifying principle to regulate the sale of natural gas; 'the oil—gas price equivalency' (see IEA (1982) pp. 11—2; and Aït-Laoussine (1980b) pp. 64—5). However this implies that consumers concede to producers a super-profit margin similar to those on crude oil sales. It would be necessary to discern whether conditions in the natural gas market are such as to justify such extraprofits. As a matter of fact, because of the abundant availability of natural gas (and especially the large amounts of natural gas still being burnt, in the absence of any potential use) we are here confronted with a market whose supply side development precedes demand. The installation of an integrated network of gas pipelines and/or liquefaction and regasification plants, should increase the degree of competition among producers, even if it will still be oligopolistic competition, by creating a more unified market. What is even more important from the present standpoint, is the development of an international market for natural gas, in step with crude oil. It should stimulate − even if to a limited extent − the competition among the two sources of energy, and should thus produce reductions in the degree of oligopolistic control that has been enjoyed by producing countries in crude oil markets up to the present time. The increase in the competitive pressure on oil-exporting countries is not likely to be disruptive, because the group of natural gas-exporting countries by and large coincides with the group of oil-exporting countries. It should, however, be significant, since the geographical distribution of natural gas reserves does not coincide with that of oil reserves, and also because the degree of external dependency of some important consuming areas will be reduced. There is, however, a much more important outcome of the development of natural gas. Contrary to the dark forecasts of an impending exhaustion of oil, which will bring with it the transition to energy sources such as coal and nuclear, which are highly dangerous and increase pollution, it is likely that the eventual (due to the size of probable reserves) reduction in the share of energy consumption satisfied by oil will be accompanied by an increase in the share of a 'cleaner' energy source such as natural gas.[10]

IV. THE LONG-TERM SCENARIOS

The elements discussed in the previous section, concerning the changing structure of the international petroleum market, provide the basis for examining long-term prospects for oil prices. Let us start by recalling that in the long run oil prices depend on average production costs (inclusive of an allowance for exploration and development costs), plus a profit margin related to 'barriers to entry' or, in other words, to the degree of oligopolistic control over the market by oil companies and producing countries (see above, Chapter 3, section IX). As a first approximation, let us assume that production costs in real terms are not going to change substantially: the need to exploit more and more difficult oilfields is counterbalanced, over historical time, by on-going technical progress. In addition, the difference between prices and production costs today is such that it is entirely plausible to expect that the main changes in the situation will come from this difference, rather than from costs. This is because the petroleum market is now undergoing the great transformation process discussed above. We are now in a stage of transition which should finally lead to a new equilibrium structure.

In this section we examine three possible equilibrium structures for the petroleum market. The first is the 'fully competitive scenario', which might follow from the 'breakdown scenario' discussed above in section II. A complete collapse of the control of the market by producing countries and oil companies would be accompanied by a dramatic growth of the role of spot markets, which now represent around 10 per cent of internationally traded oil.[11] Under the present institutional financial framework, a 'deep' spot market is a necessary and sufficient condition for the growth of future markets for crude oil and oil products. This, in addition to the high ratio of fixed to variable costs at all stages of activity within the oil sector (an element on which see above, Chapter 3, sections V and VIII), should give rise to continuous instability of prices and quantities. After a while the dramatic effects of such instability for international currency and financial markets, and hence on industrial development as well as on inflation rates within both producing and consuming countries, are likely to induce some government intervention, at a multinational level, in order to stabilise the market.

The second scenario, which might be considered the most likely one, at least for the medium term (namely for the 1980s), might be called the 'informal "As Is" scenario', since it would repeat, in a sense, the 'As Is' Agreement of 1928, in which major oil companies agreed to keep their market shares in oil products in major consuming countries constant (see above, Chapter 4, section III). Given the spread of anti-trust policies by governments in consuming countries, there is certainly no room for a formal agreement of this kind among companies. But the markets for the main refined products can be described as 'differentiated oligopoly' (see above, Chapter 2, section VI, and Chapter 3, section IX), with barriers to entry due not so much to the large optimal size of plant compared to the size of the market, as to the role of trademarks and the relative stickiness of seller—buyer relationships.

Thus, if there is no full-range disruption of the market, major companies are likely to maintain their relative market shares in product markets, also stabilising — more or less — the relative shares of producing countries in the market for crude oil, as part of their attempt to keep 'order' in the international petroleum market. This would take place through a system of long-term agreements between producing countries and oil companies, accompanied, as in the past, by a subsidiary network of long-term deals between crude-short and crude-long oil companies, i.e. between companies with less crude than they need and companies in the opposite position. Producing countries would have to avoid selling a large proportion of their oil on spot markets, and to favour sales to larger companies rather than to newcomers, who would be obliged to put a downward pressure on product prices in order to ensure themselves an enlarged share of those markets, corresponding to their increased availability of crude. There is room, instead, for government-to-government agreements, especially for those consuming countries which have a well-established State oil company, as is the case for Italy.

Saudi Arabia would seem to favour this line of development, which is, in fact, fully acceptable for producing countries, once they recognise the intrinsic weaknesses of OPEC as a cartel. It would also be acceptable to the largest consuming countries, the United States, for at least two reasons. First, it is the home-country for most major oil companies, as well as an important producer; hence in the United States there are strong internal pressure groups favouring policies conducive to relatively high and stable oil prices. Second, the presence of large internal oil production means that the US economy as a whole enjoys a competitive advantage in comparison to other industrialised countries — such as Japan, Germany, etc. — in need of oil imports at world prices; and this advantage is larger, the higher crude oil prices.

The problems with this scenario arise because of the existence of a certain degree of competitive pressure within both producing countries and oil companies. It is likely to provoke a process of change — even if a slow and gradual one — of the relative share of companies in product markets, with an increasing share for smaller companies and the 'newcomers'. Analogously, the major companies' efforts to reconstitute a sufficiently high degree of vertical integration through the acquisition of own resources of crude in countries not members of OPEC, together with the process of energy savings and substitution of oil with other energy sources, are bound to provoke a decrease in OPEC's weight in the international petroleum market and the increase of competitive pressures within OPEC itself. It is difficult to say whether these pressures will build up over time to the point of bringing about the first scenario, the 'fully competitive' one; but for a medium-long period (3 to 10 years) this second scenario — 'Informal As Is' — could well survive such competitive pressures, and the current behaviour of the 'leaders' within each of the three groups (United States, Saudi Arabia, Exxon) is such as to make it the more likely.

Over a longer period, in reaction to market instability or even directly, as the outcome of better international political relationships, a third scenario might be possible: a 'triangular compromise', i.e. a joint agreement for the planning of (or at least a good degree of control over) developments in the oil sector connecting the most important, if not all, amongst producing and consuming countries, and oil companies. This might be the consequence of the actual experience, or the fear, of the instability problem arising in the first and possibly at the conclusion of the second scenario. Because of the international nature of the oil market, the instability of crude oil prices is bound to be reflected in instability of exchange markets and international financial markets: a situation conducive to a collapse of the international financial system, and thus to a new Great Depression. Avoiding this outcome requires not only co-operation in establishing a new and stable international monetary system, and in ensuring the smooth operation of international financial markets; it also requires, in perspective, co-operation in the stabilisation of the crude oil market. Sketching the details of a co-operative scheme would now be a pointless exercise. It is clear, however, that co-operation in the oil sector should be inserted in a wider framework of multilateral co-operation for the stabilisation of primary commodity markets. More generally, it should be part of a wide-ranging North–South agreement; perhaps along the lines found in the Brandt Report (1980).[12]

Among the dangers of the present situation is the general tendency away from this outcome, and an increasing tendency to 'underground protectionism'. The geographical locations of exploratory efforts by large oil companies and State companies of oil-importing countries, and the specificities of the energy diversification programme (with, for instance, two countries such as France and Czechoslovakia, with important internal reserves of uranium, placing much more emphasis than the others on the development of nuclear energy), seems to point to a process – albeit a gradual one – of regional segmentation of the international petroleum market. This favours a process of growing 'underground protectionism', cumulating political and economic elements (such as differential fiscal and proprietory regimes), which divert efforts of agents in the market from the minimisation of 'physical' costs of energy supplies. In this situation there is a growing risk that energy policies will be mainly based on short-term 'strategic' considerations, which do not consider the evolutionary trends in crude oil prices and the perspective changes in the structure of the market, simply extrapolating the present situation. Since for each and every country the minimisation of the costs of energy supplies is a decisive element for defending the international competitiveness of its economy, while for all countries jointly the minimisation of 'physical' costs of energy supplies is a decisive element in favouring a non-inflationary economic development, it is extremely important not to lose sight of the factors determining the evolution of the international petroleum market, which this study has tried to bring to the fore.

Appendix: Chronology of the Principal Events in the Petroleum Sector

1854   Abraham Gesner patents a process for refining kerosene and lighting gas; oil lamps come into use.

1859   (August) First oil well: Edwin Drake discovers oil at Titusville, Pennsylvania. The price of oil is $20 per barrel; but falls to 50 cents in 1861 because of storage difficulties.

1870   Creation of Standard Oil Company; Rockefeller starts his policy of concentration of the oil industry in Pennsylvania.

1882   Creation of the Standard Oil Trust.

1888   The Ottoman Empire grants a petroleum concession to a group controlled by the Deutsche Bank.

1890   Royal Dutch Petroleum Company founded.

1897   Marcus Samuel founds the Shell Transport and Trading Company.

1901   Spindletop oil strike in Texas leading to the creation of the Gulf and the Texas companies (January).

Charles D'Arcy, an Englishman, is granted a 60-year concession in Persia.

1907   Merger of Royal Dutch and Shell Transport to form Royal Dutch Shell.

1908   Oil is discovered in Persia.

1911   The development of the car industry causes the sale of petrol to exceed that of paraffin for the first time in the United States.

1911   The US Supreme Court orders the break-up of the Standard Oil Trust (May).

1912   Creation of the Turkish Petroleum Company. First use of the assembly line to produce the Model T Ford.

1913   Introduction of the 'depletion allowance' in the United States.

1914   After having converted its navy from coal to oil, the British government (in which Churchill was First Lord of the Admiralty) acquires 50 per cent of the Anglo-Persian Oil Company (from 1935 Anglo-Iranian, and from 1954 British Petroleum).

1918   Oil production starts in Venezuela.

1920   The San Remo Agreement substitutes France and Britain in place of Germany in the Turkish Petroleum Company.

1925   Creation of the Iraq Petroleum Company from the remains of the Turkish Petroleum Company, with a concession valid until the year 2000.

1926   Creation of the Azienda Generale Italiana Petroli (AGIP), the first petroleum company fully owned by a national government.

1927   Discovery of oil at Kirkuk in Iraq.

1928   The 'Red Line' Agreement regulating exploration by the major companies in the Middle East (July). At the conclusion of a price war the major companies reach the 'As Is' Agreement for collaboration in world markets (September).

1930   Socal (Standard Oil of California) obtains an exclusive concession for the State of Bahrain and discovers oil two years later.

1933   Socal obtains the first Saudi Arabian concession.

1934   Anglo-Persian and Gulf obtain a joint concession in Kuwait.

1935   The 'Connally Hot Oil Act' supporting the Texas Railroad Commission's pro-rationing scheme for oil is passed in the United States.

1936   Socal cedes to Texaco 50 per cent of its concessions in Bahrain and Saudi Arabia on the foundation of the joint company Caltex.

1937   Mexico nationalises its petroleum industry.

1938–9 Discovery of oilfields in Saudi Arabia, Kuwait and Quatar.

1948   Official termination of the 'Red Line' Agreement; Exxon and Mobil become partners of Socal and Texaco in Aramco, formal owner of the Saudi Arabian concession. First Arab–Israeli war (May).

1948   Marshall Plan introduced in Europe; post-war reconstruction of European (and Japanese) industry favours conversion to oil over coal as the basic energy source.

1950   Introduction of the 'golden gimmick' which acts in favour of the increase in royalties paid to Saudi Arabia and the other producing countries at the expense of the US taxpayer.

1951   Mossadeq assumes power in Iran and nationalises the oil industry, creating the National Iranian Oil Company (NIOC); the major companies boycott Iranian oil.

1953   Formation of the Ente Nazionale Idrocarburi (ENI). In the USA an anti-trust suit which lasts until 1968 is brought against the five major American oil companies.

1954   After the fall of Mossadeq the major American companies and some 'independents' are admitted to the Iranian consortium.

1956   Nationalisation of the Suez Canal (July); second Arab–Israeli war (October).

1959   Quotas established by the USA for the import of crude and refined products (April). Discovery of the Groningen gasfield in the Netherlands. Exploration starts (slowly) in the North Sea.

1960	Creation of the Organisation of Petroleum Exporting Countries (OPEC).
1961	Iraq expropriates 99 per cent of the areas covered by the concessions given to the Iraq Petroleum Company.
1962	Death of Mattei in an air accident. Creation of Petromin, the Saudi Arabian State Oil Company.
1967	Third Arab–Israeli war (June), Suez canal blocked.
1968	Creation of the Organisation of Arab Petroleum Exporting Countries (OAPEC). Discovery of the Prudhoe Bay oilfields in Alaska.
1969	In the Santa Barbara canal, off the coast of California, an accident produces leaks from an underwater oilfield with substantial ecological damage to the coast; US off-shore exploration is halted for several years.
1970	Production of North Sea oil starts. In May the Tapline which transports oil from Saudi Arabia to the Mediterranean is closed by an accident. In August the Libyan request for price increases is accepted by Occidental.
1971	Teheran Agreement between OPEC and the oil companies (February), Tripoli Agreement (April); nationalisation of the petroleum industry in Algeria. Declaration of the gold inconvertibility of the dollar and the introduction of internal price controls for crude and refined products in the US (August).
1972	Nationalisation of the Iraqi consortium (June); Saudi co-participation in Aramco agreed (December). Discovery of oil in the Reforma province in Mexico.
1973	Abolition of import quotas for crude and refined products in the US (April); fourth Arab–Israeli war and the oil blockade of Israeli supporters (October). First petroleum crisis: between October 1973 and January 1974 OPEC quadruples the price of crude.
1974	Oil embargo is lifted (March). Formation of the International Energy Association (IEA) under the auspices of the OECD with the objective of facing OPEC with a united front of the major industrialised countries; France and a number of other countries in favour of bilateral agreements refuse to join.
1975	International economic crisis; reduction of national income in the major industrialised countries reduces the demand for oil. Nationalisation of the Kuwait Oil Company (March). Suez Canal is reopened (June).
1976	IEA countries agree to mutual assistance plan in case of emergency. Nationalisation of Venezuelan concessions (January).
1978	Iranian revolution (September).
1979	Petrol shortages in US, especially in California. Second petroleum crisis.
1980	Iran–Iraq war (September). 'Windfall Profits Tax' is approved in the US. Saudi Arabia's nationalisation of Aramco is completed.

1981   Reduction in the price of Nigerian and Libyan crude; OPEC agrees price realignment (October).

1982   Currency crisis in Mexico (August).

1983   Sharp reduction in crude prices; difficulties within OPEC over prices and production quotas (February—March). Saudi Arabia forms Norbec, a trading company independent of Petromin and Aramco, to operate on the spot market to regulate supply.

1984   Iran and Iraq bomb tankers in Persian gulf, heightening tension in oil markets and slowing shipping through the straits of Hormuz (May).

Notes

1. *Webster's Third New International Dictionary, Unabridged* (Chicago: G. & C. Merriam and Encyclopedia Britannica, 1981).
2. The introduction of computers has brought about enormous progress in the reliability of seismic analysis. The last ten years has seen the development of a new technique called 'bright spot' which has greatly reduced the probability of dry test wells.
3. On the organisational structure of the major petroleum companies see Sylos Labini and Guarino (1956, pp. 28–31). Few substantial changes in this area have occurred since their study was published.
4. However, United States anti-trust legislation sets limits to the co-operation of the largest American oil companies in exploratory activities in US off-shore territorial waters.
5. The 'barrel' is the most commonly used unit of measure in the petroleum sector. It equals about 0.137 tonnes, or 159 litres, or 0.159 cubic metres. The flow of production is measured in barrels per day: one barrel per day equals about 50 tonnes per annum. On the various units of measure the interested reader may consult Banks (1980, pp. 2–5) or *Energy and Hydrocarbons* (1981, p. 9).
6. For an analysis of the transportation phase of the petroleum sector in the period immediately preceding the Second World War, but still of relevance today, see Frankel (1969, pp. 33–49 and 157–64). A detailed analysis of the market for charter crude oil carriers is given in Adelman (1972, pp. 103–59 and 333–7).
7. The example is the refinery of Abadan, which was constructed in the second decade of this century and for many years was the largest in the world. For most of the components that go to make up a refinery the 'law of cubed and squared proportions' applies: the cost (for example, of a reservoir) increases in proportion to the surface, that is to the square of the radius while the capacity increases in proportion to the volume, i.e., the cube of the radius. However, these economies of scale may reach a limit if the productive capacity of the plant is given by the extent of the market and the costs of transport to nearby markets are too high.
8. In the United States the diffusion of small independent refineries, which are technologically sub-optimal, was encouraged by the controls on the petroleum sector, in particular the entitlement programme under the import quota policy. According to this programme, oil import licences were granted directly to all US

144

refineries (and could be sold freely at a price equal to the difference between the internal and the imported price of oil) in proportion to the oil refined, but in higher proportion for the smaller than for the larger refineries: the so-called 'small-refiner bias'. A similar situation resulted from the 1971–81 oil price control system which differentiated between oil in place, newly discovered, and imported oil, necessitating an allocation of the different categories among the refineries. See Kalt (1981, pp. 59–61) and US Congress (1980, pp. 83–90).

9. It is none the less probable that the greatest efforts, at least initially, will be concentrated in the newly industrialised countries. See below, Chapter 7, section IV.

10. At the time of the first petroleum crisis in 1974 the United States consumed 48.1 per cent of the world's petrol production (excluding the Eastern Block countries) compared with an average of 30.8 per cent for all petroleum products (Kalt, 1981, p. 144).

11. It is in this respect that the small refineries are particularly inefficient, generally requiring crude of higher than average quality to produce a lower than average proportion of 'light' products. The US programme to favour small refineries is thus counterproductive (cf. US Congress, 1980, p. 87).

12. These installations are frequently converted to storage reservoirs for crude or refined products. The substantial increase in demand for storage facilities has not been the result of a generalised increase in consumption, but rather for strategic reasons (with most governments instituting minimum limits on stocks in order to meet any future disruption in supplies) and economic motives of a precautionary-speculative nature, induced by the sharp fluctuations in prices, as well as by the fact that the rise in prices has caused a decrease in storage costs as a proportion of price (around 10–20 per cent on average, but with wide variability).

13. See, for example, US Congress (1980, pp. 42–52) for a simple summary of the technical aspects of the refining process.

14. From the consumer's point of view the various petroleum products are either independent or substitutes, but not complements. As a consequence an increase in the price of a product will have a positive or zero, but not negative, effect on the demand for the other products. The setting of prices product by product would thus lead, after the necessary number of steps, to the same results that could have been reached by means of the joint determination of prices with the objective of maximising total receipts.

15. For reasons discussed below (Chapter 4, section IV, and Chapter 6, section III), given the prices of petroleum products it is in the interest of the vertically integrated firms to set the price of crude so that the greatest proportion of total profits accrue to the initial stage of production; the price of crude is thus linked (even more than is normally the case between the costs of inputs and the final product) to the price of the refined products. See, however, Chapter 7, section I, below.

NOTES TO CHAPTER 3: THE PRICE OF OIL

1. The quote is from the cover of Meadows *et al.* (1975), a report prepared in 1972 for the Club of Rome by a group of MIT scientists and perhaps the best-known example of this line of reasoning.

2. In this respect an interesting present-day warning may be found in Jevons's grim 1865 forecast of the impending exhaustion of coal supplies in England. As an instance of the more optimistic perspective which becomes possible when the role of technical progress is taken into account, see Kahn (1978); with reference to the energy problem, Kahn stresses the developments in technologies not based on hydrocarbons, such as breeders, solar energy, geothermy, which may render them economically profitable.

3. The role of expectations and some policy implications of the user cost principle are employed in the analysis of the problem given in Davidson, Falk and Lee (1974).

4. See Parrinello (1982, p. 191). The seminal paper on the neoclassical theory of exhaustible natural resources is Hotelling (1931); on the same lines, see, for example, Solow (1974), Sweeney (1977), Pindyck (1978), Dasgupta and Heal (1979), Levhari and Pindyck (1981).

5. Nordhaus (1973) (see also Nordhaus, 1979, 1980) develops in this respect the concept of the 'backstop technology' ('roughly, a substitute process with infinite resource base') as a less high-brow, more realistic basis for empirical studies of the energy sector. Even if Nordhaus (1980, p. 352) states that 'the oil price of the mid-1970s could not be justified by its intrinsic scarcity', the underlying theory is still the marginalist one; see the criticisms in Davidson, Falk and Lee (1974, pp. 413–14).

6. See Nordhaus (1973, pp. 534–8); Davidson, Falk and Lee (1974, pp. 414–20).

7. Nehring (1978, pp. 54ff.). The data collected in the book refer to 31 December 1975, with some additional references to fields discovered in 1976 and 1977. But if we look, for example, at the statistics presented in the *Oil and Gas Journal*, year end issues from 1976 onwards, we can see that the rate of discovery of new giant and large fields is again increasing, after the fall in the years 1970–5. (According to Nehring's definition, giant oilfields are those containing at least 500 million barrels of recoverable crude.) Nehring's estimates seem especially conservative for Siberian and inland Chinese reserves. For a comparison of different estimates, see Foley (1976, p. 138).

8. As already stressed, we should distinguish this fact from the possibility that through mistaken evaluations of an imminent exhaustion of oil resources, induced by captious propaganda, decisions might be made assuming an impending scarcity problem. But unless there is a concomitant oligopolistic or monopolistic control of the market, which – within limits – allows major operators to influence the course of events, market forces would quickly restore a more realistic attitude among operators.

9. Adelman (1972, p. 253); see also Adelman (1976, 1979): 'What lies

ahead in the late twenty-first century, nobody knows, but a shortage of oil reserves is less to be feared than a shortage of drinkable water or breathable air'. See also Davidson (1979a, 1979b).

10. 'Ricardian' models of differential rent for natural resources are presented in Parrinello (1982, pp. 196ff.). However, Parrinello stresses, the Ricardian theory of differential rent is a static one, while 'when exhaustible natural resources exist in short supply, the choice of the system of production and therefore the determination of prices cannot be reduced to a problem of choice of techniques in a single period of time' (p. 208). This is but a different way of saying that the theory of differential rent cannot explain directly — *especially in a non-competitive situation* — the gap between price and cost.

11. See Penrose (1968, pp. 150–72); Blair (1976, pp. 29–53 and 98–120).

12. Adelman (1972, pp. 15 and 169–70). Penrose (1968, pp. 46–7) perceives Frankel's point as referring to the stability or instability of the oil market; this should rather be seen, in fact, as a corollary of Frankel's thesis on the prevalence of non-competitive (oligopolistic) conditions.

13. Adelman (1972, p. 6). The analytical procedure followed by Adelman recalls the equality, in equilibrium, of the extensive and intensive margin of the productivity of land in the theory of differential rent.

14. Furthermore, as has been argued in the previous section, Adelman's reasons for increasing costs are strictly valid only within a static framework; over time technical progress (both in exploration and in production) may counterbalance, and more than counterbalance, any static tendency to increasing costs. Adelman does not provide any evaluation of the pace of technical progress.

15. It should be stressed, however, that notwithstanding this legal framework (which only applies to the United States), control over pipelines and refineries is still used as a basis for controlling the market; see, for example, Blair (1976, pp. 137–9 and 246–52).

16. Penrose's approach is followed by Luciani (1976), who also points to the role played by the August 1971 crisis of the international monetary system in paving the way for the 1973–4 oil price explosion. This is, however, an element that acted on all primary commodities in 1971–3 (see Sylos Labini, 1982, pp. 50–2) and cannot explain the comparatively much higher path followed by oil prices.

17. There may be various sets of 'correct' decisions; and each set will bring out a different equilibrium configuration of the market. In other words, equilibrium under oligopolistic conditions is 'plurideterminate', not 'indeterminate'. For the distinction between 'indeterminacy' and 'multideterminacy' in relation to oligopolistic markets, see Sylos Labini (1969).

18. The historical roots of this approach can be traced back to Marshall's vision of the biological evolution of firms (see Marshall, 1961). A fundamental contribution to the development of the managerial approach was given by Penrose herself (see Penrose, 1959, 2nd edn 1980; M. Slater's 'Foreword' to this edition discusses the influence of Penrose's thought on the modern theory of the firm).

19. On the distinction between the two approaches, see Roncaglia (1978).
20. See Chevalier (1975, p. 12; 1977, p. 129). Chevalier (1977, pp. 132–3) explicitly refers to Marx; but in Marxian analysis, as in that of Classical economists, the concept of surplus is only defined with reference to the economic system as a whole, while it has no meaning independently of relative prices and distribution if referred to an individual sector, where the product (or products) is heterogeneous from the means of production. In other words, it is impossible to provide a theoretical explanation of the level (or at least the limits) of the realised value of refined products taking as given production conditions and distribution in other sectors, since these will not only influence, but also be influenced by, the results of the struggle among the three contending groups in the oil sector. The 'realised value' of oil is defined by Chevalier (1975, pp. 13–4; 1977, p. 129) by referring to the prices of the next-best substitutes of oil products; but as we saw after 1973, and as is theoretically obvious, such prices – like all prices in the system – are influenced by the price of a basic commodity such as oil. Moreover, since a number of refined products are jointly derived from oil, and each of them has a number of possible uses, the 'next-best substitute' cannot have a precise definition. This concept can find a better use in analysing the degree of 'external' competition in the market of each refined product. These criticisms also apply to Nordhaus's concept of the 'backstop technology' discussed above. In fact, what Chevalier calls 'surplus' is but the sum of monopoly rents and differential rents for the oil sector; the struggle over these rents was already considered the basic issue in the evolution of the oil market by, for example, Davidson (1963) and Posner (1973).
21. Chevalier (1975, pp. 59–65, 108–9, 211; 1977, pp. 141–5, 153).
22. Chevalier (1975, p. 15). The year 1970 is taken as the dividing line of two very different phases of the oil market throughout the whole book; see also Chevalier (1977, p. 142). The period of increasing costs is, however, referred to as beginning in 1971 in Chevalier (1977), p. 141n and p. 142n. Chevalier (1975, pp. 64–5; 1977, p. 145) recalls the massive explorations started around 1970–1 in Alaska, the Arctic, the North Sea, and generally offshore as pointing to a new phase of increasing costs. As a matter of fact, exploration both in Alaska and the North Sea began earlier: the price level prevailing in the 1960s was probably in current terms already sufficient to make exploitation of both areas profitable (especially if we consider for Alaska the fact that the internal US price was higher than the price prevailing in international markets and, for the North Sea, its proximity to important consuming areas).
23. Chevalier (1975) p. 15; see also pp. 99ff.; and Chevalier (1977) pp. 146–7.
24. The elements on which Chevalier relies (see note 22 above) refer to the sector as a whole and can affect the individual firm only in so far as competition does not prevail in the sector; but in this case the size of the barriers to entry is more important, in determining the equilibrium price of crude oil at any given point in time, than the tendency

of costs either to increase or to decrease over (historical) time for the sector as a whole. In fact, with his notion of the 'cost in evolution', Chevalier collapses two different problems into one: the determination of oil prices at any given point in time and the determination of their changes over time. It should be added that following Chevalier's reasoning, the period of decreasing costs prior to 1970 should have been characterised by *negative* rents!

25. For a criticism of marginalist theories of non-competitive market forms, and in particular of the so-called game-theoretic approach based on 'reaction curves' and 'conjectural variations', see Sylos Labini (1969) pp. 19–20.

26. This concept does not coincide with Adelman's 'Maximum Economic Finding Costs' discussed above (section IV), since Adelman refers to the more costly among fields in operation, which if generalised free competition prevailed would be expelled from the market, since world demand can be met by enlarging production in the cheapest areas, *imprimis* Middle East (including still-to-be-located oilfields). As already noted, in the present situation it is the high current price of crude oil which explains the exploitation of currently marginal oilfields, and not vice versa.

NOTES TO CHAPTER 4: THE OIL COMPANIES

1. See Sampson (1976) p. 71n. The 'Seven Sisters' are: BP (British Petroleum, ex Anglo-Iranian), Exxon (Standard Oil of New Jersey), Gulf, Mobil (Standard Oil of New York), Royal Dutch Shell, Socal (Standard Oil of California), and Texaco. Apart from BP (English) and Shell (English, Dutch), the others are multinational companies with the US as their home country.

2. On the evolution of the US legal system, see Sylos Labini and Guarino (1956) pp. 3–26.

3. For an analysis of the US and anti-monopoly laws, see Neale (1970).

4. See Sampson (1976) p. 41. As the Report of the Federal Trade Commission (1952, p. 207) notes, this situation is the logical result of the way in which the sentence of the Supreme Court was executed: by distributing to the shareholders of the Standard Oil Company of New Jersey (later Exxon), which was the holding company, the share capital it owned in the other 33 subsidiary and affiliate companies of the group. The low degree of competition prevailing in the sector is also revealed by the high rates of return, especially in the transport stage. For instance, in 1913 the investments in pipelines within the United States show an average return of 41.5 per cent: namely, just a bit over two years is necessary to recover the cost of building the pipelines (Solberg, 1976, p. 65).

5. For a synthetic account, rich in statistical data, of the development of the main oil companies, and for specific bibliographical references on each of them, see Penrose (1968) pp. 87–149.

6. Churchill on this occasion showed himself the faithful disciple of

Adam Smith's liberalism. The principle of the non-intervention in the economy on the side of the State had in fact developed as a critique of the feudal remnants (such as internal custom barriers, public monopolies, etc.); but among the exceptions admitted by Smith himself were those concerning the military safety of the State. Furthermore, active public intervention against concentrations of *private* power is part of the liberal position supporting competition. See Smith (1971) vol. I, pp. 406–15.

7. Analogously to what happened in the case of Standard Oil, and possibly even more strongly, economies of scale in the transport stage decisively contributed to the acquisition of market power on the part of Shell and BP, jointly with the advantages of an integrated network of production and distribution on an international scale.

8. Specifically, in 1927–8 there was a price war between Standard Oil of New Jersey (now Exxon) and Shell. The price war was favoured by the availability of low-priced Soviet oil; it was initially confined to the Indian market, but soon it had repercussions in other markets all over the world. See Sampson (1976) pp. 82–5.

9. On the working of the pro-rationing scheme, see Sylos Labini and Guarino (1956) pp. 18–21. As the Report of the Federal Trade Commission (1952, p. 218) notes, the policy of conservation through rationing of production, officially presented as a reply to the perspectives of exhaustion of oil, is in fact supported by oil companies only when it becomes clear that the situation is completely different, with abundant proven reserves and an excess of productive capacity.

10. Here as elsewhere the companies' present names are used, which may be different from those used in the periods under discussion.

11. It was Gulbenkian who, after prolonged discussions, finally took a red pencil and drew on a map what were, in his opinion, the boundaries of the ex-Ottoman Empire.

12. The companies' relative shares were subject to change as a consequence of political upheavals, as for instance in the case of Iran after Mossadeq's fall. Immediately before the oil crisis (January 1972) the respective shares of the 'Seven Sisters' and CFP in Middle East consortia were as follows:

	Iraq	Iran	Saudi Arabia	Kuwait	Qatar	UAE
BP	23.75	40	–	50	23.75	23.75
Shell	23.75	14	–	–	23.75	23.75
Exxon	11.875	7	30	–	11.875	11.875
Mobil	11.875	7	10	–	11.875	11.875
Gulf	–	7	–	50	–	–
Texaco	–	7	30	–	–	–
Socal	–	7	30	–	–	–
CFP	23.75	6	–	–	23.75	23.75
Others	5	5	–	–	5	5

SOURCE: Al-Chalabi (1980) p. 12; Penrose (1968) p. 151.

13. The regulations concerning crude oil liftings in the various consortia have generally been an exceptionally well-kept secret. It is possible, however, to deduce their general magnitude from other information: see, for example, Penrose (1968) pp. 155–64. There are then long-term agreements concerning crude supplies from crude-long companies to crude-short ones. On such agreements, see the Federal Trade Commission (1952) pp. 137–62 (and pp. 47–136 on Middle East consortia).

14. See Blair (1976) pp. 98ff. An extremely meaningful instance of the companies' ability to regulate crude world supplies is offered by the Iranian events, when Iranian crude was boycotted on world markets as a reaction to the nationalisations decreed by Mossadeq in 1951. On that occasion, Iranian crude was substituted, within the time span of a week, by crude from other Middle East oilfields. Again, after Mossadeq's fall, liftings of crude elsewhere in the Middle East were reduced in order to make room for Iranian crude. In these events it was apparent, among other things, that Middle East consortia had wide margins of unused productive capacity available, in keeping with the best practice of oligopolistic firms.

15. Achnacarry Castle, in the Scottish Highlands, had been rented under pretense of hunting wood grouse and fishing trout by Henry Deterding, Shell's boss. His guests for the occasion were the Cadmans (BP), Exxon's Walter Teagle with three consultants, and some representatives of other companies, among these one of the Mellons for Gulf.

16. The main findings of this inquiry are presented in Federal Trade Commission (1952). The report is mainly the work of John Blair.

17. The Achnacarry Agreement provides for two top-level co-ordinating committees, one based in London and one in New York, plus national committees for sharing consumers among the companies operating in each country. The Swedish committee, for instance, met 55 times in 1937, 49 times in 1938, and 51 times in 1939, making resolutions on more than two thousand issues, for instance reaching an agreement over bids to be submitted for public auction concerning diesel oil supplies to the Stockholm Tramways Company (Federal Trade Commission (1952) pp. 280ff.; Blair (1976) p. 67). According to the oil 'majors', the agreement was terminated with the outbreak of the Second World War, in September 1939; but according to Blair (1976, p. 63), the London and New York committees were still operating in 1971. On the occasion of the Iranian crisis in 1951, and of the negotiations with Libya twenty years later, the oil companies again held meetings in order to work out a common strategy, obtaining for this purpose clearance from US anti-trust laws under the justification of the emergency situation (see, for example, Sampson (1976) pp. 154–5, 258–60).

18. Obviously this requires a complex system of price differentials in order to take into account quality differences, and a generally accepted system for the computation of transport costs. See Federal Trade Commission (1952) Chapter X; Penrose (1968) Chapter VI; Adelman (1972) Part 2. It is under these conditions that 'posted prices' come to be generally accepted. They are defined as those prices officially

announced by oil companies, at which the companies are willing to sell crude to anyone wanting to buy it. Transport costs are then added to these prices. In the case of ocean transport, such costs are computed on the basis of a tariff system (AFRA) designed for this purpose (besides the works quoted above, see Waddams (1980) pp. 39–45). Thus oil companies were able to declare to the fiscal authorities of consuming countries that the prices set for crude oil imports had an objective basis; but in fact all agents in the oil sector knew very well that 'only fools and affiliates pay posted prices', while all other transactions — especially those concerning long-term agreements between crude-long and crude-short companies — took place at much lower prices (see, for example, Adelman (1964) p. 143).

19. See Adelman (1972) Appendices II.a–II.i, pp. 279–320.
20. See, for example, Solberg (1976) pp. 190–3; Adelman (1972) pp. 138–9. See below, Chapter 6, section I, in particular note 9.
21. Blair (1976) p. 50. The profit rate is computed as the ratio of profits to net assets. Company publications often present profitability data referring to ratios of profits to share capital at market prices; but stock exchange prices will reflect profits resulting from the companies' market power, so that their profitability appears to be equivalent with companies in other sectors. In other words, since the stock exchange is a competitive market, there should be no advantage to buyers of the shares of a company enjoying a monopolistic position in its own sector of activity, compared with the shares of a company meeting strong competition in its own market. Rates of return computed over share capital at market prices as a consequence will appear to be 'normal', and systematically lower than those computed over net assets. Rather — as Waddams (1980, p. 46) points out — profit rates for vertically integrated companies should be computed with reference to the whole productive cycle. Once this is done, the exceptional profits of the production stage are reduced to more normal proportions by the very modest book-keeping results of the affiliates operating in the distributive stage. However, even once this correction is made, large oil companies will turn out to have enjoyed oligopolistic extra-profits. This is true notwithstanding the drastic fall, in the late 1950s, in the rate of return over foreign investments of US multinational oil companies (on which see Jacoby (1974) pp. 245–7). In those years, in fact, the entry into the European market of US 'independent' oil companies, of State companies such as ENI, and of Soviet oil, eroded the oligopolistic structure of control of the 'Seven Sisters' (as it is shown by Jacoby (1974) pp. 172–212). It must also be recalled that by showing in the accounts that profits are mainly (if not fully, or more than fully) obtained in the production stage, the companies minimise their fiscal payments, so that their net after-tax profits turn out to be only slightly lower than their pre-tax profits.
22. See Penrose (1968) pp. 183–5; Adelman (1972) pp. 131ff. Penrose, however, is much more prudent than Adelman, in that she stresses that crude oil prices, because of the vertically integrated structure of oil companies, cannot be given much importance (Penrose, 1968, p.

185). A clearer indication, in this regard, is provided by the decrease in the rate of return over the investments of US multinational oil companies suggested in the previous note.

23. Federal Trade Commission (1952) pp. 360ff.

24. Adelman (1972) pp. 89–100 (the passage quoted is on p. 94).

25. The 'transfer price' is that price which, in the case of vertically integrated multinational companies, is charged by the affiliate operating in a given country and in a given stage of the productive process on sales to some other affiliate operating in another country and in another productive stage. The literature on 'transfer prices' is very extensive; see, for example, Verlage (1975).

26. For example, by Frankel (1969) Part II; see also Penrose (1968) pp. 46–7; Jacoby (1974) pp. 17–9.

27. On the 'golden gimmick' see below, Chapter 6, section III. The 'depletion allowance', a specific fiscal deduction granted to crude oil producers, first introduced in the United States in 1913 and for a long time equal on average to 27 per cent of the value of crude oil produced, was abolished as from January 1975 as far as the larger oil companies are concerned. Together with the 'golden gimmick' (officially known as a 'foreign tax credit'), the 'depletion allowance' constitutes a strong incentive for oil companies to set high prices for crude oil, given the realised value of a barrel of refined products, because in this way fiscal deductions are maximised. Vertical integration is here identified with multinationalisation. As a matter of fact, this is generally true in the petroleum industry; but in principle we might have companies which are vertically integrated but not multinational, or which are multinational but not vertically integrated. In the first of these two cases, the above-mentioned advantages can proceed from rules allowing for special fiscal deductions for specific production stages, such as the 'depletion allowance' for the stage of crude oil production. In the second of the two cases, in the absence of any vertical integration, the mechanism of 'transfer prices' cannot play any role, so that the reasoning in the text would not apply any longer. It should be noted that in the case of a State company such as ENI the fiscal charge net of deductions is proportionately much higher than for large private companies, yielding correspondingly lower profits net of tax payments (see ENI, 1982).

28. The relevance of this factor might be denied by applying the neoclassical theory of perfect competition to financial markets, for this approach suggests that there is perfect equivalence between internal and external financing. This thesis was the object of critiques, and countered by arguments purporting internal financing to be by far more convenient: see, for example, Sylos Labini (1969) p. 142, and Wood (1975) pp. 17ff.

29. After 1974, Petromin (Saudi Arabia), NIOC (Iran) and KNPC (Kuwait) entered the top seven crude oil-producing companies in the world.

30. Particularly, jointly with State companies of oil-importing developing countries: see, for instance, the articles collected in UNCNRET (1980); and Hartshorn (1980).

31. The target of low prices on refined products for final consumption in internal markets may be present or not, and is generally subordinated to the other targets. Analogously, the target of favouring fuller employment, which is the priority target for most of public intervention in the economy, is here only indirectly pursued through minimisation of the costs of energy supplies, since it favours the international competitiveness of the national manufacturing sector and, by constraining the value of imports, loosens the constraint of the trade balance, which is often decisive in forestalling the adoption of expansionary macroeconomic policies.

32. Concerning the State companies of producing countries, apart from the works quoted above (note 30), see Al-Chalabi (1980); their role and strategies are implicitly analysed when discussing the role and strategies of producing countries: see below, Chapters 5 and 7.

33. At least in principle, the existence of a State oil company should also provide public authorities with more information on the oil sector, particularly costs, thus favouring control over 'transfer prices' applied to crude oil imports on the side of affiliates of foreign multinationals, and over the prices of refined products in internal markets.

34. The two most widely debated cases are the 1955 agreement with Egypt and the 1957 agreement with Iran. In both cases ENI assumed responsibility for the financing of exploratory costs, but if oil was found the government of the producing country reimbursed half of these costs, and participated with a 50 per cent share of the subsequent development costs, obtaining 75 per cent of the profits (50 per cent as an associate in the venture, plus half the profits of AGIP, i.e. an additional 25 per cent, as royalties). As can be seen, in contrast to widespread opinion, such conditions are not in fact much more attractive for producing countries than the traditional ones. Producing countries obtain a large share of the profits only because they participate in the financing of the venture: see Frankel (1966) pp. 115–18. On the strategy of ENI in the Italian context, see below, Chapter 6, section VII.

35. For some information on the most important of these companies (Arabian Oil Company – Japanese; Petrofina – Belgian; Conoco, namely Continental Oil Company; Marathon; Standard Oil Company of Indiana; Phillips Petroleum; Getty Oil; Atlantic Richfield, etc.), see Penrose (1968) pp. 133–44, and the sources quoted there. Following pressures on the side of the US government, a selected group of 'independents' associated in Iricon was accepted, with a 5 per cent share, in the new Iranian consortium formed after the fall of Mossadeq. At least partly, however, these companies have connections with the larger oil companies, through the common ownership of majority shareholdings (see the appendix to this chapter). Furthermore, recently some 'independents' have been the object of takeovers, thus officially losing their independence.

36. On the role of the small chains of petrol retailers in the American market, see Blair (1976) pp. 237ff., who also provides an interesting interpretation of how the larger companies inflicted a hard blow to

these annoying small competitors, taking advantage of the difficulties connected with the oil crisis.

37. Exploitation of Libyan oil resources began on the basis of a 1955 'petroleum law', modified in 1961 and again in 1965. This law favoured a multiplicity of concessions to different companies and groups of companies, rather than to a unique consortium. The bargaining position of the Libyan government was thereby substantially strengthened. This strengthening in turn constituted a decisive prerequisite for the Libyan government's success in its 1970–1 bargaining with oil companies. On the history of Libyan oil, which is thus a crucial aspect of the history of the petroleum market in the post-war period, see Waddams (1980).

38. In 1950 the eight largest companies (the 'Seven Sisters' plus the French CFP) controlled 99.4 per cent of crude oil production outside North America and the communist countries; in 1957 this percentage was already down to 92 per cent. It fell to 68.4 per cent in 1970 and reached 49.3 per cent in 1979, if the 'buy back' crude provided for in the participation agreements is added to own-production and to crude acquired on the basis of long-term agreements (Waddams, 1980, pp. 33–4; *Energy and Hydrocarbons*, 1981, Table 133b). The decrease in the market share of large companies is particularly stressed by Jacoby (1974); for more recent studies, see Fassina (1981) and ENI (1982).

39. The confrontation between the Libyan government and the oil companies in 1970–71, which constituted a decisive step towards the victory of OPEC, is in fact characterised by the feeble bargaining position of some of the small independent oil companies, for which Libyan crude was the sole supply source. The Libyan government took advantage of this opportunity to break the companies' front (see, for example, Sampson, 1976, pp. 250–5).

40. The development of medium-sized firms, at the expense of the market share of larger firms, thus cannot be considered by itself a sufficient condition guaranteeing an improvement in the situation from the consumers' point of view (although Jacoby (1974) maintains otherwise). It is also possible — and as a matter of fact this is what has occurred since 1971 — that the reduced degree of control over the market on the side of larger companies will be to the advantage of producing countries. The development of medium-sized companies is remarkable: for instance, the companies engaged in exploratory activities in the Middle East increased from 9 in 1940 to 126 in 1976 (Turner, 1980, p. 92). Libya was the first producing country to bet on medium-sized companies. In applying the 1955 petroleum law, in the following year 51 concessions were attributed to 17 different oil companies (Stobaugh, 1979, p. 25).

41. The phenomenon of 'internal' or 'captive markets' is one of the main reasons favouring the existence of large conglomerates. The best-known instance is provided by ITT: see Sampson (1973).

42. On the development in these fields of large oil companies, see ENI (1982) and US House of Representatives (1978).

43. See Eichner (1976) and Wood (1975).
44. At least in part, these takeovers may originate in speculation. Once the controlling share of the equity capital in a company owning coal reserves is acquired at prices only slightly higher than current stock exchange prices, part of these reserves can then be sold to third parties, at prices reflecting the increases of crude oil prices in the immediately preceding period. A company following this line of action indicates its evaluation that the capitalised value of coal companies on the stock exchange does not fully reflect the new situation following the crude oil price increases, although considering the future trend in crude oil prices. Obviously this line of speculation is no longer open, given the clear downward tendency of crude oil prices.

    With respect to Occidental, it may be interesting to note that it is also the company which has been leading the policy for 100 per cent US-based energy sources.
45. In this respect at least the concrete application of the Clayton Act was not very strict; the prevalent criterion was that what was forbidden was only the presence of the same person in the boards of directors of companies operating within the same sector. See Neale (1970) pp. 201–2.
46. The phenomenon has by now acquired such relevance as to be the object of a specialised monthly periodical, *Institutional Investor*, and of inquiries conducted by US Congressional commissions (see, for instance, US House of Representatives, 1968).
47. On the importance of institutional investors, and more generally on the existence of a web of relationships connecting large corporations and mirrored in the phenomenon of 'interlocking directorates', see Blumberg (1975) who gives an interesting analysis of the power structure of US corporations.
48. The US Senate inquiry is in any case sufficiently representative for our purposes. It considers 122 corporations, the larger ones among those listed in the Stock Exchange. On the whole, they represent 41 per cent of the equity value of all companies listed in the Stock Exchange, and include all the largest companies from the various sectors of the economy.
49. See the lively description given by Sampson (1973).
50. Reprinted as an appendix in Thurow (1975). This enquiry represents a good point of reference for us, precisely because it refers to a period immediately preceding the abandonment of the gold exchange standard in 1971 and the 1973 oil crisis. A more recent study, published in *Forbes* (13 Sept., 1982), does not suggest that any substantial changes are necessary in our discussion above.
51. In the case of airline companies the requirements for bank financing acquire special relevance. This is why airlines have been singled out for special consideration in the two Senate inquiries utilised in this appendix (US Senate, 1978a, pp. 18–97, 525–33; US Senate, 1978b, pp. 186–213).
52. On the role of 'interlocking directorates' in the petroleum sector, see also Federal Trade Commission (1952) pp. 29–33. Sampson (1976,

specifically on pp. 197–9) and Turner (1980, pp. 104–5, 160) also stress the role of John McCloy, 'the key figure in oil diplomacy' and 'a kind of chairman of the American Establishment'; as a lawyer, 'he represented the anti-trust interests of all seven of the Seven Sisters' and 'was, by 1973, representing the interests of at least twenty-six of the world's oil companies'.

53. See Federal Trade Commission (1952) pp. 119–29.
54. This was publicly known only twenty years later: see US Senate (1975) pp. 47–8.
55. In order to explain this event it is not sufficient to recall generically the spirit of oligopolistic collaboration established since the 1930s among the major oil companies. The discovery of exceptionally large oilfields, with exceptionally low production costs, such as those in the Arab peninsula, constituted a drastic change in the previous situation in the world petroleum market. In no other period might a price war have appeared so attractive to any of the Seven Sisters. (On the conditions in which a price war may be convenient, see Sylos Labini, 1969, pp. 44–50). It should also be recalled that the major oil companies themselves declare that after the end of the Second World War the 'As Is' agreement signed at Achnacarry in 1928 for joint control over petroleum markets was no longer considered to be valid. Concerning the Socal and Texaco decision, we should also recall that the US government declared the entry of Exxon and Mobil into Aramco to be in the national interest; because of this, it was considered not to be in conflict with anti-trust laws. According to Jacoby (1974, p. 39), it was, in fact, the US State Department which urged the entry of Exxon and Socal into Aramco, in order to strengthen the US presence in Saudi Arabia.

NOTES TO CHAPTER 5: THE OIL-PRODUCING COUNTRIES AND OPEC

1. Since oil can be exported both as crude and as refined products, we should subtract from gross internal production of crude, not the quantity of crude refined within the country, but the crude oil equivalent of the national consumption of refined products. The difference between the two balances will become increasingly relevant if OPEC countries persist in their strategy of expanding the domestic refining of their crude oil production.
2. The United States' share in world crude oil production, excluding communist countries, was about 64 per cent in 1910; remaining stable in 1920 and 1930, it reached 66 per cent in 1945, and declined in subsequent years: 51 per cent in 1955, 42 per cent in 1960, 34 per cent in 1965, 27 per cent in 1970, 23 per cent in 1973; over the past few years it has been around 20 per cent (Federal Trade Commission, 1952, p. 38; *Energy and Hydrocarbons*, 1981, pp. 61–2).
3. See Solberg (1976) pp. 23–6.
4. Data on the size and year of discovery for main oilfields are available in Nehring (1978).

5. Solberg (1976) pp. 56–8.
6. Nehring (1978) p. 37.
7. More precisely, in territories included within the present boundaries of Iran and Iraq. See Nehring (1978) pp. 14ff.
8. At the end of the nineteenth century, Russia and the United States produced around 90 per cent world crude production (Jacoby, 1974, p. 25).
9. The quantity of oil imported into or exported from any country, however, may exceed such a difference, both because imported oil can be utilised for refining of products which are then exported (and vice versa), and because the qualities of national crude may not correspond to the qualities required by the refineries. See below, Chapter 5, section VI and note 37.
10. See *Energy and Hydrocarbons*, various years.
11. See, for example, Smart (1975) p. 271; Smart also stresses the role of the Yom Kippur war against Israel in favouring the unity of Arab countries. Mikdashi (1975, pp. 207–8) stresses that 'if one applies the definition of export cartels used in Western countries (for example, the Webb–Pomerene Act of the United States), the OPEC organization does not pass the test'.
12. The OPEC Secretariat in Vienna edits a number of publications, some occasional and some periodic, furnishing information about the Organisation's activities. In the first group, the following are of particular interest: *Statute of OPEC, OPEC National Oil Companies Profiles, OPEC Official Resolutions and Press Releases 1960–80*. In the second group, among others, of interest are: *OPEC Review, OPEC Bulletin, OPEC Annual Statistical Bulletin*, and the *Annual Reports*.
13. The importance of this factor is stressed, for example, by Girvan (1975).
14. On this, see below, Chapter 6. See also Darmstadter and Landsberg (1975, particularly pp. 27–32). Libyan bargaining power, because of its proximity to European markets, was strengthened by the interruption of the Tapline, the pipeline bringing Saudi crude to the Mediterranean.
15. We refer here to the so-called 'golden gimmick': see below, Chapter 6, section III.
16. This element is considered 'central to an explanation of the events of the seventies' by Vernon (1975, p. 4) among others. On 'independent' oil companies and ENI, see above, Chapter 4, section V.
17. Gheddafi's Libya profited from precisely such circumstances: see above, Chapter 4, section V and Appendix. We will not enter here into the details of OPEC's history, nor into the chronology of its success in 1971–3. See Sampson (1976), Penrose (1975), Rustow and Mugno (1976), Al-Chalabi (1980), and the OPEC publications quoted above (note 12).

   With respect to the chronology of events and particularly to price movements, see the very detailed Appendices in Rustow and Mugno (1976) pp. 125–51 (statistical tables) and pp. 152–65 (chronology). Rustow and Mugno are very careful to avoid the mistake, common to many news reports of that time, of focusing attention on 'posted prices' which, as already stressed, are simply notional reference prices. For oil companies, the cost of crude produced under a concessionary agreement is equal to

$$0.125P + c + 0.5\ (P - 0.125 - c) = 0.05625P - 0.5c$$

assuming a 12.5 per cent royalty and 50 per cent taxes ('fifty—fifty agreements'), and where P indicates the 'posted price', and c the technical cost of production (which is generally equal to a few cents per barrel). For a given and unchanged P, fiscal receipts of producing countries per barrel of crude, and hence the 'tax paid cost' for the oil companies, varies when the fiscal share changes, as occurred in 1970—1, or with the 'expensing' of royalties (namely, when royalties are no longer deductible from P before computing the profits on which income tax is applied). Further complications arise with joint-ventures, in which a share of the oil produced is recognised as property of the producing countries, who then sell it back to the participating oil companies or to third parties. In the transition years after 1973, joint-venture agreements provided for the crude belonging to producing countries ('equity oil') to be sold compulsorily; in part to the oil companies who were the former proprietors of the producing consortia and who now share in the joint-venture agreements ('bridging oil'), in order to help the companies to meet their long-period obligations, and in part sold to the companies on the simple request of producing countries ('phase-in oil') so as to avoid a sudden surge of supply in the international oil market. The cost of oil supplies to the companies will then depend on the shares of 'bridging oil', 'phase-in oil' and direct purchase of the producing countries' free shares, and on the price charged for each type of oil (see Al-Chalabi, 1980, pp. 43ff.). Over time, as the proportion of direct sales by the producing countries gradually increases, the average cost of company supplies will approach official prices. However, in the early phases the divergence is substantial. For example, the 'posted price' of $10.84 per barrel of Arabian Light (the quality usually used as the 'reference price') in actual fact represented a 'tax-paid cost' of $7 a barrel to the companies, which was the actual objective of OPEC at the time (see Al-Chalabi, 1980, p. 87). Naturally, such conditions mean that the prices paid by the larger companies with concessionary rights are much lower than the official OPEC prices paid by the smaller companies. The additional profits that arise from this arrangement — in particular to the members of Aramco — have been considered by some commentators as a *de facto* indemnisation conceded to the companies who had owned the nationalised consortia by the producing countries (on the surplus profits of the Aramco partners, see US Senate, 1980, pp. 60—2).

18. The importance of the factor is highlighted by, for example, Penrose (1975) and Luciani (1976). See above, Chapter 3, note 16.
19. The overall importance of this factor in determining the structure of

the oil market which can already be noted in the 1940s has been strongly emphasised by Frankel (see above, Chapter 3, section V). On the relation between such factors and the power of OPEC, see Rustow and Mugno (1976, pp. 70–8).

20. For a comparison between OPEC's successes and the much less brilliant results obtained from attempts by the producing countries of various other primary products to form cartels see Smart (1975), in particular pp. 264–75. Smart reports the success of Morocco and Tunisia in quadrupling the price of the mineral phosphate, but the list of failures is much longer.

21. In a 'seller's market' such as 1979–80 the failure of OPEC to secure the necessary co-ordination of their sales policies is less important, yet the reduction of the proportion of OPEC crude sold through the oil majors points to the increasing importance of the problem. See Al-Chalabi (1980) p. 144.

22. Various commentators maintain that the second petroleum crisis, i.e. the sharp increases in prices in 1979–80, was not only or even mainly the result of Khomeini's Islamic revolution and the subsequent Iran–Iraq war, but also and primarily the result of the massive increases in stocks of crude oil and refined products by the industrialised countries. In fact, Saudi Arabia adjusted its production in order to meet the shortfalls due to the reduction in Iranian production. See Said (1980); Al-Chalabi (1980) p. 144, and in particular the highly detailed analysis given by Genco (1981). Other authors (in particular Verleger, 1979) emphasise the responsibility of US energy policies.

23. This proposal has not been discussed after the second petroleum crisis of 1979–80. It is possible that Saudi Arabia considered the price level reached in 1980 to be excessive with respect to its medium- to long-term objectives, and that during 1981–3 its short-term goal was to bring about a gradual reduction in prices, on the one hand employing the occasion to reduce the bargaining power of the 'hawks' inside OPEC, and on the other avoiding a too rapid downward adjustment. It seems reasonable to conclude that the 'Yamani formula' should again become relevant at the conclusion of the adjustment phase. See Chapter 7, section III below.

24. Perhaps this fact explains and/or is explained by the care and ease which accompanied the transfer of control of Aramco, which minimised the reduction in investment and thus the reduction in availability of potential supplies which has characterised the transition phase in other cases.

25. See CIA (1977) and Nehring (1978). In fact Soviet proven reserves, after doubling between 1965 and 1970, have declined since 1973 (*Energy and Hydrocarbons*, 1981, p. 55). The limited value of statistics on proven reserves should not be forgotten in this context (see above, Chapter 2, section II, and Chapter 3, section II). In fact, oil production has increased by 41 per cent between 1973 and 1980 to account for 20 per cent of world production (*Energy and Hydrocarbons*, 1981, p. 63).

26. See, for example, Odell (1979) pp. 48–700. Klinghoffer (1977, pp.

280–8) takes an intermediate position. It is most probable that the future impact of the USSR will be in the natural gas market, especially on completion of the giant gas pipeline linking the Siberian gasfields to Western Europe. Natural gas reserves in the USSR increased by a factor of five between 1965 and 1970, and then doubled between 1970 and 1980. Production has followed a similar pattern, reaching 28 per cent of world production (*Energy and Hydrocarbons*, 1981, pp. 57, 65).

When discussing 'socialist' oil, one should not forget the excellent position of China, whose proven reserves have increased five-fold between 1965 and 1970, after that date remaining more or less constant despite a five-fold increase in production between 1970 and 1980 (*Energy and Hydrocarbons*, 1981, pp. 55, 63). A number of Western oil companies are currently involved in a massive exploration programme of the Chinese off-shore fields. On the prospective position of Chinese production, see, for example, Foster (1980).

27. See Goldman (1975), Kaser (1980), Martellaro (1981) and above all Klinghoffer (1977).
28. The prices charged to the communist countries for Soviet crude have been traditionally higher than the prices at which it is supplied to the 'non-aligned' developing countries and Western countries. The determination of prices which should rule for a full five-year planning period did represent an advantage to the Comecon countries importing Soviet oil in the period after the oil crisis of 1973. See Klinghoffer (1977) pp. 90–3.
29. See Klinghoffer (1977) pp. 130–4, 233–6.
30. For the importance of Soviet oil in the development of ENI, see Klinghoffer (1977) pp. 220–1, and Magini (1976) pp. 147–9. Imports of Soviet oil reached a maximum in 1961 when they provided 72 per cent of ENI's supplies and 23 per cent of Italy's total imports. Other authors (for example Colitti, 1979; Frankel, 1966) seem to underestimate this aspect, instead concentrating their attention on ENI's attempts to expand in the Middle East and the sales tactics used to gain a satisfactory market share in the distribution stage in the Italian market.
31. During the Arab oil embargo in 1973 the Soviet Union continued to sell, at ever higher prices, oil to the Western countries who were the victims of the action while at the same time declaring – as it had on previous occasions – solid support for the Arab countries (Klinghoffer, 1977, p. 173). Once again, in the conflict between political and economic objectives, Soviet oil policy was primarily determined by the latter aspect.
32. Estimates for research costs and development of North Sea wells can be found in MacKay and Mackay (1975) pp. 37–40, 46–7, 68–75.
33. To the purely technical problems and the problems of finance which involve the international financial markets (e.g. loan guarantees and export credits) that concern governments, one must also add the ecological impact. All of these problems are present in the case of the Alaskan pipeline:

In Alaska the white snow reflects so much of the energy falling on it that the water-logged ground beneath it never thaws. This is the permafrost. One of the fears which delayed the construction of the Alaska oil pipeline was that a break in the pipe would spread black oil over a large area. This would alter the amount of radiation reflected, reducing it amost to zero. It would increase the amount of energy absorbed, raise the temperature of the ground, melt the permafrost, and cause large-scale land erosion and collapse of the pipeline.   (Foley, 1976, p. 29)

34. See, for example, Tiratsoo (1972).
35. See Solberg (1976) pp. 179–80.
36. The explosion of an off-shore well with disastrous ecological consequences played a part in this case as well.
37. For example, this seems to be the case with North Sea oil which is of good quality and produces a high proportion of petrol and thus is more suited to the American than to the British market (see MacKay and Mackay, 1975, pp. 2–3). Similar considerations alongside minimisation of transport costs and deficient refinery capacity apply to the case of China (see Klinghoffer, 1977, p. 275).
38. This is the case of the export of Alaskan crude to Japan balanced by imports from the North Sea, Libya or West Africa to the heavily populated and high energy using East coast of the United States.

NOTES TO CHAPTER 6: THE US AND OTHER CONSUMING COUNTRIES

1. In 1955 the United States was still absorbing over half of world crude consumption; by the beginning of the 1970s the figure had fallen to a little less than a third, and in 1981 to a bit more than a quarter (25.9 per cent). See *Energy and Hydrocarbons* (1982), pp. 22 and 24).
2. For a lively discussion of this relationship, rich in literary citation about an America that 'keeps going', see Solberg (1976, pp. 108–48). In 1980 road transport accounted for 28 per cent of final energy consumption in the US and an eighth of the world's total crude oil consumption (see *Energy and Hydrocarbons*, 1982, p. 31). As a consequence of this particular composition of consumption, refineries in the United States are constructed to produce a higher proportion of petrol than in other countries (see US Congress, 1980).
3. See Yergin (1979, p. 143). According to other assessments (*Energy and Hydrocarbons*, 1981, pp. 22, 25), Canadian consumption has surpassed the United States both as a proportion of national income and, from 1974, in relation to population. Climatic conditions and the composition of industrial output, as well as the level and composition of final consumption, account for this result.
4. See *Energy and Hydrocarbons* (1981, pp. 26ff.). Subsequent years

show a slight reduction in the weight of the United States as a result of important savings in the consumption of petroleum.

5. For example, the 16 per cent reduction of petroleum consumption achieved in the United States between 1978 and 1981 constitutes 4.7 per cent of world consumption in 1978. In absolute terms the reduction in United States consumption between 1978 and 1980 was slightly higher (94 million tonnes against 85) than the reduction in overall world consumption (see *Energy and Hydrocarbons*, 1982, pp. 22 and 24).

6. See Stobaugh (1979, p. 50).

7. It is, in fact, the interests of the 'Seven Sisters' to assure control and rapid development of the European markets rather than the bargaining power of the American officials responsible for implementation of the Marshall Plan which explains why the petroleum companies were so willing to accept modification in the pre-war mechanism of price fixing based on the price of Texas oil, introducing a new Saudi Arabian 'base point' (however, with a price more than ten times the cost of extraction). See *Federal Trade Commission* (1952, pp. 372–8), Penrose (1968, pp. 183–5) and Adelman (1972, pp. 134–48).

8. See Solberg (1976, pp. 186–7). Recently a number of authors have suggested that the political element dominates in large technological choices which determine the evolution of the division of labour and the social structure (see in particular Marglin, 1974). It should not be forgotten, however, that the political element cannot overturn the fundamental element in technical choice: the comparison of relative profitability; it may, however, exert influence by modifying the basic inputs used in the economic calculation of profitability (see Villetti, 1978a). The higher risk of union action in the coal mines is today considered as one of the major obstacles to a 'return to coal' in the aftermath of the petroleum crisis (see Horwitch, 1979, pp. 86, 94–7).

9. Obviously the problem takes on this aspect in a period in which internal production is tendentially (i.e. given the 'rules of the game' in absence of any political intervention) insufficient to satisfy internal demand. It is thus a problem that concerns the United States in its role as a large consuming country; it is for this reason that the problem is discussed here rather than in the preceding chapter. The problem appears in these terms in the United States primarily in the post-war period. It is perhaps necessary to point out that despite the fact that the balance of payments is one of the primary objectives in the resolution of this problem, such an objective need not have an unfavourable effect on oil imports. For example, remittance of profits from foreign investments must be taken into consideration; for the petroleum sector these may be substantial. The foreign investments of American petroleum companies comprise a third of the US total. It is thus also possible that, as occurred in the United States in 1973, measures which lead to increasing imports of oil (elimination of the Mandatory Oil Import Policy) should produce an improvement rather than a deterioration in the balance of payments (see Odell, 1979, p. 25).

10. See above Chapter 2, section II, and Chapter 3, section II on the concept of 'proven reserves'.
11. See, for example, Bohi and Russell (1978).
12. See Kalt (1981, pp. 156–61). US Congress (1980, p. 73) estimates the difference between domestic US and imported oil prices caused by import controls at about $1.00 per barrel. One of the consequences of this situation is that natural gas, with its price restrained by government regulation, acquired a share of the United States energy market (especially in domestic heating) substantially above that observed in other countries (see Odell, 1979, p. 38).
13. The prices of domestic crude oil and finished petroleum products were frozen by the Nixon administration's wage and price freeze introduced in August 1971 (together with the abandonment of the gold convertibility of the dollar). In 1973 a complicated multi-price system was introduced. Finally, in 1980 a programme of gradual liberalisation of prices was adopted, accompanied by an even more complicated system of differential taxes (see Kalt, 1981). The policy of domestic crude oil price control at precisely the time when international prices were increasing dramatically led to a sharp reversal in the competitivity of US industry with respect to relative energy input costs.
14. This aspect is overlooked by the majority of commentators who concentrate their attention on OPEC, on the Arab embargo and/or on the scarce natural resource aspect of crude oil to explain the dramatic increase in prices in 1973–4. An important exception is to be found in the group of essays collected in a special issue of *Daedalus* (Autumn 1975) dedicated to the oil crisis. Other authors (Sampson, 1976; Penrose, 1977; Adelman, 1972, p. 254; Kalt, 1981, p. 230) all emphasise the role of the US State department in supporting the increase in the bargaining power of OPEC in the negotiations in 1971–3.
15. *Energy and Hydrocarbons* (1981, p. 81).
16. The Egyptian attack on Israel occurred on 6 October 1973. According to various sources, the Egyptian president, Sadat, had already informed King Faisal of Saudi Arabia of the imminent attack in May, who in turn gave hints to the Aramco partners (Exxon, Mobil, Socal and Texaco) during a reunion in Geneva on 23 May (see, for example, Stobaugh, 1979, p. 27). It should be added, however, that if Israel was indeed caught by surprise by the attack the American government must not have realised the full significance of the signals that were coming from the Saudi Arabians.
17. See, for example, Sampson (1976, pp. 334ff.).
18. Certain 'accidental' factors such as the breakdown of the Tapline due to an incident in the Syrian desert also played a role. The Tapline is a pipeline that was opened in 1950 to carry 500,000 barrels of Saudi crude per day to the Mediterranean. Its interruption increased the geographical advantage of Libyan oil and was of enormous benefit to the Libyans in their bargaining with the companies in 1971–3.
19. See Sampson (1976, pp. 155–6), Blair (1976, pp. 193–204) and US Senate (1975). Among recent discussions of the tax credit see Davidson

(1978) and Safer (1979, pp. 75–85, 135–49).
20. The following table summarises the numerical examples discussed in this section. The first case corresponds to conditions prevailing before the introduction of the 'golden gimmick' in 1950. The second is a hypothetical case in which royalties are transformed into taxes by the producing country without any change in its total receipts. The third case exemplifies what occurred in 1950 when the introduction of the 'golden gimmick' was accompanied by an increase in Saudi Arabian taxes. As can be seen in the passage from the first to the third case, the increase in taxes is accompanied by a reduction in taxes paid to the United States, while the companies' net profits remain unchanged. In the fourth case, which may be considered as representative of conditions in the early 1970s, an increase in producer-country taxes is accompanied by an increase in posted prices. With respect to the third case, the receipts of the producing country increase while taxes paid to the US decrease. Because the companies compensate for the higher taxes paid to the producing country by increasing prices by an equivalent amount, the reduced tax payments to the United States government goes directly to increasing company net profits.

	I Pre-1950	II Golden Gimmick	III Post-1950	IV (1970–4)
1. Price	$1.00	$1.00	$1.00	$1.20
2. Cost of production	.20	.20	.20	.20
3. Royalties	.20	–	.20	.20
4. Producing-country tax	–	.20	.20	.20
5. (= 3 + 4) Producing country receipts	.20	.20	.40	.60
6. (= 1 – 2 – 3) US taxable income	.60	.80	.60	.80
7. (= 6 x .50) US tax assessment	.30	.40	.30	.40
8. (= 7 – 4) US tax	.30	.20	.10	–
9. (= 1 – 2 – 5 – 8) net profits	.30	.40	.30	.40

21. On 'transfer prices' see above, Chapter 4, note 25. By varying transfer prices the multinational can redistribute profits among its affiliates without affecting the total gross profits of the group. Transfer prices are set with the objective of minimising the overall tax assessment of the group.
22. Davidson (1978). It should be emphasised that the recourse to the 'golden gimmick' is not a necessary consequence of the elimination of

'double taxation'; petroleum companies operating in the United States have traditionally paid 'royalties', not 'taxes', to the owners of the land from which they pump petroleum.

23. It is not necessary that this should occur. If all the companies operate under the same conditions, and in the absence of collusive behaviour, the increase in price could be inferior – just sufficient to maintain the companies' net profits unchanged. But, if the taxes to be paid to Saudi Arabia are calculated on the basis of 'posted prices', and if that price is used to value the transfer of crude to their affiliates and in sales to third parties, the result will be the same as that given in the example.

24. See Table 135ff. of *Energy and Hydrocarbons*, various years. In part, the increase in profits in a period of increasing prices is due to re-valuation of stocks and proven reserves (see Turner, 1980, pp. 141–2). Stobaugh and Yergin (1979, p. 217) give a figure of $800 billion for the revaluation of US proven reserves of oil and gas.

25. See Sampson (1976, pp. 180, 292–4) and Turner (1980, pp. 155–7).

26. Federal Trade Commission (1952). This report is in large part the work of J. M. Blair; see Sampson (1976, p. 171).

27. Court proceedings were initiated in April 1953 against the five largest American petroleum companies. They were resolved during the 1960s by means of consent decrees in the case of Exxon, Gulf and Texaco and the withdrawal of charges against Socal and Mobil in 1968. To a certain extent even cosmetic measures such as the entry of a selected group of 'independents' into the Iranian consortium in 1955 could have had a significant influence in reducing the degree of monopoly control in the market, introducing the independents to the delights of low cost Middle East production (on the selection of the independents for the Iranian consortium see Sampson, 1976, pp. 182–5). The multinationalisation of the independents who had acquired foreign supply sources with the intention of using them to supply US markets was then accelerated, as noted above, by the regulations placed on imports of oil into the United States in 1957.

28. For numerous examples, see Federal Trade Commission, 1952, pp. 228–348; Blair, 1976, pp. 56–71; and Chapter 4, section III above.

29. See MacKay and Mackay (1975, pp. 24–30) for a discussion of the policy followed by the British government in the case of the North Sea.

30. See US House of Representatives (1978) and the bibliography given there.

31. See above, Chapter 4, section V. On the timid moves indicating a re-awakening of anti-monopoly policy within the EEC and in Japan, see Sampson (1976, pp. 374–7).

32. In this way US diplomacy seems to have ignored the role of the major companies. For a description of the United States position (and in particular that of Kissinger, who was then Secretary of State) see Kissinger (1979, 1982).

33. Australia, Austria, Belgium, Canada, Denmark, Germany, Great Britain, Greece, Japan, Ireland, Italy, Luxembourg, the Netherlands,

New Zealand, Norway, Spain, Sweden, Switzerland, Turkey and the United States. The members of the OECD who chose not to join are Finland, France, Iceland and Portugal. The Organisation for Economic Co-operation and Development, created in 1960 with headquarters in Paris, which groups the major Western industrialised countries, is a study centre for the co-ordination of the economic policies of the member countries. It does not have any supra-national powers, however. On the role of the IEA, see Lantzke (1975).

34. The primary aims of the IEA are reprinted on the first page of all its publications (among which its annual reports on *Energy Research, Development and Demonstration in IEA Countries*, and *Energy Policies and Programmes of IEA Member Countries*, are of special interest).

35. A scheme of this type was proposed by Adelman in testimony before the Energy subcommittee of the US Senate (12 January 1977) and was reported in *The Economist*, 8 April 1978. For a modified version, integrated with recommendations concerning the fiscal treatment of the petroleum companies, see Davidson (1979a). On similar lines see also Safer (1979) which develops his submission to the Senate Energy subcommittee (Safer, 1980). For the discussion provoked by these proposals see, for example, US Congress (1979) and US Senate (1980).

36. This is not meant to signify that sharp changes in economic policy are necessarily injurious. For example, the gradual pace of the freeing of prices of domestically produced crude oil generated forecasts of continuous increases in prices, leading producers to slow their production (because crude in the ground was expected to increase in value more rapidly than financial assets acquired from pumping and selling it). This created conditions which were just the opposite of those intended.

37. Nor is it likely that they should be in the foreseeable future, given the opposite interests of the large petroleum companies and the behaviour of the Reagan administration toward the business world (one should also add the obvious foreign policy consideration: the risk of 'pushing OPEC into the arms of the Soviet Union').

38. It is precisely these 'windfall gains', only partially reflected in the stock market prices of the companies, which explain the wave of 'takeovers' which has swept over the oil and coal sectors in the last few years (obviously on the assumption that coal reserves have also revalued, although in lesser proportion than crude reserves): see Chapter 4, section VI, above, and Chapter 7, section IV, below.

39. In fact, this is what is already occurring as a result of the decline in prices in recent months, although on a greatly reduced scale compared to what might occur as a result of a full-scale collapse in prices. See, for example, the supplement to the *Financial Times* of 10 November 1982 on the 'World Oil Industry'.

40. The proposal, originally developed by Thomas Enders, the oil expert of the State department, was launched by Henry Kissinger in February 1975. In the face of opposition from other industrialised countries it was abandoned in March (see Sampson, 1976, p. 407; Solberg, 1976, p. 262).

41. The estimates of the costs of developing the major alternatives to oil (coal, nuclear, solar, oil sands, bituminous schist, geothermal, etc.) vary substantially. Among the most recent, see those given in Stobaugh and Yergin (1979) and in Mabro (1980). It is interesting to note that $7.00 was also OPEC's objective for the tax yield per barrel in 1974 (see Al-Chalabi, 1980, p. 51).

42. An analogous problem may be discerned in the English economy in the beginning of the nineteenth century. As a result of the Continental blockade imposed by Napoleon, the price of grain soared and many landowners, considering the new prices as permanent, invested substantial sums to bring marginal land with high costs of production into cultivation. After the Napoleonic wars the collapse of the price of grain on the domestic market was avoided, or at least postponed, by means of the 'Corn laws' which isolated the English market from the competition of Polish grain (see Sylos Labini, 1979, pp. 48–9).

43. In the United States, and in various other countries, house owners who install solar energy apparatus receive, via fiscal credits, a contribution amounting to about a third of the capital costs (see Maidique, 1979).

44. See IEA, *Energy Research, Development and Demonstration in IEA Countries*, various years. In addition, the development costs of nuclear technology have in large part been supported by military research. Perhaps solar energy would today be a more competitive alternative if the same time, money and effort had been utilised as has been the case of nuclear energy for military and civil purposes.

45. See IEA, *Energy Research, Development and Demonstration.*

46. Consider the optimism of the otherwise well-documented study of the US House of Representatives (1978).

47. With reference to Sylos Labini's theory of oligopoly (1969) we could say that the co-ordination of the development of the various energy sectors reduces the price-elasticity of demand of each energy source. This is one of the factors determining the level of the barriers to entry and the degree of oligopolistic control of each sector. Such co-ordination is favoured, among other things, by the habit of forming consortia for energy projects of large size.

48. See Magini (1976, p. 96): 'The Iranian political crisis gave a decisive boost to the expansion of refinery capacity in Italy [in 1951]. . . . The major petroleum companies at that time adopted a policy line which was to make Italy the refinery of Middle East oil for distribution to South and Central Europe'. The motives of such a policy, undoubtedly influenced by the Iranian crisis, were however of a more general nature: the greater ease in transporting crude, the greater political stability with respect to the developing countries, and the greater fiscal 'flexibility' with respect to the developed countries, of a country of delayed industrialisation such as Italy.

49. Increased use of natural gas cannot be considered as 'diversification'. The composition of Italy's demand for energy is given in *Energy and Hydrocarbons* (1982, pp. 124–5).

50. For statistics of the market share of the major oil companies in the

Italian market see Table 220b, ibid., and ENI (1981c, p. 80).
51. This aspect is emphasised by Colitti (1979, pp. 197—9) who recalls both the slogan '*supercortemaggiore*, the powerful Italian petrol' and the distribution of service stations along all major highways with food and hygienic facilities in place of simple pumps. See also Frankel (1966, pp. 98—9) and Magini (1976, pp. 141—6).
52. Purchases started in 1957. By 1971, 72 per cent of ENI's supplies came from the USSR. The NATO sanctions against trade with the Soviet Union introduced in 1962 do not seem to have had any effect on this trade (see Klinghoffer, 1977, pp. 220—1). On the price of the Soviet oil, see also Adelman (1972, pp. 407—10) and Jacoby (1974, p. 163).
53. In particular, the attempt, criticised by Frankel (1966, pp. 121, 129—30), to expand into Central Europe with its own refineries and distribution network, defying the major companies outside its own national base.
54. See Colitti (1979, pp. 235—41). A reconstruction of the tragic disappearance of Mattei, which supports the thesis of sabotage, may be found in Franco Rosi's 1970 film *The Mattei Affair*.
55. Shell ceded its Italian distribution network and some refineries to the Monti group (which used the trade name 'Mach'). The major part of these interests ended up under ENI's wing with the crisis of Monti's empire in 1980.
56. The National Energy Plan was only approved by Parliament in October 1981. It took eight years after the oil crisis before fiscal incentives for the use of solar power were introduced, while attempts to reduce the consumption of gasoil for domestic heating had little effect. For an outline of Italian energy policy see ENI (1981c, pp. 116—18).

NOTES TO CHAPTER 7: SOME LIKELY FUTURE SCENARIOS

1. For a critical survey of some of the main econometric models of the petroleum market, and more generally of the energy market, see Koreisha and Stobaugh (1979).
2. See, for instance, the table on the component elements of the price of a barrel of refined products sold in Europe, and their changes from 1965 to 1978, in Al-Chalabi (1980) p. 112.
3. For a generalisation of this theory to the entirety of economic relationships, as well as to the totality of the Arab world, see ENI's 'Project Interdependence' (ENI, 1981a, and ENI, 1981b).
4. 'At the world level, the reduction in the share of oil in energy consumption between 1973 and 1980 (from 47.2 per cent down to 44.5 per cent) takes on an increased importance, if we notice that it represents a sharp reversal of the trend of the previous 30 years' (ENI, 1981c, p. 14).
5. The decrease in crude oil prices, considered in dollar terms, may turn out to be quicker when the dollar goes up in exchange markets, and conversely slower when the dollar goes down.

6. The increase in royalties paid to producing countries under the form of taxes was, in fact, at least in part counterbalanced, via the 'golden gimmick', by an increase in allowable deductions from taxable incomes in the United States. See above, Chapter 6, section III.
7. 'Even if [OPEC countries] cut their output to zero, they could not for long keep the world price of crude at 10 dollars a barrel. Well before that point the cartel would collapse' (Milton Friedman, *Newsweek*, 4 March 1974).
8. For an analysis of the relationships between companies and Arab countries, see Luciani (1981).
9. This percentage is systematically lower for the Arab country members of OAPEC, which go from 30.7 per cent in 1973 to 52.8 per cent in 1979. In the same years, the percentages for Saudi Arabia are 14.3 per cent and 29.9 per cent respectively (OAPEC, 1981, p. 45).
10. Among other things, we may recall that below certain depths the presence of gasfields is more likely than that of crude oilfields. Thus in recent years the increase in proven gas reserves has been more rapid than the increase in oil reserves (Jensen, 1980, p. 43). In the short to medium term, an exception may be provided by the US market, where the share of energy provided by natural gas is already relatively high (see above, Chapter 6, note 12).
11. For some information on the evolution of the spot market see Abu-Khadra (1980). It is shown there how the development of the spot market after 1974 benefited from US regulations favourable to small refiners (see above, Chapter 2, section V), which stimulated demand for crude on the spot market; it was also favoured by the nationalisations of crude production operations in Middle East and African countries. Before 1974 the spot market mainly dealt in refined products.
12. Odell (1979, pp. 21—2) also favours this scenario, through the establishment of an apposite international agency. In Brandt (1980) see especially Chapters IX, X (on the energy issue) and XII.

Bibliography

Abdel-Fadil, M. (ed.) (1979), *Papers on the Economics of Oil: A Producer's View* (Oxford University Press).

Abu-Khadra, R. M. (1980) 'The Spot Oil Market: Genesis, Qualitative Configuration and Perspectives', *OPEC Review*, vol. 4, no. 1 (1980) pp. 105–15.

Adelman, M. A. (1964) 'Oil Prices in the Long Run (1963–75)', *Journal of Business*, vol. 37, no. 2 (Apr.) pp. 143–61.

_____(1972) *The World Petroleum Market* (Baltimore: Johns Hopkins Press).

_____(1976) 'The World Oil Cartel', *Quarterly Review of Economics and Business*, vol. 16, pp. 7–18.

_____(1979) 'Reply to Harkin', *Challenge*, Nov.–Dec., pp. 70–1.

Aït-Laoussine, N. (1980a) 'Gas: Recent Developments and Problems of Supply', in R. Mabro (ed.) (1980a) pp. 27–42.

_____(1980b) 'Towards a New Order in Gas Pricing', *OPEC Review*, vol. 4, no. 2, pp. 50–72.

Al-Chalabi, F. (1980) *OPEC and the International Oil Industry: A Changing Structure* (Oxford University Press).

Al-Janabi, A. (1979) 'Determinants of Long-term demand for OPEC Oil', in M. Abdel-Fadil (ed.) (1979) pp. 35–53.

Al-Sabah, A. K. (1979) 'Oil in the 1980s', in M. Abdel-Fadil (ed.) (1979) pp. 54–9.

Banks, F. E. (1980) *The Political Economy of Oil* (Lexington, Mass.: Lexington Books).

Berle, A. A. and G. C. Means (1933) *The Modern Corporation and Private Property* (New York: Macmillan).

Blair, J. M. (1976) *The Control of Oil* (New York: Pantheon Books).

Blumberg, P. I. (1975) *The Megacorporation in American Society* (Englewood Cliffs, N.J.: Prentice-Hall).

Bohi, D. R. and M. Russell (1978) *Limiting Oil Imports* (Baltimore: Johns Hopkins Press).

Brandt, W. *et al.* (1980) *North–South: A Programme for Survival* (London: Pan Books).

Breglia, A. (1965) *Reddito sociale* (Rome: Edizioni dell'Ateneo).

Chevalier, J. M. (1975) *La nuova strategia del petrolio* (Milan: Il Formichiere; original edn Paris: Calmann-Levy, 1974).

_____(1977) 'Elementi teorici d'introduzione all'economia del petrolio: l'analisi dei rapporti di forza', in G. Merzagora (ed.) (1977) pp. 127–55 (original in *Revue d'économie politique*, 1975).

CIA (Central Intelligence Agency) (1977) *Prospects for Soviet Oil Produc-*

tion, ER 77–10270, Washington, D.C. (Apr.).

Colitti, M. (1979) *Energia e sviluppo in Italia* (De Donato, Bari).

———(1981) 'Size and Distribution of Known and Undiscovered Petroleum Resources in the World, with an Estimate of Future Exploration', *OPEC Review*, vol. 5, no. 3, pp. 9–65.

Darmstadter, J. and H. H. Landsberg (1975) 'The Economic Background', *Daedalus*, vol. 104, no. 4, pp. 15–37.

Dasgupta, P. and G. Heal (1979) *Economic Theory and Exhaustible Resources* (Cambridge University Press).

Davidson, P. (1963) 'Public Policy Problems of the Domestic Crude Oil Industry', *American Economic Review*, vol. 53, pp. 85–108.

———(1972) *Money and the Real World* (London: Macmillan).

———(1978) 'The United States Internal Revenue Service: Fourteenth Member of OPEC?', *Journal of Post Keynesian Economics*, vol. 1, no. 2, pp. 47–58.

———(1979a) 'What is the Energy Crisis', *Challenge*, July–Aug., pp. 41–6.

———(1979b) 'Reply to Harkin', *Challenge*, Nov.–Dec., pp. 71–2.

———(1979c) 'Natural Resources', in A. S. Eichner (ed.) *Post-Keynesian Economics* (White Plains, N.Y.: Sharpe) pp. 151–64.

———, L. H. Falk and H. Lee (1974) 'Oil: Its Time Allocation and Project Independence', *Brookings Papers on Economic Activity*, no. 2, pp. 411–48.

Eichner, A. S. (1976) *The Megacorp and Oligopoly* (Cambridge University Press).

Energy and Hydrocarbons (Rome: ENI (Yearbook of Energy Statistics), various years).

ENI (1981a) *The Interdependence Model*, 3 vols (Rome).

ENI (1981b) *Development Through Co-operation: Proceedings of a Seminar between OPEC and South-European Countries*, 2 vols (Rome).

ENI (1981c) *Rapporto sull'energia*, prepared with the collaboration of ENEL, CNEN and CNR, presented to the CNEL Assembly, Rome, 16 Dec.

ENI (1982) *I mutamenti in atto nell'industria petrolifera*, 2 vols, mimeo, Rome, Jan.

ENI (1983) *Strategie delle compagnie petrolifere: elementi di analisi*, mimeo, Rome, Jan.

Fassina, E. (1981) 'Una analisi del comportamento delle maggiori imprese petrolifere multinazionali nell'ultimo trentennio', *Rivista internazionale di scienze sociali*, vol. 89, no. 2, Apr.–June, pp. 138–64.

Federal Trade Commission, Staff Report (1952) *The International Petroleum Cartel* (Washington, D.C.: Government Printing Office).

Foley, G. (1976) *The Energy Question* (Harmondsworth: Penguin Books).

Foster, J. (1980) 'Petroleum Prospects of the People's Republic of China', in R. Mabro (ed.) (1980) pp. 257–65.

Frankel, P. H. (1966) *Mattei: Oil and Power Politics* (London: Faber & Faber).

———(1969) *Essentials of Petroleum*, 2nd edn (London: Frank Cass: 1st edn, 1946).

Genco, P. (1981) 'Il mercato internazionale petrolifero dopo la crisi iraniana', *Economia delle fonti di energia*, vol. 24, no. 14, pp. 45–93.

Girvan, N. (1975) 'Economic Nationalism', *Daedalus*, vol. 104, no. 4, pp. 145–58.

Goldman, M. I. (1975) 'The Soviet Union', *Daedalus*, vol. 104, no. 4, pp. 129–43.

Hartshorn, J. E. (1980) 'The Special Characteristics of OPEC and Importing Countries' National Oil Companies', in R. Mabro (ed.) (1980) pp. 157–66.

Horwitch, M. (1979) 'Coal: Constrained Abundance', in R. Stobaugh and D. Yergin (eds) (1979) pp. 79–107.

Hotelling, H. (1931) 'The Economics of Exhaustible Resources', *Journal of Political Economy*, vol. 39, Apr., pp. 137–75.

IEA (International Energy Agency), *Energy Policies and Programmes of IEA Member Countries* (Paris, yearly reports).

_____, *Energy Research, Development and Demonstration in IEA Countries* (Paris, yearly reports).

_____ (1982) *Natural Gas: Prospects to 2000* (Paris: OECD Publications).

Jacoby, N. H. (1974) *Multinational Oil* (New York: Macmillan).

Jensen, J. T. (1980) 'World Natural Gas Reserves and the Potential for Gas Trade', in R. Mabro (ed.) (1980) pp. 43–69.

Jevons, W. S. (1865) *The Coal Question* (London: Flux, 1906; 1st edn, 1865).

Kahn, H. (1978) *The Next 200 Years* (London: Abacus).

Kalt, J. P. (1981) *The Economics and Politics of Oil Price Regulation* (Cambridge, Mass.: MIT Press).

Kaser, M. (1980) 'The Energy Policies of the Soviet Union', in R. Mabro (ed.) (1980) pp. 247–56.

Keynes, J. M. (1936) *The General Theory of Employment, Interest and Money* (London: Macmillan).

Kissinger, H. (1979) *White House Years* (Boston, Mass.: Little, Brown).

_____ (1982) *Years of Upheaval* (Boston, Mass.: Little, Brown).

Klinghoffer, A. J. (1977) *The Soviet Union and International Oil Politics* (New York: Columbia University Press).

Koreisha, S. and R. Stobaugh (1979) 'Limits to Models', in R. Stobaugh and D. Yergin (eds) (1979) pp. 234–65.

Lantzke, U. (1975) 'The OECD and its International Energy Agency', *Daedalus*, vol. 104, no. 4, pp. 217–27.

Levhari, D. and R. S. Pindyck (1981) 'The Pricing of Durable Exhaustible Resources', *Quarterly Journal of Economics*, vol. 96, no. 3 (Aug.) pp. 365–77.

Luciani, G. (1976) *L'OPEC nella economia internazionale* (Turin: Einaudi).

_____ (1981) *Compagnie petrolifere e paesi arabi* (Bologna: Il Mulino).

Mabro, R. (ed.) (1980) *World Energy Issues and Policies* (Oxford University Press).

MacKay, D. I. and G. A. Mackay (1975) *The Political Economy of North Sea Oil* (London: Martin Robertson).

Magini, M. (1976) *L'Italia e il petrolio tra storia e cronologia* (Milan: Mondadori).

Maidique, M. A. (1979) 'Solar America', in R. Stobaugh and D. Yergin (eds) (1979) pp. 183—215.

Marglin, S. A. (1974) 'What Do Bosses Do? Origins and Functions of Hierarchy in Capitalist Production', *Review of Radical Political Economy*, vol. 6, no. 2.

Marshall, A. (1961) *Principles of Economics*, 9th (Variorum) edn (London: Macmillan).

Martellaro, J. A. (1981) 'Soviet Energy Resources: Present and Prospective', *Economia Internazionale*, vol. 34, no. 1 (Feb.).

Meadows, D. H. *et al.* (1975) *The Limits to Growth*, 2nd edn (New York: New American Library).

Merzagora, G. (ed.) (1977) *Petrolio e crisi* (Milan: Feltrinelli).

Mikdashi, Z. (1975) 'The OPEC Process', *Daedalus*, vol. 104, no. 4, pp. 203—16.

Neale, A. D. (1970) *The Anti-Trust Laws of the U.S.A.*, 2nd edn (Cambridge University Press).

Nehring, R. (1978) *Giant Oil Fields and World Oil Reserves* (Santa Monica, Calif.: RAND Corporation).

Nordhaus, W. (1973) 'The Allocation of Energy Resources', *Brookings Papers on Economic Activity*, no. 3, pp. 529—70.

_____(1979) *The Efficient Use of Energy Resources* (New Haven, Conn.: Yale University Press).

_____(1980) 'Oil and Economic Performance in Industrial Countries', *Brookings Papers on Economic Activity*, no. 2, pp. 341—88.

OAPEC (1981) *Secretary General's Seventh Annual Report, A.D. 1980* (Kuwait: OAPEC).

Odell, P. R. (1979) *Oil and World Power*, 5th edn (Harmondsworth: Penguin Books).

OPEC, *Annual Reports* (Vienna).

_____ *Annual Statistical Bulletin* (Vienna).

_____*OPEC Bulletin* (Vienna).

_____*OPEC Review* (Vienna).

_____(1980) *Statute of OPEC* (Vienna).

_____(1981) *OPEC National Oil Companies Profiles* (Vienna).

_____(1981) *OPEC Official Resolutions and Press Releases 1960—80* (Oxford: Pergamon Press).

Parrinello, S. (1982) 'Terra', *Dizionario di economia politica*, ed. G. Lunghini, vol. 1 (Turin: Boringhieri) pp. 179—211.

Pasinetti, L. L. (1981) *Structural Change and Economic Growth* (London: Cambridge University Press).

Penrose, E. (1959) *The Theory of the Growth of the Firm* (Oxford: Blackwell; 2nd edn, 1980).

_____(1968) *The Large International Firm in Developing Countries* (London: Allen & Unwin).

_____(1971) *The Growth of Firms, Middle East Oil and Other Essays* (London: Frank Cass).

_____(1975) 'The Development of Crisis', *Daedalus*, vol. 104, no. 4, pp. 39—57.

_____(1977) 'Le compagnie petrolifere multinazionali nel Medio Oriente e la "crisi del petroli"', in G. Merzagora (ed.) (1977) (originally published in *Mondes en developpement*, no. 5, 1974).

Pindyck, R. S. (1978) 'The Optimal Exploration and Production of Non-Renewable Resources', *Journal of Political Economy*, vol. 86, no. 5 (Oct.) pp. 841–61.

Posner, M. V. (1973) *Fuel Policy: A Study in Applied Economics* (London: Macmillan).

Ridolfi, M. (1972) 'Aspetti del sistema teorico di Alfred Marshall: una revisione critica di interpretazioni moderne', *Annali della Facoltà di Scienze Politiche*, University of Perugia, no. 12, pp. 119–204.

Roncaglia, A. (1978) *Sraffa and the Theory of Prices* (New York: Wiley).

Rustow, D. A. and J. F. Mugno (1976) *OPEC: Success and Prospects* (London: Martin Robertson).

Safer, A. (1979) *International Oil Policy* (Lexington, Mass.: Lexington Books).

———(1980) *A Strategy of Oil Proliferation*, Joint Economic Committee, US Congress (Washington, D.C.: US Government Printing Office).

Said, A. (1980) 'The Double-Edged Sword of Stockpiles', *OPEC Bulletin*, vol. 11, no. 15 (June) pp. 13–17.

Sampson, A. (1973) *Sovereign State: The Secret History of ITT* (London: Hodder & Stoughton).

———(1976) *The Seven Sisters* (New York: Viking Press, Bantam edn; 1st edn London: Hodder & Stoughton, 1975).

Smart, J. (1975) 'Uniqueness and Generality', *Daedalus*, vol. 104, no. 4.

Smith, A. (1971) *The Wealth of Nations* (London: Dent, Everyman's edn).

Solberg, C. (1976) *Oil Power* (New York: New American Library).

Solow, R. M. (1974) 'The Economics of Resources or the Resources of Economics', *American Economic Review*, vol. 64, pp. 1–14.

Sraffa, P. (1925) 'Sulle relazioni fra costo e quantità prodotta', *Annali di economia*, vol. 2, pp. 277–328.

———(1926) 'The Laws of Returns Under Competitive Conditions', *Economic Journal*, vol. 36, pp. 535–50.

Steindl, J. (1952) *Maturity and Stagnation in American Capitalism* (Oxford: Blackwell).

Stobaugh, R. (1979) 'After the Peak: the Threat of Imported Oil', in R. Stobaugh and D. Yergin (eds) (1979) pp. 16–55.

———and D. Yergin (eds) (1979) *Energy Future* (New York: Random House).

Sweeney, J. L. (1977) 'Economics of Depletable Resources: Market Forces and Intertemporal Bias', *Review of Economic Studies*, vol. 55 (Feb.) pp. 125–41.

Sylos Labini, P. (1969) *Oligopoly and Technical Progress*, 2nd edn (Cambridge, Mass.: Harvard University Press; 1st Italian edn, 1957).

———(1970) 'Sulla struttura delle grandi imprese industriali', in *Problemi dello sviluppo economico* (Rome–Bari: Laterza) pp. 217–51.

———(1979) *Lezioni di economia*, vol. 1 (Rome: Edizioni dell'Ateneo).

———(1982) 'Rigid Prices, Flexible Prices and Inflation', *Banca Nazionale del Lavoro Quarterly Review*, no. 140 (Mar.) pp. 37–68.

_____ and G. Guarino (1956) *L'industria petrolifera* (Milan: Giuffre).

Tarbell, I. (1904) *The History of the Standard Oil Company* (New York: Macmillan).

Thurow, L. (1975) *Generating Inequality* (New York: Basic Books).

Tiratsoo, E. N. (1972) *Natural Gas*, 2nd edn (Beaconsfield: Scientific Press).

Turner, L. (1980) *Oil Companies in the International System*, 2nd edn (London: Allen & Unwin).

UNCNRET (UN Centre for Natural Resources, Energy and Transport) (1980) *State Petroleum Enterprises in Developing Countries* (Oxford: Pergamon Press).

US Congress (1979) Congressional Research Service, *Oil Imports: A Range of Policy Options* (Washington, D.C.: US Government Printing Office).

_____ (1980) *US Refineries: A Background Study* (Washington, D.C.: US Government Printing Office).

US House of Representatives (1968), Staff Report for the Subcommittee on Domestic Finance, *Commercial Banks and their Trust Activities: Emerging Influence on the American Economy* (Washington, D.C.: US Government Printing Office).

_____ (1978) Staff Report of the Subcommittee on Monopolies and Commercial Law, *Competitive Aspects of Oil Company Expansion into Other Energy Sources* (Washington, D.C.: US Government Printing Office).

US Senate (1974) Subcommittee on Multinational Corporations (Church Committee), *Multinational Petroleum Companies and Foreign Policy*, volumes 4–7 (*Hearings*) (Washington, D.C.: US Government Printing Office).

_____ (1975) *Multinational Oil Corporations and US Foreign Policy* (Washington, D.C.: US Government Printing Office).

US Senate (1978a) Subcommittee on Reports, Accounting and Management, *Voting Rights in Major Corporations* (Washington, D.C.: US Government Printing Office).

_____ (1978b) *Interlocking Directorates among the Major US Corporations* (Washington, D.C.: US Government Printing Office).

US Senate (1980) Subcommittee on Energy Regulation, *Limiting Oil Imports* (*Hearings*) (Washington, D.C.: US Government Printing Office).

Verlage, H. (1975) *Transfer Pricing for Multinational Enterprises* (Rotterdam University Press).

Verleger, H. (1979) 'The US Petroleum Crisis of 1979', *Brookings Papers on Economic Activity*, no. 2, pp. 463–76.

Vernon, R. (1975) 'An Interpretation', *Daedalus*, vol. 104, no. 4, pp. 1–14.

Villetti, R. (1978a) 'Lavoro diviso e lavoro costrittivo', in R. Villetti (ed.) (1978b) pp. xliii–xliv.

Villetti, R. (1978b) *Socialismo e divisione del lavoro* (Quaderni di Mondoperaio) no. 6 (Rome).

Waddams, F. C. (1980) *The Libyan Oil Industry* (London: Croom Helm).

Wood, A. (1975) *A Theory of Profits* (Cambridge University Press).

Yergin, D. (1979) 'Conservation: the Key Energy Source', in R. Stobaugh and D. Yergin (eds), (1979) pp. 136–82.

Index

Index